A SHORT HISTORY OF MARRIAGE

A SHORT HISTORY
OF MARRIAGE

BY

EDWARD WESTERMARCK

PH.D., HON. LL.D. (ABERDEEN)

MARTIN WHITE PROFESSOR OF SOCIOLOGY IN THE UNIVERSITY OF LONDON;
PROFESSOR OF PHILOSOPHY AT THE ACADEMY OF ÅBO (FINLAND)

HUMANITIES PRESS

New York 1968

First published in 1926

Reprinted 1968 by

HUMANITIES PRESS, INC.
New York, N. Y. 10010

Printed in U.S.A. by
NOBLE OFFSET PRINTERS, INC.
NEW YORK 3, N. Y.

FOREWORD

THIS book is based on the fifth edition of my *History of Human Marriage,* in which may be found references to nearly all of the authorities consulted, but is not intended to be an abridged edition of it. I am here dealing with marriage as a social institution, in the strict sense of the term, and have consequently omitted various topics discussed in the larger work.

E. W.

Burpham,
Guildford.
June 1926.

CONTENTS

CHAPTER I

THE ORIGIN OF MARRIAGE

Definition of marriage as a social institution, p. 1 *sq.*—The institution of marriage has probably developed out of a primeval habit, p. 2 *sq.*—The relations between the sexes and parental care among the lower animals, p. 3 *sq.*—Among the Quadrumana, p. 4.—Why in certain species male and female remain together till after the birth of the offspring, p. 5 *sq.*—The need of marital and paternal protection among the man-like apes, p. 6 *sq.*—The family consisting of parents and children, with the father as its protector, in mankind, p. 7.—Criticism of the hypothesis of promiscuity, pp. 7-20.—A few cases in which the husband is said not to live with his wife, p. 20.—Cases in which the mother's brother is said to have greater rights over a child than the father, p. 20 *sq.*—Paternal rights among matrilineal peoples, p. 21 *sq.*—Dr. Hartland's hypothesis that the authority of the father is the result of later development, p. 22 *sq.*—That the functions of the husband and father in the family involve the duties of protecting and supporting the wife and children, testified by an array of facts, p. 23.—A man often prohibited from marrying until he has given some proof of his ability to fulfil these duties, p. 23 *sq.*—The more or less durable union between man and woman and marital and paternal care probably due to instincts once necessary for the preservation of the species, p. 24 *sq.*—The social conditions of savages who know neither cattle-rearing nor agriculture, unless perhaps of the most primitive kind, p. 25 *sq.*—Unreasonable to suppose that primitive men were more permanently gregarious than many modern savages, p. 26 *sq.*—The family in mankind presumably an inheritance from the parent species out of which the Anthropoids and the Hominides gradually developed, p. 27.—The tendency of habits to become rules of conduct, p. 28.—The marital and parental instincts, p. 28 *sq.*—They give rise not only to habits but to rules of custom, or institutions, p. 29.—Marriage rooted in the family rather than the family in marriage, p. 29 *sq.*

CHAPTER II

THE FREQUENCY OF MARRIAGE AND THE MARRIAGE AGE

Among the uncivilised races, as a general rule, nearly every man endeavours to marry when he has reached the age of puberty and practically every woman gets married, p. 31.—Unmarried persons looked upon as unnatural beings or objects of contempt or ridicule, *ibid.*—Among savages girls married at an earlier age than among the peoples of

[vii]

CONTENTS

CHAPTER III

ENDOGAMY

CHAPTER IV

EXOGAMY

CONTENTS

CHAPTER V

MARRIAGE BY CAPTURE

CONTENTS

CONTENTS

CHAPTER VIII

MARRIAGE RITES

[xi]

CONTENTS

CONTENTS

A SHORT HISTORY OF MARRIAGE

CHAPTER I

THE ORIGIN OF MARRIAGE

MARRIAGE is generally used as a term for a social institution. As such it may be defined as a relation of one or more men to one or more women which is recognised by custom or law and involves certain rights and duties both in the case of the parties entering the union and in the case of the children born of it. These rights and duties vary among different peoples and cannot, therefore, all be included in a general definition; but there must, of course, be something which they have in common. Marriage always implies the right of sexual intercourse: society holds such intercourse allowable in the case of husband and wife, and, generally speaking, even regards it as their duty to gratify in some measure the other partner's desire. But the right to sexual intercourse is not necessarily exclusive. It can hardly be said to be so, from the legal point of view, unless adultery is considered an offence which entitles the other partner to dissolve the marriage union; and this is by no means always the case.

At the same time, marriage is something more than a regulated sexual relation. It is an economic institution, which may in various ways affect the proprietary rights of the parties. It is the husband's duty, so far as it is possible and necessary, to support his wife and children, but it may also be their duty to work for him.

As a general rule he has some power over them, although his power over the children is in most cases of limited duration. Very often marriage determines the place which a newly-born individual is to take in the social structure of the community to which he or she belongs; but this cannot, as has been sometimes maintained, be regarded as the chief and primary function of marriage, considering how frequently illegitimate children are treated exactly like legitimate ones with regard to descent, inheritance, and succession.[1] It is, finally, necessary that the union, to be recognised as a marriage, should be concluded in accordance with the rules laid down by custom or law, whatever these rules may be. They may require the consent of the parties themselves or of their parents, or of the parties as well as of their parents. They may compel the man to give some consideration for his bride, or the parents of the latter to provide her with a dowry. They may prescribe the performance of a particular marriage ceremony of one kind or other. And no man and woman are regarded as husband and wife unless the conditions stipulated by custom or law are complied with.

- As for the origin of the institution of marriage, I think that it has most probably developed out of a primeval habit. We have reason to believe that, even in primitive times, it was the habit for a man and a woman (or several women) to live together, to have

---

[1] In China, for instance, all sons born in the household have an equal share in the inheritance, whether the mother be the principal wife or a concubine or a domestic slave; and according to Muhammadan law no distinction in point of inheritance is made between the child of a wife and that borne by a slave to her master, if the master acknowledge the child to be his own.

sexual relations with one another, and to rear their offspring in common, the man being the protector and supporter of his family and the woman being his helpmate and the nurse of their children. This habit - was sanctioned by custom, and afterwards by law, and was thus transformed into a social institution. I shall state my reasons for the belief in the existence of such a habit among our earliest human ancestors and try to find out its origin.

Similar habits are found among many other species of the animal kingdom. Not, however, among the very lowest. In the great sub-kingdom of the Invertebrates the relations between the sexes are generally of the most fugitive nature, and even the mothers are exempted from nearly all anxiety as regards their offspring; and in the lowest classes of the Vertebrates parental care is likewise almost unheard of. But the case is very different with the large majority of Birds. Among them male and female keep together not only during the breeding season, but also after it, and the parental instinct has reached a high degree of intensity on the father's side as well as on the mother's. Dr. Brehm, the well-known student of the habits of animals, believes that most birds, with the exception of those belonging to the Gallinaceous family and some other species, when pairing, do so once for all till either one or the other dies. He is so filled with admiration for their exemplary family life, that he enthusiastically declares that "real genuine marriage can only be found among birds."

Nothing of the kind can be said of most of the Mammals. The mother is, no doubt, very ardently concerned for the welfare of her young, generally nursing them with the utmost affection, but in the majority of species the relations between the sexes are restricted to the pairing season. Yet there are various species in which the union between male and female is of a more durable character and the male acts as the protector of the family. This is frequently the case among the Quadrumana. The anthropoid apes are of particular interest to us. As to the orang-utan the statements are conflicting. According to one of our informants this ape lives in families consisting of male, female, and one or sometimes two young ones; according to others, the old males are always found alone, whereas a female may be seen with two young ones, one a nursing infant and the other one a year or two old. Wallace never saw two full-grown animals together; but as he sometimes found either females or males accompanied by half-grown young ones, we may, from his account also, draw the conclusion that the offspring of the orang-utan are not devoid of all paternal care. More unanimous in this respect are the statements we have regarding the gorilla. From the various accounts it appears that it lives in family groups, consisting of one adult male (according to one account sometimes two), one or more females, and one or more young ones of different ages, and that the adult male, or father, guards, warns, and protects his family, and apparently builds a nest for them. The habits of the chimpanzee are said to be very similar. Von Koppenfels states that the chimpanzee, like the gorilla, builds a nest for the young and female on a forked branch, and that the male himself spends the night lower down in the tree.

If we ask why in certain animal species male and

female remain together not only during the pairing season but till after the birth of the offspring, I think that there can be no doubt as regards the true answer. They are induced to do so by an instinct which has been acquired through the process of natural selection because it has a tendency to preserve the next generation and thereby the species. This is shown by the fact that in such cases the male not only stays with the female and young, but also takes care of them. Marital and paternal instincts, like maternal affection, are necessary for the existence of certain species, although there are many other means by which a species may be enabled to subsist. Where parental care is lacking, we may be sure to find compensation for it in some other way. Among the Invertebrates, Fishes, and Reptiles an immense proportion of the progeny succumb before reaching maturity; but the number of eggs laid is proportionate to the number of those lost, and the species is preserved nevertheless. If every grain of roe spawned by the female fishes were fecundated and hatched, the sea would hardly be large enough to hold all the creatures resulting from them. The eggs of Reptiles need no maternal care, the embryo being developed by the heat of the sun; and their young are from the outset able to help themselves, leading the same life as the adults. Among Birds, on the other hand, parental care is an absolute necessity. Equal and continual warmth is the first requirement for the development of the embryo and the preservation of the young ones; and for this the mother almost always wants the assistance of the father, who provides her with necessaries and sometimes relieves her of the brooding. Among

Mammals the young can never do without the mother at the tenderest age, but the father's aid is generally by no means indispensable. In some species, as the walrus, the elephant, and the bat, there seems to be a rather curious substitute for paternal protection, the females, together with their young ones, collecting in large herds or flocks apart from the males.

In the case of the man-like apes there are some obvious facts which may account for the need of marital and paternal protection. One is the small number of young; the female brings forth but one at a birth. Another is the long period of infancy; the orang-utan is said to be full-grown only at the age of fifteen. If the family life of this ape, nevertheless, is more defective than that of the gorilla and chimpanzee, the reason may perhaps be that it is exposed to fewer dangers; except man, the orang-utan in Borneo has no enemy of equal strength. Finally, none of these apes can be called gregarious animals. In this respect they differ from the smaller monkeys; and the reason for this is presumably just their larger size, which on the one hand makes the protection afforded by gregariousness less necessary, and on the other hand makes it more difficult to live in larger herds owing to the greater quantities of food required. It is said that the gorilla hardly ever spends two nights on the same spot, each family roaming about in the bush from place to place in search of food. Dr. Savage tells us that the chimpanzees are more numerous in the season when the greatest number of fruits come to maturity, which seems to indicate that the solitary life in separate family groups generally led by this ape is due chiefly to the difficulty it has in getting food at other times of the year. And if the chimpanzee in Kamerun, as we are told by native informants, lives in bands, its greater sociability may have something to do with the fact that "the immense forests furnish an abundance of varied food, so the chimpanzee usually experiences little trouble in satisfying its hunger."

When we from the highest monkeys pass to man, we meet with the same phenomenon. Among the lowest savages, as well as the most civilised races of men, we find the family consisting of parents and children, and the father as its protector and supporter. There are, it is true, statements to the effect that certain peoples live or have lived in a state of promiscuity without any family ties; there are various customs which have been interpreted as survivals of such a state in the past; and the hypothesis has been set forth that promiscuity prevailed universally among primitive men. But neither the statements in question nor the supposed survivals of earlier promiscuity seem to me to possess any evidentiary value at all.

After examining in detail all the cases which are known to me of peoples said to live in a state of promiscuity, I have arrived at the conclusion that it would be difficult to find a more untrustworthy collection of statements. Some of them are simply misrepresentations of theorists in which sexual laxity, frequency of separation, polyandry, group-marriage or something like it, or absence of a marriage ceremony or of a word for "to marry" or of a marriage union similar to our own, is confounded with promiscuity. Others are based upon indefinite evidence which may be interpreted in one way or other, or on information proved to be inaccurate. And not a single statement can be said to be authoritative or even to make the existence of promiscuity at all probable in any case. That no known savage people nowadays is, or recently was, living in such a state is quite obvious; and this greatly discredits the supposition that promiscuity prevailed among any of the peoples mentioned by classical or mediæval writers in their summary and vague accounts. Considering how uncertain the information is which people give about the sexual relations of their own neighbours, we must be careful not to accept as trustworthy evidence the statements made by classical writers with reference to more or less distant tribes in Africa or Asia of which they evidently possessed very little knowledge. In the very chapter where Pliny states that among the Garamantians men and women lived in promiscuous intercourse he tells us of another African people, the Blemmyans, that they were said to have no head and to have the mouth and the eyes in the breast. I have never found this statement quoted in any book on human anatomy, and can see no reason to assume that our author was so much better acquainted with the sexual habits of the Garamantians than he was with the personal appearance of the Blemmyans. Moreover, the statements in question are so short and ambiguous that different constructions may be put on them. The community of women mentioned in them does not necessarily imply general promiscuity within the horde or tribe, but may mean group-relations similar to those which are known to prevail among certain modern savages; and if the existence of marriage is denied, we must remember that the

word "marriage" may have many meanings. The
same may be said with regard to the promiscuity
ascribed by mediæval writers to certain Slavonic
peoples. But even if we could be induced to believe
that an Aryan people a few centuries ago had no
marriage, we should certainly have to admit that it
had lost something which its ancestors possessed in
the past.

It has been argued by advocates of a primitive
stage of promiscuity that, side by side with marriage,
promiscuity is found among savages in all parts of
the world, and very frequently not as a mere fact
but as a practice permitted by custom; and this, we
are told, shows that sexual intercourse must originally
have been unchecked. Now it is a well-known fact
that among many uncivilised peoples both sexes
enjoy perfect freedom previous to marriage. But if
we look at the facts a little more closely we soon find
that many of them could not, in any circumstances,
be regarded as relics of primitive promiscuity—either
because they are known to be of later growth, or
because they do not represent promiscuity at all.
Pre-nuptial freedom does not mean that an unmarried
woman is constantly changing her lovers or an
unmarried man the objects of his love, or that they
can do so without reproach. Sexual connections
between a boy and a girl are very frequently a preliminary to their marriage. They may be a regular
method of courtship, or they may be a trial before
establishing more permanent relations. Among many
peoples there is a regular marriage upon trial before
the union becomes definite, the bridegroom either
taking the girl to his own house or going himself to

stay with her parents for a certain length of time. Something of the kind existed even in Scotland prior to the Reformation, as a genuine custom known as "hand-fasting." "At the public fairs men selected female companions with whom to cohabit for a year. At the expiry of this period both parties were accounted free; they might either unite in marriage or live singly." A similar custom existed in Ireland, in a very rude form; and the Welsh, according to an old writer, did not marry until they had tried, by previous cohabitation, the disposition and particularly the fecundity of the person with whom they were engaged. Among many uncivilised peoples the free intercourse between unmarried persons generally leads to marriage if the girl becomes pregnant or gives birth to a child, or a seducer or lover is in such a case compelled to marry the girl or otherwise has to pay a fine. All this presupposes that the father of the child is known—which remains something very different from promiscuity.

I certainly do not mean to say that pre-nuptial relations among simple peoples always have this character; we have too many and too positive statements to the contrary to allow us to doubt that promiscuity outside marriage does exist. Yet I do not hesitate to affirm that promiscuity among the unmarried is after all an exception in the customs of unadulterated savages. Messrs. Hobhouse, Wheeler, and Ginsberg have in their book on *Material Culture and Social Institutions of the Simpler Peoples* come to the conclusion that among the cases examined by them —about 120 in number—those in which pre-nuptial relations are condemned are nearly as numerous as those in which they are condoned; and although I prefer giving no figures, partly on account of the indefiniteness of many of the statements, I may say that my own collection of facts convinces me that the standard of savage chastity has at any rate not been overrated by those authors. But then we have to consider the deteriorating influence which contact with civilisation has in so many cases exercised on the lower races, and the still more important fact that "pre-nuptial unchastity" includes all kinds of sexual relations previous to formal marriage, however exclusive and constant they may be.

Moreover, when we examine how far the condemnation or condonation of pre-nuptial unchastity among the simpler peoples is correlated with economic advance, it is found that the standard of pre-nuptial chastity in a tribe is not proportionate to its degree of culture. On the contrary, it seems that in the lowest tribes chastity is more respected than in the higher ones. This is also what might be expected if marriage is the natural and normal relation between the sexes in mankind. Pre-nuptial chastity or unchastity largely depends on the age when marriages are contracted. At the lower stages of culture celibacy is much rarer and marriage is entered into at an earlier age than among ourselves; but even in savage life there are circumstances which may compel adult persons to live unmarried for a longer or shorter time. A man may be too poor to maintain a wife, or where he has to buy her he may be unable to pay the price, or the polygyny of some may lead to the celibacy of others. These obstacles, however, would occur chiefly where some advancement in culture has been made, and in a much smaller degree under more primitive conditions, where consequently there would be less reason for pre-nuptial unchastity. Extra-matrimonial relations can thus be easily explained without recourse to the hypothesis that in the beginning all relations between the sexes were promiscuous. When we consider that in our own midst prostitution has shown a tendency to increase in a higher ratio than population, and that in spite of the general infertility of prostitutes there are towns in Europe where the illegitimate births outnumber the legitimate ones, it is nothing less than absurd to speak of the unchastity of unmarried savages as a relic of an alleged primitive stage of promiscuity.

The hypothesis of promiscuity or "communal marriage," as Lord Avebury called it, is supposed to derive much support from certain customs which are interpreted as acts of expiation for individual marriage. In many cases, we are told, the exclusive possession of a wife could be legally acquired only by a temporary recognition of the pre-existing communal rights. As a recognition of this kind is regarded the so-called *jus primæ noctis* not infrequently accorded to a priest, king, or nobleman, who is then looked upon as a representative of the community after the ancient right was taken away from its male members in general. Yet before we are entitled to make such an inference we have to consider whether the right in question may not be accounted for by feelings or ideas among peoples who recognise it or are addicted to practices of a kindred nature. This is the method which should be adopted in the study of any custom, and is particularly called for in a case like the present one, where a custom is used as evidence for the existence of a previous state which is itself entirely hypothetical.

The first fact, then, which attracts our attention is a frequent reluctance on the part of a bridegroom to deflower the bride, or to do so in the manner indicated by nature. Indeed, among various peoples young women or girls are deflowered by extra-matrimonial intercourse in circumstances which clearly show that the act by no means implies the exercise of a right on the part of him who performs it, but is an operation which the husband is anxious to avoid. The chief reason for his reluctance is no doubt superstitious fear, and this feeling seems in many cases at least to be closely connected with the widespread fear of hymeneal blood. A priest or a medicine-man, on the other hand, may do with safety what is perilous to other persons; and if, as Dr. Karsten observes in his recent book on *The Civilization of the South American Indian,* there is an apprehension that evil spirits might interfere at the first sexual intercourse, such a man knows how to deal with them, and therefore knows "how to deflower the girl without her being supernaturally harmed, and without her husband being harmed afterwards." More positive benefits may also be expected from his embrace; sexual intercourse with a holy person is frequently held to be highly beneficial. And what is or has been merely a habit may be interpreted as, or actually become, a right. The same may be said of the *jus primæ noctis* of a chief or king, whose services may be sought for on grounds similar to those which have led to defloration by priests. In an old manuscript, which contains a collection of pieces in the Irish language compiled about A.D. 1100, it is said that Conchobar, King of Ulster, who lived at the time when Christ was born, deflowered all the virgins of his kingdom, and it is indicated that the defloration of maidens was a duty incumbent upon him. At the same time the *jus primæ noctis* of a chief may also, no doubt, have the same origin as the right of certain chiefs to cohabit with their female subjects at any time. But whether the *jus primæ noctis* belonging to a chief or priest ultimately springs from ordinary persons' fear of defloration, or from hope of benefits resulting from intercourse with a holy or superior person, or from the sexual appetite of the man who has the right—it is always the consequence of his own personal qualities or authority, and cannot, therefore, be regarded as the relic of an ancient communal right.

Another custom which has been adduced as evidence of former communism in women is that which requires a man to offer his wife or one of his wives to a guest. To Lord Avebury it seems to involve the recognition of "a right inherent in every member of the community, and to visitors as temporary members." Were this so, we should certainly have to conclude that "communal marriage" has been widespread in the human race, the custom of lending wives being found among many peoples in different parts of the world. But we might as well look upon the offer of a meal or a bed to a guest as a relic from a time when no man had any food or shelter which he could call his own. For I think there can be no doubt that the custom which requires a host to lend his wife to his guest is only an incident of the general rule of hospitality, which in some form or other seems to prevail universally at the lower stages of civilisation. It is not always the wife who is offered: it may be a daughter, a sister, or a servant. This sort of hospitality is frequently mentioned in Irish heroic tales, and there are several cases in French mediæval literature which point to the former existence of it in France. Like other forms of hospitality, the lending of wives to visiting strangers may also be connected with superstitious beliefs; for the unknown stranger, as everything unknown and everything strange, arouses a feeling of mysterious awe in simple minds. When properly treated, he may bring with him blessings, but on the other hand he is also a potential source of evil. He is commonly believed to be versed in magic; and the evil wishes and curses of a visiting stranger are greatly feared, owing partly to his quasi-supernatural character and partly to his close contact with the host and his belongings, which makes it easy for him to transfer evil to them. The custom which requires a host to lend his wife to a guest becomes more intelligible when we consider the supposed danger of the stranger's evil eye or his curses, as also the benefits which may be supposed to result from his love.

Among a large number of uncivilised peoples descent is reckoned through the mother, not through the father; and this custom, often called "mother-right," has been explained by McLennan and various later writers as the result of uncertain paternity due to sexual promiscuity. Yet no one has been able to exhibit any general coincidence of what we consider moral and immoral habits with the prevalence of patrilineal and matrilineal descent among existing savages. There are peoples among whom inheritance goes through the mother only, although adultery is said to be extremely rare; whereas patrilineal descent prevails among others, who lay little restraint of any kind on sexual intercourse either before or after marriage. Dr. Hartland, who shares my view that we cannot ascribe matrilineal descent to uncertain paternity, justly observes that mother-right "is found not merely where paternity is uncertain, but also where it is practically certain," whereas father-right "is found not merely where paternity is certain, but also where it is uncertain and even where the legal father is known not to have begotten the children. Nay, the institutions of father-right often require provision for, and very generally permit, the procreation by other men of children for the nominal father." I do not deny that mother-right may have directly something to do with child-birth, with the fact that the child comes from the mother, whatever ideas be held about fatherhood; but I think there can be little doubt that both father- and mother-right at least in a large measure depend on social conditions. However impossible it might be to explain their prevalence in each separate case, even if our knowledge of the lower races were far less incomplete than it is at present, we can, I believe, with a considerable degree of probability indicate in a general way the chief causes, or at least some of them, which have led to the system of mother-right, apart from any consideration of blood-relationship.

Among savages in particular the tie between mother

and child is much stronger than that which binds the child to its father. The savage mother is for a long time seen carrying the child at her breast, the suckling period lasting for two, three, or four years or even more. In cases of separation the infant children always follow the mother, and so, very often, do the children more advanced in years. In polygynous families it is a frequent arrangement that each wife has a hut for herself, in which she lives with her children; and even where this is not the case, mother and children naturally keep together as a little sub-family. Moreover, among many peoples it is the custom for a man on marrying to quit his home and go to live with his wife's people, and in nearly all these cases mother-right prevails. One cause of it seems, therefore, to be matrilocal marriage. This conclusion is corroborated by the fact that when matrilocal and patrilocal marriages occur side by side among the same people, descent is—at least in some instances—reckoned through the mother if the husband goes to live with his wife's people, and through the father if he takes her to his own home.

I think it may be said without hesitation that not one of the customs alleged as relics of an ancient state of indiscriminate cohabitation of the sexes, or "communal marriage," presupposes the former existence of such a state. The numerous facts put forward in support of the hypothesis of promiscuity do not entitle us to assume that promiscuity has ever been the prevailing form of sexual relations among a single people, far less that it has constituted a general stage in the social development of man, and least of all that such a stage formed the starting-point of all human history. Nay, the hypothesis of promiscuity not only lacks all foundation in facts, but is actually opposed to the most probable inference we are able to make as regards the early condition of man.

Darwin remarked that from what we know of the jealousy of all male quadrupeds, armed, as many of them are, with special weapons for battling with their rivals, promiscuous intercourse is utterly unlikely to prevail in a state of nature; but the lines of evidence afforded by Morgan, McLennan, and Lubbock led him to believe that almost promiscuous intercourse at a later time was extremely common throughout the world, and a similar view is held by some other writers. Now, if the facts adduced as evidence of former promiscuity really had proved that it was general at some stage of human development, we should, of course, be compelled to admit that jealousy on the part of the men could have been no serious hindrance to it. But the case is entirely different if we have no reason whatever to suppose that there was a stage of promiscuity at any time. Then the prevalence of male jealousy both among the anthropoid apes and among the existing races of men constitutes a strong *primâ-facie* evidence of its prevalence in mankind in earlier ages as well. That masculine jealousy is a general human characteristic may be inferred not only from the direct statements of observers, but from customs or laws concerning adultery, which make the seducer or the unfaithful wife or both liable to punishment of some sort, inflicted either by the injured husband himself or by the society of which he is a member, or at all events give him power to divorce his wife.

There are certainly savage peoples who have been

said to be almost devoid of jealousy. This has often been inferred from the practice of lending, exchanging, or prostituting wives. But such an inference cannot be accepted if sexual jealousy simply means, as I take it to mean, the angry feeling which is aroused by the loss, or the fear of the loss, of the exclusive possession of an individual who is the object of one's sexual desire. First, who can exactly tell what a savage feels when he, for reasons stated above or simply in compliance with the customs of his people, lends his wife to a visitor? And secondly, a person may have a tendency, and even a strong tendency, to experience a certain feeling although on some special occasions it fails to make its voice heard. A desire may be silenced by another desire, which for the moment at least is the stronger of the two. A man may, generally speaking, be quite jealous of his wife and yet, under the influence of love of money, prostitute her to a stranger or, as negro husbands sometimes do, use her for entrapping other men and making them pay a heavy fine. Moreover, sexual jealousy presupposes some degree of sexual love, and neither a savage nor a civilised man always loves his wife. One reason why a man exchanges his wife for that of another man is that he has got thoroughly tired of her.

By all this I certainly do not mean to deny that there are people who are remarkably little addicted to jealousy. This is said of many who practise polyandry. But these peoples cannot on that account be quoted in support of the theory of promiscuity, since polyandry, as will be seen, owes its origin to specific causes which would never have produced general communism in women. It is also in the present connection important to note that polyandry has been mainly found, not among savages of the lowest type, but among peoples who have flocks and herds or who practise agriculture and some of whom cannot be called savages at all. These facts do not speak in favour of McLennan's statement that "polyandry must be regarded as a modification of and an advance from promiscuity." Nor could the practice of prostituting wives in any case be taken as evidence of primitive lack of jealousy. It has certainly not the flavour of primitiveness, and among many peoples it is known to have arisen through their contact with a "higher civilisation." It may be added that if the hypothesis of an animal pairing time in the infancy of mankind holds good—as I have elsewhere tried to show—we may assume that jealousy at that stage was no less intense than among other mammals.

While there are no known instances of peoples living in a state of promiscuity, there are undoubtedly peoples among whom a child stands in a more intimate relation to its maternal uncle than to its father. In a few exceptional cases—among the Orang Mamaq in Sumatra, among the kindred Malays of the Padang Highlands in the same island, among the Syntengs of the Jaintia Hills in Assam, and among the Nayars of Malabar—it is said to be the custom for the husband not to live with his wife at all, but merely to pay her visits in the place where she dwells with her maternal relatives; and the children she bears then remain with her. More frequently it is said that the mother's brother has greater rights over a child than the father, or that the latter's authority is very slight or even *nil,* although the children live with their parents, at least in earlier years. Yet I think it is necessary to receive with some caution statements which attribute unqualified power to the maternal uncle to the exclusion of the father. Travellers are naturally impressed by the difference between the European family system and that of the people they visit, and may therefore be liable to emphasise this difference somewhat more than is justified by the actual facts. In this way we may explain certain inconsistencies occasionally found in their accounts—as when a writer says that among the Lobi in French West Africa the children belong to their uncle, although they live with their parents, and in the next page that "there is no authority but that of the father of a family"; or when an authority on the Ewhe-speaking peoples of the Slave Coast tells us in one place that "the eldest brother is the head of the family," but speaks in another place of the father as the "owner or master of the household," and says that when a man wants to marry a certain girl the negotiations are made with her parents. In any case the elementary paternal duties seem to be recognised universally while the children live in their father's house, however limited be his rights over him.

But it must not be supposed to be a general rule among matrilineal peoples that the maternal uncle or any other member of the mother's kin has more authority over the children than the father. Among all Australian tribes, whether patrilineal or matrilineal, the father is most distinctly the head of the family. The same is the case in many parts of Melanesia where descent is traced through the mother; as Dr. Codrington puts it, "the house of the family is the father's, the garden is his, the rule and government are his." Concerning the matrilineal Algonkin of North America, Charlevoix says that even though the father "is not regarded as father, he is always respected as the master of the cabin." And of the Iroquois—who, on the authority of Morgan, have been represented as one of the few instances of mother-right "in its most typical form," where the father has no authority in the household—an earlier authority tells us that the mother superintends the children, but that the word of the father is law and must be obeyed by the whole household. These are only a few instances of a very widespread right granted to the father among peoples who have the matrilineal system of descent.

Dr. Hartland—to mention only the latest exponent of "mother-right"—regards the authority of the father as the result of later development, and maintains that the family consisting of father, mother, and children has everywhere been preceded by a social organisation of mother-right where the father was a wholly subordinate personage. The main arguments on which this theory is based have already been mentioned. Among a few peoples, not even half a dozen in number, it is said to be the custom for husband and wife to remain permanently in their own communities, apart from each other, and for the children to stay with the mother. Among various other peoples the mother's kin, and particularly the maternal uncle, are said to have greater rights over the children than the father, if not exclusive rights over them; whereas among many matrilineal peoples the father's power is paramount. I can find no reason whatever to assume that these peoples, also, had full-fledged mother-right in former times. If a certain institution is highly developed among some peoples and much less developed among others, it does not follow that it was once highly developed among the latter as well. In the present case any such conclusion is particularly illegitimate, considering that the fullest mother-right prevails among agricultural tribes, whereas the matrilineal system is nowhere feebler than among the Australian aborigines, who still live in the hunting and food-collecting stage. This is very significant on account of the close connection which exists between the family organisation and factors of an economic character. Nor can I accept the statement that "mother-right everywhere preceded father-right"; if it had done so we might expect to find it particularly prevalent among the most primitive savages, which is not the case. Those who advocate a primitive stage of mother-right without paternal rights and paternal duties are faced by the formidable fact, which will be dealt with presently, that among those very low savages who chiefly or exclusively subsist on game and such products of nature as they can gather without cultivating the soil or breeding domestic animals, the family consisting of parents and children is a very distinct social unit, with the father as its head and protector.

That the functions of the husband and father in the family are not merely of the sexual and pro-creative kind, but involve the duties of supporting and protecting the wife and children, is testified by an array of facts relating to peoples in all quarters of the world and in all stages of civilisation. Indeed, many savages set an example to ourselves by not allowing a man to marry until he has given some proof of his ability to fulfil those duties. Among the Macusis of British Guiana, before a young man is permitted to choose a wife, "he must prove that he is a man, and can do man's work. Without flinching, he suffers the infliction of wounds in his flesh; or he allows himself to be sewn up in a hammock full of fire ants; or by some other similar tests he shows his courage. And he clears a space in the forest to be planted with cassava, and brings in as much game and fish as possible, to show that he is able to support himself and others." Among the Siberian Yukaghir "the prospective father-in-law would go to the woods and fell as thick a tree as he could find. The bridegroom had to drag the trunk of the tree to the house of his future father-in-law, and throw it upon the tent, so that it would fall. Then the father-in-law would say, 'This is a good man; he will be able to support us and to care for our safety.'" Among some of the Wapokomo in British East Africa too early marriage is prevented by the rule that no man may marry until he has killed a crocodile, and given a part of the flesh to the woman to eat. Among the Bechuana and Kafir tribes south of the Zambesi a youth is allowed to take a wife only after he has killed a rhinoceros. And of various head-hunting tribes in south-eastern Asia we are told that no man can marry without having first procured at least one human head as a token of his valour.

When we find in mankind a habit, like that of living in families, which it has in common with many other animal species, including those most nearly related to it, we naturally ask whether it may have a similar origin in all these cases. May we suppose that the more or less durable union between man and woman and the care which the man takes of the woman and their common offspring are due to instincts which were once necessary for the preservation of the human race? We found reasons to believe that the marital and paternal relations among the anthropoid apes are the results of instincts which are needed for the subsistence of the offspring, because their number is small, the period of infancy is long, and the kind of food on which the species lives and the quantity of it required prevent a gregarious mode of life. Now there can be no doubt whatever that in mankind, also, the number of children has always been comparatively very small and the period of infancy comparatively very long. We have, moreover, good reasons to believe that our earliest human or half-human ancestors subsisted on essentially the same diet —chiefly but not exclusively vegetable—and required about the same quantities of food as the man-like apes. Is it not likely, then, that the same causes have produced the same results in either case? The objection will perhaps be raised that man, unlike the anthropoid apes, is now an extremely social animal and therefore, like other social animals, might easily have dispensed with those marital and paternal ties which for some reason or other exist, but could hardly have been needed for the subsistence of the species. But this objection loses its force when we consider the social conditions of savages who know neither cattle-rearing nor agriculture—unless perhaps of the most primitive kind—and exclusively or almost exclusively subsist on what nature directly gives them —game, fish, fruit, roots, and so forth.

From a careful examination of available facts it appears that among such savages in different parts of the world the family consisting of parents and children is a very well-marked unit. It is certainly not the only association among them; if travellers speak of the family tie as the only one which joins individuals with one another, they without doubt use the term "family" in a wider sense. Closely related families not only hold friendly relations with each other, but live together in smaller or larger groups; and there may be social organisations of a more comprehensive character, as among the Australian natives. At the same time, it is repeatedly stated that the families belonging to the same group do not always keep together, but often disperse in search of food, and may remain separated even for a considerable time; and this is the case not only in desolate regions where the supply of food is unusually scarce, but even in countries highly favoured by nature. Now I ask: is it reasonable to suppose that primitive men were more permanently gregarious than many modern savages? The answer must be: they were undoubtedly less. Let us remember that all savages now existing stand high above our earliest human ancestors. Man, as we know him, has—to quote Darwin—"invented and is able to use various weapons, tools, traps, etc., with which he defends himself, kills or catches prey, and otherwise obtains food. He has made rafts or canoes for fishing or crossing over to neighbouring fertile islands. He has discovered the art of making fire, by which hard and stringy roots can be rendered digestible, and poisonous roots or herbs innocuous." In short, he has gradually found out many new ways of earning his living which his ruder ancestors had no idea of, and has thus more and more emancipated himself from direct dependence on surrounding nature. If this notwithstanding there are still so many savage peoples among whom the separate families often are compelled to give up the protection afforded them by living together, in order to find the food necessary for their subsistence, I think we have reason to believe that the family, implying marital and paternal care, was hardly less indispensable for primitive man than it is for the gorilla and chimpanzee. If this was the case, the family may have been an inheritance from the parent species out of which the Anthropoids and the Hominides gradually developed. It may be supposed to have been so if that hypothetical species lived on the same diet as the man-like apes, or even on a diet somewhat more animal than that of the chimpanzee, and also, being of a comparatively large size, required about the same quantities of food as they; if, further, it gave birth to the same small number of young; and if its offspring were in need of parental care for a comparatively long period. I want to emphasize that it is on such factors, and not merely on the habits of the gorilla and the chimpanzee as they are, that I base my supposition that the family consisting of parents and children existed among primitive men.

I have so far spoken of habits, not of institutions.

But there is an intimate connection between them. Social habits have a strong tendency to become true customs, that is, rules of conduct in addition to their being habits. A habit may develop into a genuine custom simply because men are inclined to disapprove of anything which is unusual. But in the present case the transition from habit to custom has undoubtedly a deeper foundation. It is an instinct that induces the male to remain with the female and to take care of her even after the sexual relations have ceased. We may assume that the tendency to feel some attachment to a being who has been the cause of pleasure, in the present case sexual pleasure, is at the bottom of this instinct. Such a feeling may originally have caused the sexes to remain united and the male to protect the female though the sexual desire was gratified; and if procuring great advantage to the species in the struggle for existence, conjugal attachment would naturally develop into a specific characteristic. An instinct must also be the cause of the care which the father takes of his offspring; the paternal feeling seems to be hardly less prevalent among savages than among civilized men. This feeling, however, and also the kindred feeling of maternal love are not quite adequately defined as the affection which attaches a creature to its young. Though most frequently and most strongly displayed in this relation, the so-called parental feeling is really excitable apart from parenthood, as Spencer justly observed. According to him, the common trait of the objects which arouse it is always relative weakness or helplessness. But this explanation contains only part of the truth; even in a gregarious species mothers make a distinction between their own offspring and other young. To account for the maternal sentiment we must therefore assume the existence of some other stimulus besides the signs of helplessness, which produces, or at least strengthens, the instinctive motor response in the mother. This stimulus, so far as I can see, is rooted in the external relationship in which the helpless offspring from the beginning stand to the mother, being in close proximity to her from their tenderest age. And the stimuli to which the paternal instinct responds are apparently derived from the same circumstances as those which call into activity the maternal instinct, that is, the helplessness and the nearness of the young. Wherever this instinct exists the father is near his offspring from the beginning, living together with the mother. Of course I here speak of the parental feelings only in their original simplicity; later on they become more complex, through the association of other feelings, as those of property and pride, and tend to extend themselves beyond the limits of infancy and childhood.

In mankind these instincts give rise not only to habits, but to rules of custom or institutions. Social beings endowed with such instincts, as also with a sufficiently developed intellect, would feel moral resentment against a man who forsakes the woman with whom he has conjugal intercourse and the offspring resulting from it. And, as I have observed in another work, public or moral resentment or disapproval is at the bottom of the rules of custom and of all duties and rights.[1]

From what has been said above it appears that

[1] *The Origin and Development of the Moral Ideas.*

marriage and the family are most intimately connected with one another: it is originally for the benefit of the young that male and female continue to live together. Indeed, among many peoples true married life does not begin for persons who are formally married or betrothed, or a marriage does not become definite, until a child is born or there are signs of pregnancy; while in other cases, as already pointed out, sexual relations which happen to lead to pregnancy or the birth of a child are, as a rule, followed by marriage or make marriage compulsory. We may truly say that marriage is rooted in the family rather than the family in marriage.

CHAPTER II

THE FREQUENCY OF MARRIAGE AND THE MARRIAGE AGE

AMONG the uncivilised races of men marriage not only exists, but is much more frequent than among ourselves. As a general rule nearly every man endeavours to marry when he has reached the age of puberty—if he has not been betrothed before—and practically every woman gets married. Among some savages priests or magicians have to remain single; and there are inverts, male and female, who avoid sexual intercourse with the opposite sex. Very frequently we are told that a person who does not marry is looked upon as an unnatural being or is an object of contempt or ridicule. Among the Santals in Bengal a man who remains single "is at once despised by both sexes, and is classed next to a thief, or a witch; they term the unhappy wretch 'No man.'" Among the Kafirs a bachelor has no voice in the kraal. The Kachins of Burma perform derisory funeral rites on the death of bachelors and old maids. According to Fijian beliefs, he who died wifeless was stopped by the god Nanggananggga on the road to Paradise and smashed to atoms.

The frequency of marriage depends, of course, largely on the age when people generally marry. Although in the latter respect, as well as in the former, statistical data are entirely lacking so far as savages are concerned, I think we may safely say that among all of them the girls marry at an earlier age than among the peoples of Western civilisation, and the same is probably in most cases true of the men. Early marriage must frequently seem almost indispensable to a man. Among many uncivilised peoples he cannot easily, or cannot at all, gratify his sexual desire but in the married state or in relations which normally lead to marriage; and even where he can freely indulge in extra-matrimonial intercourse, marriage will before long become a necessity for him. He must have a female companion who takes care of his house: she procures wood and water, lights and attends to the fire, prepares the food, dresses skins, makes clothes, gathers roots and berries, and among agricultural peoples very frequently cultivates the soil. He must have a woman who bears to him children, and nurses and looks after them; for a man without offspring is an unfortunate being under savage conditions of life, where safety and welfare depend upon family ties and the old have to be supported by the young. The childless man may even have to suffer after his death for lack of offspring. The Eskimo about Bering Strait "appear to have great dread of dying without being assured that their shades will be remembered during the festivals, fearing if neglected that they would thereby suffer destitution in the future life"; and among the Bagesu of British East Africa marriage is said to be "a matter of expediency rather than love, because children are the means of assisting the ghost after death."

The young savage will also find little difficulty in supporting a family. It has been said, with special reference to some aboriginal tribes in Farther India, that "where a youth of activity has equal means with the older persons of the tribe of subsisting himself by the chase or by fishing, he finds nothing to prevent his marrying early," and that "he soon perceives it to be his real interest to enter into that state"; and something similar may be said of pastoral and agricultural tribes. Far from being a burden to a man, wife and children are frequently a source of prosperity. In his description of some Indians of Canada, Heriot observes that children form the wealth of savage tribes.

There are, however, even in savage life circumstances which may compel persons to live unmarried for a longer or shorter time. When the wife has to be bought, it may be difficult for a young man to provide the necessary price to be paid for her. In fact, of many simple peoples we are told that the necessity of paying a bride price is a more or less frequent obstacle to early marriages or even a cause of lasting celibacy. But we must not exaggerate the importance of this obstacle. When a young man is not able to buy a wife for himself, he may in many cases acquire her by working for some time with her parents or by eloping with her. Moreover, as Lord Avebury justly remarks, the price of a wife is generally regulated by the circumstances of the tribe, so that nearly every industrious young man is enabled to get one.

A poor man may find it particularly difficult, if not impossible, to procure a wife where the males outnumber the females, as is the case in many savage communities. When such a disproportion between the sexes is combined with the practice of polyandry it need not, of course, lead to celibacy among the men, but when it occurs among a non-polyandrous people there must inevitably be a certain number of men who are unable to marry. This must, for instance, be the case in many of the South Sea Islands, where there is often a striking excess of males over females. Among the Australian aborigines there are likewise, as a rule, more males than females, the old men appropriate to themselves a plurality of women, especially young ones, and in consequence the younger men have generally to wait a long time until they can marry.

Polygny, in connection with an unequal distribution of property, is very frequently reported to cause celibacy among the poorer and younger men. Among the Boloki on the Upper Congo, says Mr. Weeks, "there was a constant complaint amongst the young and vigorous men of the middle and lower orders that it was almost impossible for them to procure wives. Thus we found a small number of men possessing nearly all the women in a town, having from four or five up to twenty-five and thirty each, and a large number of young men who could not secure wives." So also among the maritime tribes of Southern Guinea, where polygny flourishes, "a very large proportion of the younger male members of society have no wives." Among the Kutchin Indians, according to Hardisty, there are but few young men who have wives—unless they can content themselves with some old cast-off widow—on account of all the chiefs, medicine-men, and those who possess rank acquired by property having two, three or more wives. Polygyny may be a cause of male celibacy even where there are many more females than males. Dr. Felkin states that among the Baganda, owing to the frequency of polygyny, a large number of the poorer men were unable to marry although the proportion of females to males was as 3½ to 1. On the other hand it must not be supposed that, wherever polygyny occurs, it necessarily or even generally leads to compulsory celibacy for a considerable number of men. Among most peoples practising polygyny it is restricted to a small minority of the population, and very often it is combined with a surplus of females, which makes it possible for practically every man to procure a wife although there are some who have more than one. Among the polygynous Waguha of Lake Tanganyika, for example, as I am informed by Mr. A. J. Swann, unmarried grown-up men do not exist, the females being more numerous than the males. It should also be noticed that polygyny could hardly have been a potent cause of celibacy at the lowest stages of civilisation, where it was little practised; nor is it likely that men had to remain unmarried on account of poverty in those primitive conditions where there was no accumulated property worth speaking of.

While polygyny may lead to celibacy among the men, its effect upon the women is exactly opposite. As Junod observes in his description of the life of a South African tribe, "every girl finds a husband in the land where polygamy flourishes." And it seems that in countries unaffected by European civilisation polygyny is practised whenever the women are in the majority; hence the almost complete absence of old spinsters among savage races. For it must not be supposed that polyandry in some countries leads to that which polygyny prevents in others. Apart from the fact that among peoples practising polyandry the males are, often at least, more numerous than the females, it is among many of them quite an exceptional form of marriage; and in no case is it known to be the exclusive form, monogamy, polygyny, and sometimes group-marriage being practised side by side with it.

The difficulties experienced by the men in procuring wives, or young wives, may be one cause of the practice of infant- or child-betrothal, which is widely spread among the simpler peoples. Its apparently universal prevalence among the Australian aborigines is no doubt connected with the great demand for women in their tribes. To acquire a girl in her childhood may also be a matter of economy, as a little girl may be bought cheaper than an older one. The child-betrothal may further be a means of preserving the virginity of the girl, which among many peoples is a highly valued quality in a bride. Finally, very frequent motives for such betrothals are the wishes of two families to be drawn together or to cement and perpetuate their friendship, and a desire to become connected with a family of importance. In many cases they are said to be particularly prevalent among people of consequence or wealth or among chiefs, and may thus be alliances of political moment.

Among many simple peoples younger sons or daughters, or both younger sons and daughters, must not marry before the elder ones as long as there is a chance of the latter getting married; or it is at any rate considered improper for them to do so. Such customs are also found in China, where children are married according to seniority, and among Semitic and Aryan peoples. We read in Genesis: "Laban said, It must not be so done in our country, to give the younger before the firstborn." Among the Vedic people it was considered proper that the younger brothers and sisters should not anticipate their elders by marrying before them; and in the ancient law-books of India a transgression of this rule is punished with damnation or, at any rate, has to be atoned for by the performance of a penance. In modern Greece it is held wrong for the sons to marry until all the daughters have been disposed of, and the latter must marry in order of seniority. In Ireland it was like-wise usual that girls should be married in order of age, beginning with the eldest; and reminiscences of the same rule survive in English, Welsh, and Scotch marriage ceremonies. Brand quotes a statement to the effect that "if the youngest daughter in a family should chance to be married before her elder sisters, they must all dance at her wedding without shoes. This, it is held, will counteract their ill-luck, and procure them husbands." The same custom, which is also alluded to in Shakespeare's *Taming of the Shrew,* is still observed or remembered in Shropshire and the north of England. In the neighbourhood of Balmoral, when a younger sister marries before the elder, the latter is forcibly made to wear green garters at the wedding, and any young man who takes them off is destined to be her future husband. It is obvious that these customs are ultimately based on the idea that men and women should marry as soon as they arrive at the proper age, and that it is un-natural for an elder brother or sister to remain unmarried when a younger one becomes marriageable.

Among peoples of archaic culture, as among most uncivilised races, celibacy is a great exception and marriage is regarded as a duty. "Almost all Chinese," says Dr. Gray, "robust or infirm, well-formed or deformed, are called upon by their parents to marry as soon as they have attained the age of puberty. Were a grown-up son or daughter to die unmarried, the parents would regard it as most deplorable." Hence a young man of marriageable age, whom consumption or any other lingering disease had marked for its own, would be compelled by his parents or guardians to marry at once. So indispensable is marriage considered by the Chinese that even the dead are married, the spirits of all males who died in infancy or in boyhood being in due time married to the spirits of females who have been cut off at a like early age. To die without leaving a son to perpetuate the family cult is considered one of the greatest misfortunes that could befall a man, and at the same time an offence against the whole line of ancestors. For it would doom father, mother, and all the ancestry in the Nether-world to a pitiable existence without descendants enough to serve them properly, to worship at the ancestral tombs, to take care of the ancestral tablets, and duly to perform all rites and ceremonies connected with the dead. According to Confucius no crime is greater than filial impiety; and Mencius said that "there are three things which are unfilial, and to have no posterity is the greatest of them." Consequently there can be no greater crime that a man can commit than to remain single. And if his wife has reached her fortieth year without bringing him a son, it is an imperative duty for him to take a concubine.

The doctrine of the Chinese moralists on marriage was also taught in Japan for more than a thousand years. The consequence of it was that, although celibacy was not positively forbidden by law, it was denounced by public opinion; indeed, according to Professor Hozumi, the obligation to marry was so effectively insisted upon by the latter that there was no need of enforcing it by legislation. But he adds that the customary prohibition of celibacy only extended to the present or future head of a family. As to the other members of it, on the contrary, celibacy was, as a rule, obligatory. Before the Restoration of 1868 only the house-head, his eldest son, who was the presumptive heir, and his eldest grandson, who would become the presumptive heir after the eldest son, were allowed—or obliged—to marry, but younger sons could not lawfully contract marriage. There was no need for the latter to marry and have children, because they had no apparent hope of ever becoming house-heads and continuators of the cult. This rule was strictly followed among the *samurai,* or military class; for permission was not given by their feudal lords for the marriage of younger sons.

Among the Semites we meet with the idea that a dead man who has no children will miss something in Shĕol through not receiving that kind of worship which ancestors in early times appear to have received.

The Hebrews looked upon marriage as a religious duty. According to the Shūlhān 'Ārūkh, the recognised Jewish code, he who abstains from marrying is guilty of bloodshed, diminishes the image of God, and causes the divine presence to withdraw from Israel; hence a single man past twenty may be compelled by the court to take a wife. The Mishna regards eighteen as the normal age of marriage for a man, while girls were treated as marriageable from the beginning of their thirteenth year, when they attained their majority. But at various times very youthful marriages have prevailed among the Jews: by the thirteenth century a large proportion of Jewish girls were married during their minority, and in the second half of the seventeenth century the bridegroom was frequently not more than ten years old and the bride was younger still.

Although Islam considers marriage a civil contract, it enjoins it as a religious duty "incumbent on all who possess the ability." "When a servant of God marries, verily he perfects half his religion." It is related in the Traditions that the Prophet once asked a man if he was married, and being answered in the negative, said, "Art thou sound and healthy?" When the man replied that he was, the Prophet said, "Then thou art one of the brothers of the devil." In Morocco I was told that a married man is blessed in this life and goes to Paradise after death, whereas a grown-up man who dies a bachelor does not find the road to Paradise, but will rise again with the devil. In Muhammadan countries it is certainly considered improper and even disreputable for a man to abstain from marrying when he has attained a sufficient age and when there is no just impediment; and, as Niebuhr remarked, "nothing is more rarely to be met with in the East than a woman unmarried after a certain time of life."

The so-called Aryan nations in ancient times, as Fustel de Coulanges and others have pointed out, regarded celibacy as an impiety and a misfortune: "an impiety, because one who did not marry put the happiness of the manes of the family in peril; a misfortune, because he himself would receive no worship after his death." A man's happiness in the next world depended upon his having a continuous line of male descendants, whose duty it would be to make the periodical offerings for the repose of his soul. It was no doubt possible to adopt a son; but in the Rig-Veda at least that custom is plainly viewed as unsatisfactory. The old idea still survives in India: "a Hindu man must marry and beget children to perform his funeral rites, lest his spirit wander uneasily in the waste places of the earth." Marriage is a duty which every parent must perform for his children; otherwise they owe him no reverence. But although a man who is unmarried is looked upon as an almost useless member of the community and, indeed, as beyond the pale of nature, he does not disgrace his family. On the other hand, there is no greater reproach for a high-class Hindu than to have a daughter unmarried at the age of puberty. A family with such a daughter is supposed to labour under the displeasure of the gods; on a strict rendering of certain texts her unmarried state entails retrospective damnation on three generations of ancestors. Of the unmarried girls in India in general only one in every

fourteen has turned her fifteenth year, and of the
bachelors only one in twenty-four is over thirty;
and among the Hindus marriage is contracted at an
earlier age than in the population as a whole. At
the higher ages practically no one is left unmarried,
except persons suffering from some infirmity or dis-
figurement, beggars, prostitutes, concubines, religious
devotees and mendicants, and a few members of certain hypergamous groups who have been unable to
effect alliances of the kind which alone are permitted
to them by the rules of their community.

A considerable number of Hindus of both sexes
are married in their infancy, though it should be
noticed that the Hindu child-marriage does not as
a rule imply immediate cohabitation. These early
betrothals may be due to various causes, suggested
by different writers, but it appears that the most
potent of them, at all events, are the dread of future
celibacy and the preference given to virgin brides—
causes which have led to the same result in many
other parts of the world. In no case can they be
regarded as survivals of a primitive custom, either
Dravidian or Aryan; for most of the Dravidian tribes
have adult marriage, while in the early Vedic texts
marriage appears essentially as a union of two persons
of full development and child-wives first occur regularly in the Sūtra period. Many of the Indian law-
books fix a definite age for the marriage of girls;
and the later the treatise, the earlier the age which
it prescribes.

In the Zoroastrian books, as in the sacred books of
India, we meet with the idea that a man should marry
and get progeny. Ahura Mazda said to Zoroaster:

"The man who has a wife is far above him who lives in continence; he who keeps a house is far above him who has none; he who has children is far above the childless man." The greatest misfortune which could befall an ancient Persian was to be childless. To him who has no child the bridge of Paradise shall be barred; the first question the angels there will ask him is, whether he has left in this world a substitute for himself, and if the answer be "No" they will pass by and he will stay at the head of the bridge, full of grief. The primitive meaning of this is plain: the man without a son cannot enter Paradise because there is nobody to pay him the family worship. And in the eyes of all good Parsees of the present day, as in the time of King Darius and the contemporaries of Herodotus, the two greatest merits of a citizen are the begetting and rearing of a numerous family, and the fruitful tilling of the soil.

The ancient Greeks regarded marriage as a matter both of public and of private importance. In various places criminal proceedings might be taken against celibates. Plato remarks that every individual is bound to provide for a continuance of representatives to succeed himself as ministers of the Divinity; and Isæus says, "All those who think their end approaching look forward with a prudent care that their houses may not become desolate, but that there may be some person to attend to their funeral rites and to perform the legal ceremonies at their tombs." So also the conviction that the founding of a house and the begetting of children constituted a moral necessity and a public duty had a deep hold of the Roman mind in early times. Cicero's treatise *De Legibus*—

which generally reproduces in a philosophical form the ancient laws of Rome—contains a law according to which the Censors had to impose a tax upon unmarried men. But in later periods, when sexual morality reached a very low ebb in Rome, celibacy naturally increased in proportion, especially among the upper classes. Among these marriage came to be regarded as a burden which people took upon themselves at the best in the public interest. Indeed, how it fared with marriage and the rearing of children is shown by the Gracchan agrarian laws, which first placed a premium thereon; and later the *Lex Julia et Papia Poppæa* imposed various penalties on those who lived in a state of celibacy after a certain age, though with little or no result. According to the later Roman law a man could marry from the age of fourteen and a woman from the age of twelve.

A view of marriage which greatly differed from that generally held by the ancient peoples of culture was taken by a small class of Hebrews, who looked upon marriage as impure. The Essenes, says Josephus, "reject pleasure as an evil, but esteem continence and the conquest over our passions to be virtue. They neglect wedlock." This doctrine exercised no influence on Judaism, but perhaps much upon Christianity. St. Paul considered celibacy to be preferable to marriage. "He that giveth her (his virgin) in marriage doeth well; but he that giveth her not in marriage doeth better." "It is good for a man not to touch a woman. Nevertheless, to avoid fornication, let each man have his own wife, and let each woman have her own husband." If the unmarried and widows cannot contain let them marry, "for it is better to marry than to burn." These and other passages in the New Testament inspired a general enthusiasm for virginity. Commenting on the words of the Apostle, Tertullian points out that what is better is not necessarily good. It is better to lose one eye than two, but neither is good; so also, though it is better to marry than to burn, it is far better neither to marry nor to burn. Marriage "consists of that which is the essence of fornication"; whereas continence "is a means whereby a man will traffic in a mighty substance of sanctity." The body which our Lord wore and in which He carried on the conflict of life in this world He put on from a holy virgin; and John the Baptist, Paul, and all the others "whose names are in the book of life" cherished and loved virginity. Virginity works miracles: Mary, the sister of Moses, leading the female band, passed on foot over the straits of the sea, and by the same grace Thecla was reverenced even by lions, so that the unfed beasts, lying at the feet of their prey, underwent a holy fast, neither with wanton look nor with sharp claw venturing to harm the virgin. Virginity is like a spring flower, always softly exhaling immortality from its white petals. The Lord Himself opens the kingdoms of the heavens to eunuchs. If Adam had preserved his obedience to the Creator he would have lived for ever in a state of virgin purity, and some harmless mode of vegetation would have peopled Paradise with a race of innocent and immortal beings.[1]

[1] This opinion was held by Gregory of Nyssa and, in a later time, by John of Damascus. It was opposed by Thomas Aquinas, who maintained that the human race was from the beginning propagated by means of sexual intercourse, but that such intercourse was free from all carnal desire.

It is true that, though virginity is the shortest way to the camp of the faithful, the way of matrimony also arrives there, by a longer circuit. Tertullian himself opposed the Marcionites, who prohibited marriage among themselves and compelled those who were married to separate before they were received by baptism into the community; and in the earlier part of the fourth century the Council of Gangra expressly condemned anyone who maintained that marriage prevented a Christian from entering the kingdom of God. But at the end of the same century a council also excommunicated the monk Jovinian because he denied that virginity was more meritorious than marriage. The use of marriage was permitted to man only as a necessary expedient for the continuance of the human race and as a restraint, however imperfect, on the natural licentiousness of desire. The procreation of children is the measure of a Christian's indulgence in appetite, just as the husbandman sowing the seed into the ground awaits the harvest, not sowing more upon it. These opinions led by degrees to the obligatory celibacy of the secular and regular clergy.

The laws of all Christian countries fix the lowest ages at which marriage is allowed for males and females. The stipulation of the Roman law, according to which a man may marry at the age of fourteen and a woman at the age of twelve, was adopted by the Church, and is, under the influence of Canon law, still preserved in various countries; but the general tendency of the later legislation has been to raise the age-limit, which may even be as high as twenty-one years for men and eighteen for women. In many countries, however, where the canonic age-limit has not been preserved, the obstacle to marrying at an earlier age than that which the law admits may be removed by dispensation. Besides the limit below which marriage is prohibited there is frequently another higher one below which a marriage can be contracted only with the consent of parents, guardians, or other persons having control of the parties.

As to the age at which people actually marry, and the frequency of marriage, in Europe, it may be generally said that modern civilisation has proved unfavourable to the latter and has raised the average age at which marriages are concluded. In Europe more than a third of the male and female population beyond the age of fifteen live in a state of voluntary or involuntary celibacy; and among them there are many who never marry. The marriage rate varies greatly in different European countries, as appears from the following figures, which give the annual number of marriages per 10,000 marriageable persons, that is, males eighteen years of age or over and females fifteen years or over who are either single, widowed, or divorced. Nearly all of these figures refer to periods which were uninfluenced by the particular circumstances connected with the Great War. The number of marriages was in Serbia (1896–1905) 1,386, in Bulgaria (1910–11) 1,223, in Russia—not including Finland and Poland—(1896–7) 921, in Rumania (1896–1903) 873, in Hungary (1906–15) 778, in Germany (1907–14) 569, in France (1910–11) 539, in Austria (1908–13) 536, in England and Wales (1907–14) 507, in Norway (the same period) 418, in Scotland (the same period) 411, in Finland (1906–15) 398, in Sweden (1908–13) 367, in Iceland (1906–15) 335, and in Ireland (1909–12) 254. The average age of the bachelors and the spinsters who enter into matrimony was in Serbia (1896–1900) 21.8 and 19.7 respectively, in Italy (1911–14) 27.2 and 23.6, in Germany (the same period) 27.4 and 24.7, in England (1906–14) 27.4 and 25.7, in Scotland (the same period) 27.8 and 25.8, in France (1906–10) 28.0 and 23.7, and in Sweden (1906–13) 28.8 and 26.4.

In recent times the proportion of unmarried people is known to have increased in various European countries and the marriage age to have risen. In England and Wales the annual number of marriages per 10,000 marriageable persons was, in 1876–85, 568; in 1886–95, 529; in 1896–1905, 531; in 1907–14, as already said, 507; but in 1911–14, a little higher than in 1906–10. The average age of bachelor-bridegrooms and of spinster-brides was, in 1876–85, 25.9 and 24.4 respectively; in 1886–95, 26.4 and 24.9; in 1896–1905, 26.8 and 25.3; in 1906–10, 27.2 and 25.6. The tendency towards increasing age at marriage in England may also be demonstrated by taking the percentages of marriages contracted at ages under twenty-five. These were, in 1896–1900, 48.2 for bachelors and 64.4 for spinsters; in 1901–5, 45.4 and 61.6 respectively; in 1906–10, 42.5 and 59.1; and in 1911–15, 40.4 and 56.9.

A very important cause of the decline of the marriage rate and the rise of the age for marriage in Europe is the difficulty of supporting a family in modern society. The importance of the economic factor has been much emphasised by statisticians. From the days of Süssmilch till the middle of the last century it was regarded almost as a statistical axiom that the number of marriages varies inversely with the price of corn. In Germany this tendency of the number of marriages to decrease when the price of rye was high and to increase when the price was low was observed until about 1860; but since then Germany has become so industrial and commercial that the price of food is only one element in the economic well-being of the masses. In the English records, at any rate so far back as 1820, no such relation is noticeable between the number of marriages and the price of corn; on the contrary, the marriage rate has often been found to vary not inversely but directly with the price of wheat. In explanation of this fact Dr. Ogle points out that increased exports and imports put up freights and thus increase the price of corn, while at the same time men marry in greater numbers when trade is brisk and the value of exports increases; the amount of exports gauges the opportunity for employment, and is therefore an index of economic prosperity. But the correspondence between the marriage rate and the general prosperity of the country, as indicated by the course of trade, is certainly not absolute: the curves show, in fact, that it is only the oscillations which are correlated. At the beginning of the present century Hooker observed that over the preceding forty years as a whole the trade curve had risen in England, whereas the marriage rate had fallen. So also Hermann's formula that "the number of marriages in any period expresses the expectation of economic prosperity prevailing at that time" has only a relative value.

That in spite of the general economic progress people have become more and more unwilling to venture upon marriage is no doubt to some extent due to the ever-increasing standard of comfort among all classes, which has led either to a retardation or to an abandonment of marriages. In this respect there is a difference between different social classes. Professor Fahlbeck has found that among the Swedish nobility 43.17 per cent. of the marriageable men and 46.15 of the marriageable women are unmarried, while the figures for the whole population of Sweden are only 31.42 and 31.54 respectively; and the number of unmarried persons has greatly increased in recent times. Generally speaking, the average age for marriage is more advanced among the upper classes than among the lower ones. A "gentleman" before marrying thinks it necessary to have an income of which a mere fraction would suffice for a married workman. He has to offer his wife a home in accordance with her social position and his own; and unless she brings him some fortune, she contributes but little to the support of the family. Moreover, from the economic point of view there is hardly any reason to put off marrying for men who earn in youth almost as much as in later life, as is the case with miners, tailors, shoemakers, artisans, and others, who have been found to marry earlier than men of the professional class. It may also be said that a man requires more time to gain his living by intellectual than by material work.

When we consider the differences in the marriage

rate and the age for marriage in the different countries of Europe, we notice that the tendency to marry is greatest in the east of Europe with its more primitive civilisation. In Russia there is an extraordinarily large number of bridegrooms under the age of twenty, and more than one-half of the brides are under that age; and the reason for this is that an enormous proportion of the population consists of small agriculturists, who are in the habit of arranging for the marriage of their sons at as early an age as possible in order to secure an additional female labourer. The exceptionally low marriage rate in Northern Europe is, partly at least, due to emigration. And the emigration of young men and women is undoubtedly the cause of Ireland having a lower marriage rate than any other country in Europe.

An economic cause of the declining tendency to marry which still remains to be mentioned is the increasing economic independence of women. At the lower stages of civilisation a woman is a helpless being who depends on the support of a man, whereas modern civilisation provides her with means of earning her living by her own efforts alone. But besides factors of an economic character there are others, equally important, which have made men and women less inclined to enter into matrimony.

A modern writer justly points out that "by the general diffusion of education and culture, by the new inventions and discoveries of the age, by the increase of commerce and intercourse and wealth, the tastes of men and women have become widened, their desires multiplied, new gratifications and pleasures have been supplied to them. By this increase of the gratifications of existence the relative share of them which married life affords has become just so much less. The domestic circle does not fill so large a place in life as formerly. It is really less important to either man or woman. Married life has lost in some measure its advantages over a single life. There are so many pleasures, now, that can be enjoyed as well or even better in celibacy." Moreover, "by the diffusion of a finer culture throughout the community, men and women can less easily find anyone whom they are willing to take as a partner for life; their requirements are more exacting; their standards of excellence higher; they are less able to find any who can justify their own ideal, and less able to satisfy anybody else's ideal."

The marriage and divorce laws of Christian countries are also responsible for a certain number of persons remaining celibates. We may assume that if the union could be more easily dissolved it would be more readily entered into. And the law of monogamy is necessarily a cause of celibacy where the adult women outnumber the adult men. If we reckon the age for marriage from twenty to fifty years, a hundred men may in Europe choose amongst a hundred and three or four women, so that about three or four women per cent. are in normal circumstances doomed to a single life on account of our obligatory monogamy.

CHAPTER III

ENDOGAMY

SOCIETY regulates marriage in various ways. First, it lays down certain rules relating to the choice of partner. There are endogamous rules, which forbid the members of a particular group to marry anyone who is *not* a member of the group, and exogamous rules, which forbid the members of a particular group to marry anyone who *is* a member of the group. These two sets of rules are by no means contradictory, in so far as they refer to different groups. Hence endogamy and exogamy occur side by side with each other among the same people. Indeed there is everywhere an outer circle—to use Sir Henry Maine's convenient expression—out of which marriage is either definitely prohibited or considered improper, and an inner circle within which no marriage is allowed.

We hear of many races that refrain from, disapprove of, or actually prohibit marriages, or sexual relations generally, with persons belonging to another race. Mr. Powers speaks of some Californian Indians who would put to death a woman for committing adultery with or marrying a white man. At various times Spaniards in Central America, Englishmen in Mauritius, Frenchmen in Réunion and the Antilles, and Danish traders in Greenland have been prevented by law from marrying natives. The Romans were prohibited from marrying barbarians. We may say that probably every race considers it a disgrace, if not a crime, to marry within a race very different from its own, at least if it be an inferior one. This feeling is particularly strong with regard to its women. As a matter of fact, in the crosses between unequal human races the father in the vast majority of instances belongs to the superior race. "Woman," says M. de Quatrefages, "refuses to lower herself; man is less delicate." In North America, for example, the cases in which white women have married coloured men are very rare, and in the Southern States such marriages are prohibited not only by custom but often even by law; hence the enormous infusion of white blood into the black race is almost exclusively due to intercourse between white men and negresses.

Racial endogamy is no doubt chiefly due to racial or national pride and lack of sympathy with, or positive antipathy to, individuals of another race; and for this reason it is particularly common in the case of races that greatly differ from each other in ideas, habits, and civilisation generally. But at the same time I believe that some sexual aversion akin to the instinctive feeling which deters animals of distinct species from pairing with each other is in many cases really felt against sexual intercourse with persons of a race having a very different appearance, and that such aversion is particularly common in women, whose sexual instinct is generally more discriminating than that of men. This, however, would not prove that mankind consists of several species; certain races of domestic or semi-domesticated animals also refuse to mingle with each other. It seems that the instinctive aversion which owes its origin to the physiological law of similarity, according to which a certain similarity between the mating gametes is necessary for reproduction or at least for a normal reproduction, may in some degree also make itself felt in relations between members of the same species who are very different from each other. It may do so even in cases where the law in question does not act and intercrossing is not accompanied with lessened fertility; but the rule that different varieties or races of the same animal or vegetable species are prolific when crossed is not a rule which is altogether without exceptions.

Among many peoples marriage very seldom or never takes place even outside the tribe or some smaller division of it, as the clan or village. Of the Oráons in Bengal we are told that "anyone marrying out of the tribe would be at once ejected from it, and could not be readmitted before leaving his foreign wife." The Abors of Pádam in Assam view with abhorrence the idea of their girls marrying out of their own clan; and Colonel Dalton was gravely assured that "when one of the daughters of Pádam so demeans herself, the sun and the moon refuse to shine, and there is such a strife in the elements that all labour is necessarily suspended, till by sacrifice and oblation the stain is washed away." Concerning the ancient Semites, Professor Barton observes that, so far as their feeling on this point can be historically traced, it was in favour of endogamy, Semitic parents always being grieved if their children married outside their tribe. At Rome any marriage of a citizen with a woman who was not herself a Roman citizen or did not belong to a community possessing the privilege of *connubium* with

Rome—which was always expressly conferred—was invalid; but in early times it was even customary for a father to seek for his daughter a husband from his own *gens,* marriage out of it being mentioned as an extraordinary thing.

Where there is little intercourse between different tribes or subdivisions of tribes marriages between their members are naturally rare if not unknown. Habitual isolation, combined with antipathy felt against people with customs and manners and a language different from one's own, readily leads to disapproval or actual prohibition of intermarriage; and so does the desire of a tribe or clan not to part with any of its members. Where endogamy exists side by side with patrilocal marriage, a reason for it is undoubtedly reluctance on the part of the group to lose any of its women. Among the ancient Arabs marrying within the village served the purpose of strengthening the kinship tie. The Berbers of the Rīf in Morocco encourage marriages between members of the same family in order to keep away alien elements from the community, and therefore deny the right of inheritance to a woman who leaves her village. Moses ordered the daughters of Zelophehad to marry men of their father's tribe so that their inheritance should remain "in the tribe of the family of their father." But the reason given in Deuteronomy for the prohibition of intermarriage with seven Canaanitish nations was a religious one: "They will turn away thy son from following me, that they may serve other gods."

The Mosaic prohibition of marriages between Israelites and Canaanites was, at any rate from Ezra onward, extended so as to include all the pagan nations of the country; and, in the spirit of Ezra's ordinance, later religious authorities in the time of the Maccabeans and in the time of the wars against the Romans interdicted matrimonial connections between Israelites and all Gentiles. This prohibition is the established law of the Talmud and the Rabbinical code; and although in the latter no special provision was made concerning intermarriage with Christians, these were actually included in the general prohibition of intermarriage with Gentiles. The great Jewish Synod convened by Napoleon in 1807 declared that marriages between Israelites and Christians are valid when contracted in accordance with the Civil code, and that they shall not entail any disciplinary punishment (anathema), "although such marriages cannot be invested with the religious forms," that is, be solemnised by the religious rites of Judaism. The Rabbinical Conference held at Braunschweig in 1844 went a step further by resolving that the intermarriage of Jews and Christians, and in general the intermarriage of Jews with adherents of any of the monotheistic religions, is not forbidden, provided that the parents are permitted by the law of the State to bring up the offspring in the Jewish faith. This decision, however, which decidedly abandoned the Talmudic standpoint, has been strongly criticised even by some of the most pronounced advocates of reformed Judaism. No section of Jewish opinion favours marriages between parties who are not of the same religion. In some European countries, such as Russia, marriages between Jews and Christians are still very rare. In Vienna there were, in 1898, 110 mixed marriages as against 847 purely Jewish marriages, while in Prague there were only 6 as against 354.

Marriages between Christians and Jews were also prohibited by the Christians—by Constantine and later emperors and by various Councils; and during the Middle Ages they were universally avoided. "The folk-lore of Europe," says Mr. Jacobs, "regarded the Jews as something infra-human, and it would require an almost impossible amount of large toleration for a Christian maiden of the Middle Ages to regard union with a Jew as anything other than unnatural." Indeed, owing to the intense Jewish hatred for the sacred name of Christ, the early Church was more opposed to wedlock with Jews than with pagans. Although St. Paul indicates that a Christian must not marry a heathen, and Tertullian calls such an alliance fornication, the Church, in early times, often even encouraged marriages of this sort as a means of propagating Christianity; and it was only when its success was beyond doubt that it actually prohibited them. When the *Decretum* of Gratian was published, in the twelfth century, the impediment *disparitas cultus* became part of the Canon law of the Church, and from that time forward all marriages contracted between Catholics and infidels were held to be invalid unless a dispensation from such marriages had been obtained from the ecclesiastical authority. Marriages between Catholics and heretics, on the other hand, were considered valid, though illicit, if a dispensation *mixtæ religionis* had not been obtained; but there had been much opposition to such unions from early times, and various Councils had legislated against them. The Council of Trent

declared all matrimonial unions between Catholics
and non-Catholics null and void, unless entered into
before the ecclesiastical authority; but by degrees
the Popes felt constrained to make various concessions
for mixed marriages. "The Church," says Taunton,
"has always abhorred these marriages both on account
of the danger of perversion and the difficulty of edu-
cating the offspring as well as on account of the *com-
municatio in sacris."* The Protestants also originally
forbade such marriages. But mixed marriages are
not now contrary to the civil law in either Roman
Catholic or Protestant countries. The case is different
in countries belonging to the Greek Church, where
the ecclesiastical restrictions have been adopted by
the State.

Islam has made religion a bar to intermarriage.
The Koran said in explicit terms, "Marry not a
woman of the Polytheists until she embraces Islam";
but it also declared that such women as are of chaste
reputation and belong to the Scriptural sects or
believe in a revealed or moral religion are lawful
to Moslems. From these and similar directions somewhat divergent conclusions have been drawn by Sunnī
and Shī'ah lawyers; but both schools prohibit a Moslem from marrying an idolatrous female, or one who
worships the stars or any kind of fetish whatsoever.
And in no circumstances is a Muhammadan woman
permitted to marry a man who is not a Moslem.

Among the Hindus religion even forbids the intermarriage of persons belonging to different castes.
Endogamy is the essence of the caste system. Nay,
not only must a Hindu refrain from marrying outside
the limits of his caste, but where, as is usually the case,

the caste is divided into sub-castes, he must ordinarily not marry outside his sub-caste, although he may sometimes marry in certain sub-castes but not in others; and there may be some sub-castes from whom he may take a girl in marriage but to whom he may not give one. Where a caste is divided into sections of different status, there may be hypergamy, or the rule whereby parents are obliged to marry their daughters into an equal or higher section, and if they fail to do so, are themselves reduced to the status of the section in which their daughter marries; whereas the men may marry girls of their own or any inferior section. Hypergamy prevails over a wide area at the present day, but is almost unknown in the south of India and in Assam. It is a modern form of a very ancient custom.

Class endogamy is found among a large number of peoples, savage and civilised, in different parts of the world. Among the Hovas of Madagascar the three great divisions—the nobles, the commoners, and the slaves—with few exceptions, could not intermarry; nor did the three different classes of slaves marry into one another. In Polynesia the commoners were looked upon by the nobility almost as a different species of beings; and in the higher ranks marriages between nobles and commoners were strongly opposed by the former. In Tahiti, if a woman of condition chose an inferior person as a husband, the children he had by her were killed. Among the Masai in East Africa the families of smiths are not allowed to marry into the families of persons who have another occupation. In Rome plebeians and patricians could not intermarry till the year 445 B.C., nor were marriages allowed between patricians and clients. Cicero himself disapproved of intermarriages of *ingenui* and freedmen, and although such alliances were generally permitted under the Emperors, a senator could not marry a freedwoman nor a patroness her liberated slave. Between freemen and slaves *contubernium* could take place, but not marriage. Among the Teutonic peoples any freeman who had intercourse with a slave was punished with slavery, and a woman guilty of such a crime might be killed. In the Scandinavian countries slavery came to an end at a comparatively early period, whilst in Germany it was succeeded by serfdom; and equality of birth continued to be regarded as an indispensable condition of lawful marriage. From the class of freemen, both in Germany and in Scandinavia, the nobility gradually emerged as a distinct order, and marriages between persons of noble birth and persons who, although free, were not noble came to be considered misalliances. In Sweden such marriages formerly entailed serious economic consequences. Even now there are traces of the former class endogamy in Europe. According to German Civil law, the marriage of a man belonging to the high nobility with a woman of inferior birth is still regarded as a *disparagium;* and the woman is not entitled to the rank of her husband, nor is the full right of inheritance possessed by her or by her children. But, as Sir Henry Maine remarks, the outer or endogamous limit within which a man or woman must marry has been mostly taken under the shelter of fashion or prejudice. "In France, in spite of all formal institutions, marriages between a person belonging to the *noblesse* and a person belonging to the *bourgeoisie* (distinguished roughly from one another by the particle 'de') are wonderfully rare, though they are not unknown."

In many cases class endogamy is evidently due to racial or national differences. Social differentiation may be the result of foreign conquest and subjugation, the conquerors becoming the nobility and the subjugated the commonalty or slaves. In England, before the Norman Conquest the aristocracy was Saxon; after it, Norman. The descendants of the German conquerors of Gaul were for a thousand years the dominant race in France, and until the fifteenth century all the higher nobility were of Frankish or Burgundian origin. Sir William Ridgeway suggests that the Roman patricians were originally a body of Sabines who had become masters of Rome, while the plebeians were the aboriginal Ligurians; and in Sparta there was an aristocracy of conquerors sharply distinguished from the subjugated Helots.

It has been argued that the Sanskrit word for caste, *varna,* which literally means "colour," indicates how the distinction of high and low caste arose in India. This word, which in the later literature is used in speaking of the four castes, is in the Rig-Veda applied to denote two classes of men, the Dāsa and the Aryan Varna, who are contrasted on account of their colour. India was inhabited by a dark people before the fairer Aryans took possession of it, entering from beyond the North-West frontier and bringing with them the Sanskrit language and the religious ideas which are expressed in the Vedas and Upanishads; and the domineering spirit of the conquerors, their bitter contempt for foreign tribes, and their strong antipathies of race and religion found vent in the sharp distinction which they drew between themselves and the conquered population, the Śūdras. Having at first too few women of their own, they were often obliged to take aboriginal girls as their wives; but later on, when this scarcity no longer existed, they closed their ranks to any further intermixture, and when they did this each group became a caste like those of the present day. It is said that even now caste largely corresponds to race, and that, in Northern India at least, the social status of a caste is indicated by its physical type, those at the top having Aryan and those at the bottom an aboriginal physiognomy. It is true that these views have not been universally accepted; according to some writers the origin of the caste system can be found only in community of function and occupation. But the theory of the ethnological basis of caste may be correct although social rank is nowadays closely connected with occupation. Racial differences would from the beginning have been accompanied with functional differences; for the conquerors would naturally have reserved for themselves the higher occupations, leaving the more primitive ones to the people of non-Aryan descent, the Śūdras.

As descendants of different ancestors, members of noble families tend to keep up their separate position and may remain almost as foreigners to the people among whom they live. Speculating on the want of sympathy between the various classes in societies where such distinctions are recognised, Count de Tocqueville observes: "Each caste has its own opinions, feelings, rights, manners, and modes of living. Thus, the men of whom each caste is composed do not resemble the mass of their fellow-citizens; they do not think or feel in the same manner, and they scarcely believe that they belong to the same human race. . . . When the chroniclers of the Middle Ages, who all belonged to the aristocracy by birth or education, relate the tragical end of a noble, their grief flows apace; whereas they tell you at a breath, and without wincing, of massacres and tortures inflicted on the common sort of people. Not that these writers felt habitual hatred or systematic disdain for the people; war between the several classes of the community was not yet declared. They were impelled by an instinct rather than by a passion; as they had formed no clear notion of a poor man's sufferings, they cared but little for his fate." It is to this exclusiveness, with all that it carries with it, that the prohibition of marriages out of the class, or the general avoidance of such marriages, owes its origin. Irregular connections outside the endogamous circle are often looked upon with less intolerance than marriage, which places the parties on a more equal footing. This is true not only in the case of class endogamy. A traveller relates that at Djidda, where sexual morality is held in little respect, a Bedouin woman may yield herself for money to a Turk or European, but would think herself for ever dishonoured if she were joined to him in lawful wedlock.

Modern civilisation tends more or less to lower or pull down the barriers which separate races, nations, the adherents of different religions, and the various classes of society. It has therefore made the endogamous rules less stringent and less restricted, it has widened the limit within which a man or woman may marry and generally marries. This process has been one of vast importance in man's history. Largely originating in race- or class-pride or in religious intolerance, the endogamous rules have in their turn helped to keep up and strengthen these feelings, whereas frequent intermarriages must have the very opposite effect.

CHAPTER IV

EXOGAMY

FROM the endogamous rules, which forbid the members of a particular group to marry anyone who is not a member of the group, we shall pass to the exogamous rules, which forbid the members of a particular group to marry any other member of it. The term "exogamy" is generally used for a prohibition of marrying inside a larger group than one merely consisting of members of the same family, particularly the clan; but neither in the etymology of the word nor in the nature of the prohibitions can I find any ground for such a restriction. On the contrary, it has the disadvantage of disassociating rules which intrinsically belong to the same class and, in my opinion, have the same foundation.

The exogamous group is in most cases composed of persons who are, or consider themselves to be, related by blood or of the same kin; and the nearer the relationship, the more frequently it is a bar to intermarriage, at least within the same line of descent. The most frequent of all exogamous rules are those which prohibit a son from marrying his mother and a father from marrying his daughter. These rules seem, in fact, to be universally prevalent in mankind. We hear, it is true, of "marriages" between parents and children among certain peoples. But in several of these cases they are expressly said to be disapproved of; and it is exceedingly doubtful whether such unions have ever been sanctioned by the customs of any people.

Hardly less universal is the exogamous rule which forbids marriages between brothers and sisters who are children of the same father and mother. Most of the reported exceptions to this rule are either obviously erroneous or of a more or less dubious character, if for no other reason, because it is uncertain whether they refer to full brothers and sisters or to such as have only one parent in common. The best authenticated cases of customary brother-and-sister marriage are generally found in the families of kings or ruling chiefs. The most definite statements relating to such marriages come from Hawaii. "A suitable partner for a chief of the highest rank," says Malo, "was his own sister, begotten by the same father and mother as himself. . . . Another suitable partner for a great chief was his half-sister, born, it might be, of the same mother but of a different father, or of the same father but of a different mother." Consanguineous marriages, however, were the special privilege of the chiefs; we are even told that in Hawaii "the fact that the first Christian teachers allowed marriage between cousins was a distinct stumbling-block when the new religion was introduced." Garcilasso de la Vega states that the Incas of Peru from the first established it as a very stringent law that the heir to the kingdom should marry his eldest sister, legitimate both on the side of the father and on that of the mother. But according to other authorities it had always been held unlawful by the Peruvians to contract marriage in the first degree until a certain

Inca at the close of the fifteenth century married his sister on the father's side, and decreed "that the Incas might marry with their sisters by the father's side, and no others." Nobody but the sovereign, however, was authorised to dispense with the law of nature so far as to marry his own sister. From ancient Egypt there is plenty of evidence that later Pharaohs married their sisters or half-sisters, and the Ptolemies followed the precedent of the Pharaohs. In the Roman age marriage of half-sisters or full sisters occurred frequently in the families of cultivators of the soil and artisans; but that such marriages were equally or even more prevalent in earlier periods in Egypt is a mere suggestion for which no evidence has been produced. Myths and legends of marriages between divine or human brothers and sisters are not uncommon among peoples who have never been known to allow or practise marriage between full brothers and sisters; but whatever be the origin of those stories, they can certainly not be taken as evidence of customs existing in the past.

Marriage with a half-sister is not infrequent, and it seems that in nearly all these cases the brother and sister have the same father. Instances of this are found both among savages and among ancient peoples of culture—such as the Japanese, Athenians, and Semites. Abraham married his half-sister Sarah, the daughter of his father; Tamar might have been legally married to her half-brother Amnon; and such unions were still known in Judah at the time of Ezekiel, although he condemned them as abominations. It has been asserted that where clan exogamy prevails a man is allowed to marry his sister either on the father's or on the mother's side, according as descent is traced through the mother or through the father; but this assertion is based on the erroneous supposition that exogamous rules depend exclusively upon the mode of tracing descent.

Among certain peoples or certain castes in India a man has a special right, or is even expected or obliged, to marry his sister's daughter, or his brother's daughter, or his father's sister, or his mother's sister; and among various other peoples such marriages are at any rate allowed. By Jewish law an uncle may marry his niece, though an aunt may not marry her nephew; but no such marriage would be performed by Jewish rites in England, because English law forbids marriage between uncle and niece. Unions of this kind, as also marriages between aunts and nephews, are, on the other hand, permitted by law in Germany, the State of New York, Peru, and Uruguay; whilst in various other countries, such as France, Italy, Belgium, Holland, and Sweden, the legal prohibition of them may be dispensed with.

Marriages between uncles and nieces and between aunts and nephews are prohibited in all those Christian countries in which cousins are forbidden to intermarry; but the reverse is by no means the case. On the contrary, the large majority of modern law-books which prohibit marriages of the two former kinds have no objection to marriages between cousins; and this is true even of the laws in such countries as Switzerland, England, and most of the North American States, where the prohibition to marry a niece or a nephew is absolute. Generally speaking, there can be little doubt that the relationships of uncle and

[69]

niece and of aunt and nephew are more frequent bars to intermarriage than the relationship of cousins. The latter are permitted to marry both by Jewish and by Muhammadan law. In Europe they are, or were until lately, prohibited from doing so in a few countries—under the influence of ecclesiastical law—notably, Russia, Austria (except among Jews), Hungary, and Spain; and in the two latter countries the prohibition may be dispensed with. Various peoples consider that marriage with a cousin is the most proper marriage, or that a man has a right to his cousin's hand, or even that it is his duty to marry her. This, however, nearly always applies to certain cousins only, whereas marriage between other cousins may be prohibited. The ancient Arabs held that a man had a right to wed his *bint 'amm,* that is, the daughter of his father's brother; and this right is still frequently recognised in the Muhammadan world. Elsewhere, again, the most proper marriage is considered to be that between a man and his father's sister's daughter or his mother's brother's daughter, a so-called "cross-cousin marriage." Cousin marriages have obvious advantages: they strengthen the kinship tie or keep together related families, they prevent dispersion of the family property, they very often incur less marriage expenses. And the frequency of cross-cousin marriages is undoubtedly connected with the fact that, where clan exogamy prevails, cousins belonging to the same clan are naturally forbidden to intermarry. This does not imply that a man is necessarily allowed to marry a cousin belonging to another clan, but very frequently he may do so.

Among peoples unaffected by modern civilisation

the exogamic rules are probably in the large majority
of cases more extensive than among ourselves. They
very often refer to all the members of the clan or
phratry or "class" (in the sense used with reference
to Australian and Melanesian exogamy) or local
community; and the rule that a man may not marry
a woman of his own clan or class is usually supple-
mented by a further prohibition of marrying other
women who are nearly related to him. The exogamous rules of the Australian aborigines are particularly complicated. The great majority of their
tribes about which we possess accurate information
are divided into two matrimonial classes (phratries
or moieties), the members of which are not allowed to
marry within their own class. In many tribes each of
these classes is composed of two exogamous sections,
and each section may again be divided into two
exogamous subsections; so that the tribes consist of
two, four, or eight exogamous classes or sub-classes,
the members of each of which are bound to seek their
husbands or wives in a class or sub-class different
from their own. In the tribes which have the four-
class system, however, a man is, as a general rule, not
merely prohibited from marrying a woman of his own
moiety, but can only marry into one of the sections
of the other moiety. The children then belong to the
sub-class neither of their father nor of their mother,
but to the other sub-class of their mother's moiety
if the descent of the moiety or class is in the female
line, and to the other sub-class of their father's moiety
if the descent of the moiety is patrilineal. Moreover,
in most of the tribes known to us there is not only class
exogamy but clan exogamy as well, each moiety or

class being subdivided into a number of exogamous totem clans; and besides class and clan exogamy there are in Australia additional rules which prohibit the intermarriage of certain relatives who otherwise would be allowed to marry each other. The exogamous rules among the Australian natives are, or were until lately, enforced with the greatest rigidity, the penalty of death being commonly inflicted on the transgressors. This is true both in the case of marriage and in the case of irregular sexual intercourse, except that in certain tribes, on occasions when ceremonial licence takes place, the prohibitory class rules are disregarded; yet even then intercourse between the nearest relatives—between parents and children and between brothers and sisters—is strictly forbidden.

In China there is a rule of exogamy attaching to family names. Large bodies of persons in that country bear the same surname; and according to the old Chinese penal code a penalty of sixty blows is inflicted on anyone who marries a person with his own name, and the marriage shall be null and void. But the punishment attached to the intermarriage of nearer relations on the father's side is much more severe: marriage or incestuous intercourse with a grand-uncle, a father's first cousin, a brother, or a nephew is punishable by death. And besides these prohibitions there are others applying within a narrower range to relatives on the female side. The Chinese code also interdicts occasional sexual intercourse with any of those relatives with whom marriage is prohibited, the punishment in both cases being the same.

EXOGAMY

The division into exogamous clans or septs is found all over India; and in various tribes a man is not only forbidden to marry a woman of his own clan, but must also refrain from marrying in some other clan or clans, for example, that of his mother or grandmother. In addition to the prohibition of marriage within the clan, or *gotra,* a Brahman must not, according to Hindu law, marry a girl of his mother's or maternal grandfather's *gotra,* or one who is *sapindā* of his father or maternal grandfather. The rule barring the marriage of *sapindās* is that two persons cannot marry if they are both as near as fourth in descent from a common ancestor, and the relationship is derived through the father of either party; whereas if the relationship of the couple is through their mothers in each case, then they cannot marry if they are third in descent from the same ancestor. But in practice marriages are held to be valid between persons fourth in descent from a common ancestor in the case of male relationship, and third in the case of female relationship, that is, persons having a common great-grandparent in the male line or a common grandparent in the female line can marry. In the sacred law-books the *sapindā* relationship is said to extend to six degrees where the common ancestor is a male, and to either six or four when the common ancestor is a female.

In ancient Rome marriages between persons under the same *patria potestas,* or paternal power, that is *cognati* related within the sixth degree (the degree of second cousins), were considered immoral and unlawful—they were *nefariæ et incestuæ nuptiæ.* These prohibitions were gradually relaxed: from the time of the Second Punic war, at least, first cousins were allowed to intermarry, and subsequently marriage with a brother's daughter was declared legal, in accordance with a decree obtained from the Senate by the Emperor Claudius. But in later times, under the influence of the ascetic ideas prevalent in the Church, the prohibited degrees were again extended. In the Eastern Church marriage was forbidden within the seventh degree according to the Roman method of computing degrees of relationship, which was to count from one of the parties up to a common ancestor and then down to the other party, so that, for example, first cousins were held to be related in the fourth degree and uncle and niece in the third. This rule is still in force in the Eastern Church. The Western Church went still further in her prohibitions. The forbidden degrees became gradually as many as seven according to the new Western reckoning, or "canonical computation," by which seven degrees were practically equivalent to seven generations; brother and sister were related in the first degree, first cousins in the second degree, second cousins in the third degree, and similarly beyond. The seventh degree seems to have been chosen by rigorous theorists who would have forbidden a marriage between kinsfolk however remote; for it seems to have been a common rule among the Teutonic peoples that for the purposes of inheritance kinship could not be traced beyond the seventh generation, and so to prohibit marriage within seven degrees was to prohibit it among all persons who for any legal purpose could claim blood-relationship with each other. The fourth Lateran Council, held in A.D. 1215 under Innocent III., reduced the prohibited degrees from seven to four, that is, marriage was permitted beyond the degree of third cousins; and since then there has been no change. The forbidden degrees of the Western Church thus almost coincide with those of the Eastern Church, the fourth degree of canonical computation corresponding to the seventh and eighth degrees of the Roman reckoning. But there is this important difference between the legislation of the two Churches, that in the Eastern Church no dispensation is held possible from any one of the prohibited degrees, whereas in the West dispensation is not only allowed but has since early times been practised on a very large scale. It does not seem, however, that the field of the Levitical prohibitions was entered upon by the Papal dispensing claims till the fifteenth century. The Reformers went in principle back to the prohibited degrees of the Mosaic law. Henry VIII. declared in 1540 that nothing, "God's law except, shall trouble or impeach any marriage without the Levitical degrees"; as the farthest of which was considered that between uncle and niece.

Besides prohibitions of marriage between blood-relatives there are other prohibitions applying to marriage between relatives by alliance or affinity. The rules relating to the latter kind of marriage vary greatly in different countries. While many uncivilised peoples allow a man to marry his wife's sisters and even give him a prior claim to their hands, there are others that either prohibit or disapprove of such marriages altogether or—which is very common—only permit marriage with a deceased wife's younger sister. The Levitical law and Islam forbid marriage with two sisters simultaneously, and the Catholic Church forbids marriage with a deceased wife's sister, though the prohibition may be dispensed with. In England such marriages were condemned by the canon law of the English Church, and their illegality was confirmed in 1835; and, as is well known, it was only after many futile attempts and in face of very strong opposition that an Act legalising marriage with a deceased wife's sister in the United Kingdom was passed in 1907. The Eastern Church even prohibits two brothers from marrying two sisters; and a similar prohibition is found in some uncivilised tribes. Again, while very many peoples permit a man to marry the widow of his deceased brother, or elder brother, and even regard it as his duty to do so, there are others that prohibit all such marriages. The Chinese penal code punished a union of this kind with strangulation, although marriage with a deceased wife's sister has always been regarded as particularly honourable in China. Marriage with a deceased brother's widow, as well as with a deceased wife's sister, was prohibited by Canon law, and is also prohibited by the laws of many, especially Latin, countries, although dispensation is easily obtained.

Christianity introduced a new obstacle to marriage by establishing the so-called *cognatio spiritualis,* or "spiritual relationship." The Emperor Justinian passed a law forbidding a man to marry a woman for whom he had stood as godfather in baptism, the tie of the godfather and godchild being so analogous to that of father and child as to make such a marriage appear improper; and to this law the Church added various other prohibitions on account of spiritual relationship, for instance, against marriage between the minister of the sacrament and the person baptised and that person's parents, between a godfather and a sister of the godchild, between two sponsors, and between a sponsor and the child of another sponsor born after the act of baptism. Similar prohibitions arose from relationships created by confirmation.

Among various peoples marriage between persons belonging to the same village or other local group is said to be prohibited or as a rule avoided. In many of these cases we are not told whether all the members of the local group are related by blood or not, but in other cases they are certainly not so. The Australian tribe, as Dr. Howitt points out, is organised in two ways. On the one hand, it is divided socially into phratries and clans; and on the other hand, it is divided geographically into hordes. The two organizations are co-existent, but the divisions of the one do not correspond with those of the other. For while all the people who belong to any given local group are found in one locality alone, those who belong to any given social group are very frequently to be found distributed among many, if not among all, of the local groups. Now, in many tribes local proximity by birth is quite an insuperable obstacle to marriage, a man being absolutely forbidden to marry, or to have sexual intercourse with, a woman of the same horde or sub-horde. "However eligible she may be in other respects, the fact that both parties belong to the same locality is held by certain tribes, the Kurnai for example, to make them 'too near each other.'" It is chiefly in tribes where the clan system has been weakened. or has become almost extinct, that the local organisation has assumed such over-whelming preponderance, but even in some of the tribes that have a vigorous clan system local restraints upon marriage are strictly enforced. Of some of the Australian natives we are told that they consider it best to procure a wife "from the greatest distance possible." In India, "apart from the restrictions based on the exogamous group and the prohibited degrees of relationship, there is often a rule that a man should not marry a girl of his own village." The Oráons of Chota Nagpur "have an aversion to marriages be-tween a young man and a girl of the same village; and such a marriage is generally believed to bode ill for one or both of the married pair." In some parts of Russia the bride is always taken from another village than the bridegroom's; and even in provinces in which no similar custom is known to exist, the bridegroom is constantly spoken of as a "foreigner," and his friends and attendants are represented as com-ing with him from a distant country, in order to take away the future spouse. In Bulgarian songs brides are invariably said to be brought from other villages.

Many attempts have been made to account for the rules of exogamy, by writers like McLennan, Herbert Spencer, Morgan, Lord Avebury, Starcke, Frazer, Durkheim, Atkinson, Andrew Lang, Hose, McDoug-all, and others. They have been ascribed to a pristine habit of female infanticide; to the vain desire of savage men to have trophies in their wives; to expe-rience of the injurious influence of in-breeding (made at an earlier stage of human development than that represented by any living savages but afterwards forgotten) ; to marriage by capture originating in the hypothetical period of primitive promiscuity; to marriage by purchase; to a superstitious belief that incest blights the crops, prevents the multiplication of edible animals, and renders the women sterile; to totemism; or to the furious jealousy of a gorilla-like ancestor. To each of these theories the gravest objections may be raised; and in addition there are other objections that may be raised to all of them. They all regard the exogamous rules as social survivals from very remote ages. They all suppose that these rules have originated in social conditions which no longer exist, or in ideas which have been found among a few savages only or which have never been found anywhere. Now, is it really possible to believe that a law like that against incest among themselves could be traced to similar sources? Is it possible to believe that a restriction barring marriages which could be more conveniently arranged than any others, requiring neither capture nor purchase nor the consent of strangers, might have been preserved through ages without being relaxed though serving no useful purpose at all? It shall be noticed that the exogamous rules have not remained unaltered; on the contrary, they differ even among peoples of the same stock, and we know that in Europe, in the course of a few centuries, they have been greatly changed in spite of the religious sanction given them by the Church. This proves that those rules are not dead fossils, but living parts of the social organism, subject to modifications according to the circumstances.

Moreover, the theories in question imply that the

home is kept free from incestuous intercourse by law, custom, or education. But even if social prohibitions might prevent unions between the nearest relatives, they could not prevent the desire for such unions. The sexual instinct can hardly be changed by pre- scriptions; I doubt whether all laws against homo- sexual intercourse, even the most draconic, have ever been able to extinguish the peculiar desire of anybody born with homosexual tendencies. Nevertheless, our laws against incest are scarcely felt as a restraint upon individual feelings. And the simple reason for this is that in normal cases there is no desire for the acts which they forbid. Generally speaking, there is a remarkable absence of erotic feelings between persons living very closely together from childhood. Nay more, in this, as in many other cases, sexual indiffer- ence is combined with the positive feeling of aversion when the act is thought of. This I take to be the fundamental cause of the exogamous prohibitions. Persons who have been living closely together from childhood are as a rule near relatives. Hence their aversion to sexual relations with one another displays itself in custom and law as a prohibition of inter- course between near kin.

The existence of a feeling of the kind suggested, or at least of sexual indifference to housemates, has been recognised by various writers as a psychological fact proved by common experience. Dr. Havelock Ellis writes: "Between those who have been brought up together from childhood all the sensory stimuli of vision, hearing, and touch have been dulled by use, trained to the calm level of affection, and deprived of their potency to arouse erethistic excitement which produces sexual tumescence." Even between lads and girls who are educated together in the same school there is a conspicuous absence of erotic feelings, according to an interesting communication of a lady who has for many years been the head-mistress of such a school in Finland. Once a youth assured her that neither he nor any of his friends would ever think of marrying a girl who had been their schoolfellow; and I heard of a lad who made a great distinction between girls of his own school and other, "real" girls, as he called them. According to other accounts boys may display erotic feelings towards younger girls in the school, but not towards girls of their own class.

The normal want of inclination for sexual inter-course between persons who have been living closely together from the childhood of one or both of them is no doubt a world-wide phenomenon. Plato observed that an unwritten law defends as sufficiently as possible parents from incestuous intercourse with their children and brothers from intercourse with their sisters, and that the thought of such a thing does not enter at all into the minds of most of them. When I asked my Berber teacher from the Great Atlas whether marriages between cousins were frequent in his tribe, his answer was, "How could you love a girl whom you have always seen?" Among the Maori of New Zealand, according to Colenso—who is considered a first-rate authority—adult brothers and sisters slept together, as they had always done from their birth, "not only without sin, but without thought of it." In India Mr. Russell and Mr. Sturrock have found various facts supporting my view that exogamy has originated in a feeling against the marriage of persons who have lived closely together from early youth. Sir Richard Burton says, "As a general rule Somali women prefer amourettes with strangers, following the well-known Arab proverb, 'the newcomer filleth the eye.' " Mr. Grubb explains the frequent unfaithfulness on the part of married men and women among the Lengua Indians of the Paraguayan Chaco by the fact that the people "mix in a very small circle, and meet with no partner with whom they could mate, except those whom they have played with from childhood. Little choice, therefore, is left them, and there is not that novelty of a fresh face and character which tends to become captivating, and eventually leads to love."

Among the lower animals, also, there are indications that the pairing instinct fails to be stimulated by companions and seeks strangers for its gratification. The Marquis de Brisay, an authority on doves, says that "two birds from the same nest rarely couple. Birds coming from the same nest behave as though they regarded coupling as prohibited, or, rather, they know each other too well, and seem to be ignorant of their difference in sex, remaining unaffected in their relations by the changes which make them adults." The honey-bee never propagates in the nest but flies out for this purpose. Among winged ants it is common for both males and females to have a "marriage flight." They leave their nest about the same time, their swarms mix with other swarms, even their hereditary enemies, ancient quarrels are forgotten, and there is nothing but joy and love-making. Among domesticated animals it has often been noticed that companionship has a dulling effect upon the sexual instinct and that preference is given to strangers. Montaigne wrote: "I was fain to turn out into the paddock an old stallion, as he was not to be governed when he smelt a mare; the facility presently sated him as towards his own, but towards strange mares, and the first that passed by the pale of his pasture, he would again fall to his importunate neighing and his furious heats as before." I myself have been told by a trustworthy person of a stallion that would not approach mares of the same stable. Mr. G. W. Harris wrote to me: "It is well known, I believe, by dog breeders, that if you bring up from puppyhood dogs and bitches together, the bitches very frequently refuse to take the dogs to which they have been accustomed from puppyhood. There is no aversion, I believe, on the part of the male, but with regard to bitches, even from my own experience, I am able in a certain measure to corroborate this." Mr. Heape thinks that all breeders will agree that animals when brought into contact with strangers experience increased sexual stimulation. Professor Seligman has kindly provided me with the following communication: "I had about half a dozen fully plumaged drakes of the common mallard, born of domesticated stock, in a good-sized pen containing a small pool and natural herbage. They got along well together, and although constantly watched (I was studying colour changes in plumage at the time) they were found to pay no particular attention to each other. Two strange drakes of the same class of bird and in the same plumage were introduced, and these were simply overwhelmed by the sexual attentions of the older inhabitants of the pen. I know this went on for two or three hours—

it may have gone on for days; but later on they had all settled down to what seemed a normal life. The time of the year was early summer, probably early June."

Sexual indifference, however, is not by itself sufficient to account for exogamous prohibitions. But such indifference is very generally combined with sexual aversion when the act is thought of; indeed, I believe that this is normally the case whenever the idea of sexual intercourse occupies the mind with sufficient intensity, and a desire fails to appear. An old and ugly woman, for instance, would in such circumstances become sexually repulsive to most men, and to many male inverts any woman, as an object of sexual desire, is not merely indifferent but disgusting. And, as I have pointed out in my book *The Origin and Development of the Moral Ideas,* aversions which are generally felt readily lead to moral disapproval and prohibitory customs or laws.

Various objections have been raised to my theory. Psycho-analysts have called it amazing. Dr. Freud maintains that the psychological assumptions on which it is based have been completely invalidated by the results of psycho-analysis, which, on the contrary, have shown that "the earliest sexual inclinations of a young person are regularly of an incestuous nature, and that such repressed inclinations play a part which can hardly be overrated in later neuroses." The belief that psycho-analysis has unearthed facts which are destructive to my theory, however, is a supposition for which I must see some evidence before I can take it seriously. I doubt whether the study of neurotic persons can be regarded as a safe guide to the proper understanding of the normal manifestations of the sexual instinct; and in Dr. Freud's terminology "sexual inclinations" may imply mental states very different from an actual desire for sexual intercourse. Dr. Jung, another well-known psycho-analyst, says, "I am able to attribute as little strength to incestuous desires in childhood as in primitive humanity." According to Dr. Jones, psycho-analysis points out that the strong and universal inclination towards incest really exists, "only that for the most part it is repressed in the unconscious." But *why has it been repressed?* I have found no satisfactory answer to this all-important question in the writings of psycho-analysts; and it is certainly a most unjustified claim to say that psycho-analysis has thrown "a flood of light" on "the almost universal horror of incest, and the extraordinarily complicated and fierce laws that have been devised in the most varied parts of the world with the object of preventing it." For what reason have those complicated and fierce laws been devised; and how have laws in this particular case, but not in others, been able almost completely to repress an innate sexual desire, especially if it was once universally felt? These are the questions which should be answered before the existence of a conscious incestuous desire in primitive men is postulated in consequence of conclusions drawn from psycho-analytical investigations relating to a few thousand civilised individuals, mostly neurotic, and from myths and cosmogonies which allow of various interpretations.

Professor Durkheim has made the objection that if close living together calls forth aversion to sexual intercourse, such aversion ought to display itself between husband and wife as well as between near relatives. But these cases are certainly not identical. What I have here spoken of is a lack of inclination for, and a feeling of aversion associated with the idea of, sexual intercourse between persons who have lived in a long-continued intimate relationship from a period of life when the action of sexual desire, in its acuter forms at least, is naturally out of the question. On the other hand, when a man marries a woman his feeling towards her is of a very different kind, and his love impulse may remain, nay increase, during the conjugal union. Yet even in this case long living together has undoubtedly a tendency to dull the sexual desire and sometimes even to lead to positive aversion. Dr. Bloch observes: "The eternal uniformity of daily companionship puts love to sleep, damps its ardour, and even gives rise to a sense of latent or open hatred between a married pair. This hatred is observed most frequently in love-matches."

It has been argued that "the noisome list" of peoples practising adelphic incest is hostile, or even fatal, to my theory of sexual aversion among young camp-mates, whether brothers and sisters or not. But, as a matter of fact, the number of peoples reported to allow marriages between the nearest relatives is infinitesimal in comparison with the number of peoples who are known to prohibit such marriages. Moreover, as we have noticed above, some of the statements refer to a few individuals only, others are obviously incorrect or of doubtful accuracy, and in many cases it is impossible to decide whether the statement refers to full or to half brothers and sisters. The distinction between these two kinds of brothers and sisters is of importance in the present connection. We have seen that where marriage with a half-sister is allowed the brother and sister in nearly every case have the same father. This is explained by the fact that the children of different mothers are not brought into the same contact with one another as the children of the same mother. In polygynous families each wife and her children form a small group, very often living in a separate hut, and hatred and rivalry are of no rare occurrence among the members of the various sub-families. Nor does the father occupy the same place in each sub-family as he does in a monogamous family. With reference to the Athenian law which permitted a man to marry his half-sister by the father, Hume made the remark that "his step-mother and her children were as much shut up from him as the women of any other family." After speaking of the marriage of half-brother and half-sister allowed among the ancient Arabs, Robertson Smith observes: "Whatever is the origin of bars to marriage, they certainly are early associated with the feeling that it is indecent for housemates to intermarry."

To the reported cases of marriages between parents and children and between brothers and sisters may no doubt be added occasional cases of non-matrimonial incestuous intercourse occurring among both savage and civilised peoples. In Europe they seem to have been more frequent in certain epochs, as in the period of the French Rococo. Mundt states that in the middle of the last century it was not very uncommon for French fathers to live in concubinage with their own daughters; and he thinks that, generally, the French nature is not repelled to the same degree as the German by the idea of sexual union between persons nearly related by blood. "At the present time among civilised people," says Mr. Mortimer, "incest is not very rare, especially among the lowest classes in large cities. . . . And in the higher classes of our community intercourse between boys and girls of the same family is not so infrequent as most parents and guardians suppose; indeed I have heard of several cases amongst brothers and sisters of twelve and a few years older, though after puberty the instances become much rarer. . . . In by far the greater number of cases of incest in civilised countries, the intercourse is restricted to children before the age of puberty."

Yet I do not understand how these facts could invalidate my theory. They are after all quite exceptional, and I have spoken of a general rule. I have no doubt that in the world generally, and in some countries particularly, homosexual practices are infinitely more frequent than incest; and nevertheless nobody would consider their frequency to be "fatal," or even "hostile," to the common view that there is normally a feeling of love between the sexes. Considering the great variability to which the sexual instinct is subject, it is not astonishing that cases of what we consider incestuous intercourse do occur; it seems to me more remarkable that the exceptions to the rule should, comparatively speaking, be so few.

We must not forget that a lack of desire, and even a positive feeling of aversion, may in certain circumstances be overcome. The sexual instinct is so powerful that when it cannot be gratified in the normal manner it may seek for abnormal gratification. Thus homosexual practices are very frequently due to the absence of women, to say nothing of masturbation and bestiality. So also sexual intercourse with a near relative may be resorted to when another, more suitable, partner is out of reach. This may account for the practice of incest in small isolated communities, like those of some Brazilian Indians, the Chukchee, and the Bushmen, if certain reports of them are true. Mr. Thomas suggests that the marriage with a half-sister at Ososo in Nigeria may be put down to a scarcity of women. In Europe at the present day, says Dr. Bloch, "incest occurs almost exclusively as the result of chance associations—as, for example, in alcoholic intoxication, in consequence of close domestic intimacy in small dwellings, in the absence of other opportunity for sexual intercourse."

As to the consanguineous marriages in royal families there can be little doubt that they are carried out with the aim of maintaining the purity of the royal blood. The suggestion has also been made that these marriages were introduced for the purpose of giving the king's son the right of succession which, under a system of female kinship, was enjoyed either by the son of the king's sister or by the husband of the king's daughter. But this explanation has the disadvantage that it presumes the earlier existence of the system of female kinship among peoples who are not known to have had it; whereas the desire to ensure the purity of the royal blood is a well-known fact. The marriage with sisters in ancient Egypt has been explained as a method of keeping property, and especially landed property, together in the family. So also we are told that the extremely rare instances of brother-and-sister marriage among the Maori "generally arose from the desire to keep lands belonging to the woman in the same line as that of the man."

Sir James G. Frazer has argued against me that if exogamy had resulted from a natural instinct there would have been no need to reinforce that instinct by legal pains and penalties; the law only forbids men to do what their instincts incline them to do, and hence we may always safely assume that crimes forbidden by law are crimes which many men have a natural propensity to commit. This argument has been quoted with much appreciation by Dr. Freud and Dr. Jones. The latter says: "No one has answered Frazer's convincing argument that laws of this order are made only for crimes towards which a strong and widespread temptation exists. The argument ends in a *non possumus;* incest could not be forbidden so stringently unless there were a general inclination towards it." This argument implies a curious misconception of the origin of legal prohibitions. Of course, where there is no transgression there is no law; I have already spoken of the great variability of the sexual instinct and recalled the well-known fact that there are circumstances in which a natural sentiment may be blunted or overcome. We find equally or even more stringent laws against other sexual offences, such as bestiality and sodomy; would they likewise be regarded as evidence of a general inclination or a strong temptation to commit these offences? Or would the exceptional severity with which parricide is treated by many law-books prove that a large number of men have a natural propensity to kill their parents? Psycho-analysts might answer this question in the affirmative, so far as parricide is concerned; for they believe, to quote Dr. Jones, "that every man cherishes in his unconscious the wish for sexual intimacy with his mother and the desire to remove by death any disturbing rival, particularly his father." But the laws against matricide are equally severe; and it is difficult to see how a son could wish to kill his mother if he were longing for sexual intimacy with her. The law expresses the feelings of the community or the legislator and punishes acts that shock them; but it does not tell us whether an inclination to commit the forbidden act is felt by many or by few.

Frazer has also raised another, more important, objection to my theory, which compels me to add some words by way of explanation. He admits that there seems to be some ground for believing in the existence of "a natural aversion to, or at least a want of inclination for, sexual intercourse between persons who have been brought up closely together from early youth"; but he finds it difficult to understand how this could have been changed into an aversion to sexual intercourse with persons near of kin, and maintains that, till I explain this satisfactorily, the chain of reasoning by which I support my theory breaks down entirely at the crucial point. In this objection, too, he has the hearty support of Dr. Freud.

My answer to this is that the transition which Frazer finds so difficult to understand is not only possible and natural but well-nigh proved by an exactly analogous case of equally world-wide occurrence and of still greater social importance, namely, the process which has led to the association of all kinds of social

[91]

rights and duties with kinship. The maternal and paternal sentiments, which largely are at the bottom of parental duties and rights, cannot in their simplest forms be based on a knowledge of blood-relationship, but, as has been pointed out above, respond to stimuli derived from other circumstances, notably the proximity of the helpless young, that is, the external relationship in which the offspring from the beginning stand to the parents. Nor is the so-called filial love in the first instance rooted in considerations of kinship; it is essentially retributive, the agreeable feeling produced by benefits received making the individual look with pleasure and kindliness upon the giver. Here again the affection is ultimately due to close living together, and is further strengthened by it, as appears from the cooling effect of long separation of children from their parents. So also fraternal love and the duties and rights which have sprung from it depend in the first place on other circumstances than the idea of a common blood; and the same may be said of the tie which binds together relatives more remotely allied. Its social force is ultimately derived from near relatives' habit of living together. Men became gregarious by remaining in the circle where they were born; if, instead of keeping together with their kindred, they had preferred to isolate themselves or to unite with strangers, there would certainly be no blood-bond at all. The mutual attachment and the social rights and duties which resulted from this gregarious condition were associated with the relation in which members of the group stood to one another —the relation of kinship as expressed by a common name—and these associations might last even after the local tie was broken, being kept up by the common name. Here we have an immense group of facts which, though ultimately depending upon close living together, have been interpreted in terms of kinship. Why, then, may we not believe that the same has been the case with the aversion to incest and the prohibitory rules resulting from it?

Frazer asks: "If the root of the whole matter is a horror of marriage between persons who have always lived with each other, how comes it that at the present day that horror has been weakened into a mere general preference for marriage with persons whose attractions have not been blunted by long familiarity? . . . Why should the marriage of a brother with a sister, or of a mother with a son, excite the deepest detestation . . . while the origin of it all, the marriage between housemates, should excite at most a mild surprise too slight probably to suggest even a subject for a farce, and should be as legitimate in the eye of the law among all civilised nations as any other marriage?" For my own part, I believe that marriage between a man and his foster-daughter or between a foster-brother and a foster-sister, in case the social relations between them have been exactly similar to those of blood relatives of corresponding degrees, would cause more than a mild surprise, and appear unnatural and objectionable. Much, of course, depends upon the closeness of the social relationship and its nearness in time. Dr. Steinmetz's argument, that "the very sensual Frenchmen often seem to marry the lady friends of their earliest youth," is certainly not to the point. Speaking of marriages between housemates among civilised peoples, Mr. Heape justly observes: "It must be

recollected that, as civilisation progresses, the continuous living together from childhood upwards of
blood strangers becomes more and more rare. It is
also true that the Male's temporary absences from
home become more and more frequent after puberty,
and that housemates before puberty thus become
strangers afterwards if considered from a sexual point
of view. In fiction, which is a wonderfully accurate
guide in such matters, the marriage of housemates is
very rare, and when it is depicted it generally follows
unsuccessful efforts of the Male to gain a stranger for
wife." I certainly do not deny that unions between
the nearest blood-relatives inspire an aversion of their
own; but it is quite natural that they should do so,
considering that from earliest times the aversion to
sexual intercourse between persons living closely
together has been expressed in prohibitions against
unions between kindred, sanctioned by custom, law,
and religion. Nor can it be a matter of surprise that
the prohibitory rules so frequently refer to the
marriage of kindred alone. Law only takes into
account general and well-defined cases, and hence
relationships of some kind or other between persons
who are nearly always kindred are defined in terms
of blood-relationship. This is true not only of the
prohibitions of incest, but of many duties and rights
inside the family circle.

At the same time, adoption or fosterage also
constitutes a very frequent bar to intermarriage.
Among various peoples marriage is prohibited even
between all persons belonging to the same village or
other local group, whether they are related by blood
or not. And innumerable facts show that the extent

to which relatives are forbidden to intermarry is nearly connected with their close living together.

Montesquieu observed long ago that marriage between cousins was prohibited by peoples among whom brothers and their children used to live in the same house. A comparison between the forbidden degrees of the Greeks and Romans is instructive. Among the former cousins and even half-brothers and sisters were allowed to intermarry, whereas among the latter marriage was prohibited also between more distantly related persons. This difference, as Rossbach remarks, was due to the fact that the family feeling of the Greeks was much weaker than that of the Romans, among whom, in early times, a son used to remain in his father's house even after marriage, so that cousins on the father's side were brought up as brothers and sisters. Later on, the several families separated from the common household, and the prohibited degrees were retrenched accordingly. Professor Kohler points out the connection between the extensive marriage prohibitions of the Hindus and their large households. The word *gotra* (clan) means a stall or cow-pen, and would thus originally signify those who lived together in one place like a herd of cattle. Many of the Southern Slavs to this day live in house communities each consisting of a body of from ten to sixty members or even more, who are blood-relations to the second or third degree on the male side, and who associate in a common dwelling or group of dwellings, having their land in common, following a common occupation, and being governed by a common chief. Sir Henry Maine remarks: "The common residence of so many persons of both sexes in the same household may be said to be only possible through their belief that any union of kinsmen and kinswomen would be incestuous." In Wales, in former days, the exogamous joint-family consisted of kindred who dwelt together within one enclosure. "So long as the head of the family lived, all his descendants lived with him, apparently in the same homestead, unless new ones had already been built for them on the family land." The ancient Teutons, on the other hand, whose exogamous prohibitions seemed to have included only the nearest relatives, are not known to have had the joint-family institution, and, according to Tacitus, lived in scattered families at some distance from each other. It is easy to explain, says Ewald, why among the Hebrews marriage between cousins was permitted though marriage between brothers and sisters was forbidden: the former did not "form one united household, and the more each house stood strictly by itself in the ancient fashion, the wider seemed the separation between cousins." I have already referred to Robertson Smith's statement that among the ancient Arabs the intermarriage of housemates was held indecent.

Among many of the simpler peoples we notice a similar correlation between close living together and the prohibited degrees of relationship. Among peoples living in small family groups, like many of the Brazilian Indians and the Bushmen, the exogamous prohibitions are restricted to the nearest relatives only. Again, an exogamous clan is very frequently a territorial group as well as a group of kindred; and, like Sir James Frazer, I hold it extremely probable that exogamous moieties or phratries and

clans have originally been local groups with their own
territories.   Yet, as a matter of fact, the members
of an exogamous clan or phratry very frequently do
not live in the same locality; indeed, the exogamous
prohibition may even refer to the members of the
same or an "equivalent" clan or phratry who are
living in different tribes or nations.   This is a natural
consequence of the fact that the aversion to sexual
intercourse between persons living closely together
from childhood has been expressed in prohibitions
against unions between kindred.   The exogamous
rules, though in the first place associated with kinship
because near relatives normally live together, have
come to include relatives who do not live together—
just as social rights and duties connected with kinship, although ultimately depending upon close living
together, have a strong tendency to last after the local
tie is broken.   Clan exogamy has its counterpart,
for instance, in the blood feud as a duty incumbent
on the whole clan, whether the members of the clan
live together or not.

In this process the influence of a common name has
undoubtedly been of great importance. As kinship
is traced by means of a system of names, the name
comes to stand for blood-relationship.   This system
is naturally one-sided.   Though it will keep up the
record of descent either on the male or on the female
side, it cannot do both at once; and the line which
has not been kept up by such means of record, even
when it is recognised as a line of relationship, is more
or less neglected and soon forgotten.   Hence the
prohibited degrees, like the social rights and duties
generally connected with clanship, extend much

farther on the one side than on the other. It should also be remembered that, according to primitive ideas, the name itself constitutes a mystic link between those who have it in common. "In Greenland, as everywhere else," says Dr. Nansen, "the name is of great importance; it is believed that there is a spiritual affinity between two people of the same name."

The feeling against incest, however, may also be opposed to intercourse between persons one of whom has or has had sexual relations with the other's relative; and, generally speaking, the feeling that two persons are intimately connected in some way or other may, through an association of ideas and feelings, give rise to the notion that marriage or sexual intercourse between them is improper or incestuous. Hence the prohibitions of marriage between relations by alliance, the prohibitions of the Roman and Greek Churches on the ground of "spiritual relationship," and certain other prohibitions previously mentioned. Every hypothesis which pretends to give a fairly full explanation of the exogamous rules must inevitably assume the operation of the law of association. Professor Durkheim, while maintaining that my theory could not apply to clan exogamy because the members of the same totem clan do not live together, is himself quite ready to resort to analogy to explain prohibitions extending outside the totem clan; as when he says that the rule of clan exogamy has been extended to near relatives belonging to different clans because these are in no less close contact with each other than are the members of the same clan.

I venture to believe that the hypothesis here advocated is in agreement with the various facts given above. It seems to me to explain how the aversion to incest may be independent of both experience and education; why the exogamous rules refer not only to relations by blood, but very frequently to persons not at all so related; why the prohibitions of consanguineous marriages vary so considerably with regard to the prohibited degrees, applying, however, almost universally to persons living in the closest contact with each other; and why these prohibitions are so commonly extended much farther on the one side, either the paternal or the maternal, than on the other. But an important question still calls for an answer: How shall we explain the lack of inclination for, leading to positive aversion to, sexual intercourse between persons who have been living closely together from childhood? Before this question has been answered my theory of the origin of exogamy is incomplete.

The sexual instinct is of such immense importance for the existence of the species that any satisfactory explanation of its normal characteristics must be sought for in their specific usefulness. That the psychical cause to which I have traced the origin of exogamy has a deep biological foundation is suggested by a multitude of facts relating both to animals and plants. These facts make it hardly possible to doubt that self-fertilisation in the case of plants and close in-breeding in the case of animals are, on the whole, injurious to the species.

Darwin watched, from germination to maturity, more than a thousand individual plants belonging to many different species, some of which had been produced by crossing and others by self-fertilisation; and in doing so he found a notable difference in height, weight, constitutional vigour, and fertility of the offspring from crossed and self-fertilised flowers, as also in the number of seeds produced by the parent-plants. Hence, whenever plants which are the offspring of self-fertilisation are opposed in the struggle for existence to the offspring of cross-fertilisation, the latter must have the advantage. That this is the case with the large majority of vegetable species constituted for cross-fertilisation is nowadays a generally accepted fact.

As for the animal kingdom, most persons who have bred animals and written on the subject have expressed the conviction that close interbreeding leads to harmful consequences. The hog is said to be particularly susceptible to the injurious influence of in-breeding, and the sheep only a little less so. Experiments made with four-horned goats have shown that much in-breeding has a weakening effect upon the bones and muscles, lowers the vital energy of the animal, and causes the loss of the sucking instinct. Low observes that dogs continually reproduced from the same litter exhibit, after a time, the aspect of feebleness and degeneracy: "the hair becomes scanty, or falls off, the size diminishes, the limbs become slender, the eyes sunk, and all the characters of early age present themselves." With regard to thoroughbred horses, which are notoriously in-bred, it is stated in one of the earlier reports of the Royal Commission on Horse-breeding that no less than 40 per cent. of the thorough-bred mares in this country fail to have foals each year; but it seems probable that this large amount of sterility is not entirely due to the in-breeding. Professor Sheldon writes: "'In-breeding,' as it is termed—that is, the breeding for a time amongst near relations—generally results mischievously on the systems and on the fertility of stock. Consanguinity, though valuable in the formation of pure-bred types, and up to a given point, is a great evil if carried too far. The effects of too close in-breeding, at all events in the bovine world, are most commonly infertility and general debility; and what is only a slight and transient form of weakness in the first parents may, and often does, become a fixed and severe form in succeeding generations—indeed, what at first is only a weakened organic formation may be developed into a disease." So also according to Professor Ewart, "nature only tolerates in-breeding up to a certain point, for while it may assist in perpetuating useful characters by inducing prepotency, it often does this at the expense of vitality—it may be of fertility as well. It is conceivable that in-breeding has played an important part in the extinction of species; it has undoubtedly been the means of deteriorating, if not actually destroying, many of the breeds and varieties artificially produced." It is true that if proper caution is observed, in-breeding may be not only harmless but beneficial. But in such cases, as Wallace remarks, "there has been rigid selection by which the weak or the infertile have been eliminated, and with such selection there is no doubt that the ill effects of close interbreeding can be prevented for a long time; but this by no means proves that no ill effects are produced." The opinion of eminent breeders is supported by many experiments made by biologists with rats, mice, rabbits, guinea-pigs, butter-flies, and moths; and Maupas has shown that among Protozoa the divided individuals die out if they do not pair with strange individuals. That in-breeding, in the long run at least, is generally productive of evil consequences of some kind or other can hardly be open to doubt.

It has been argued that incest is constantly prac-tised by wild animals and therefore, if it were injuri-ous, would lead to the destruction of the species. Our present knowledge of their habits, however, by no means justifies this proposition. Among species that live in families the young leave the family when able to shift for themselves, or are said to refrain from pairing with one another. As regards gregarious animals it is quite possible that they prefer mating with strangers, as our domestic animals are known to do. The "marriage flight" of ants and bees obviously helps to prevent in-breeding. There are yet other arrangements in the animal world serving the same purpose. Thus among hermaphrodites self-fertilisa-tion is very often prevented by the fact that the ova and the sperms in the same animal become mature at different times. It has been pointed out that the excited state of the males in the rutting season urges them to move about in search and pursuance of females, and the great strength of their passions has been accounted for as a means of securing the necessary mixture of blood. I have made the sug-gestion that the secondary sexual characters, con-sisting in colours, odours, and the production of sounds, are useful to the species not only because they facilitate reproduction by making it easier for the sexes to find each other, but also because they tend to prevent in-breeding by attracting individuals from a distance.

So far as mankind is concerned the study of the effects of close in-breeding is prevented by the general absence of marriages between the nearest relatives. It has been said that there is no proof of the physical deterioration of peoples like the ancient Egyptians and Persians, among whom such marriages did occur. But even if among these peoples close intermarrying was more frequent than we have a right to assume, it was certainly very far from being the exclusive kind of marriage; and breeders of domestic animals inform us that the mixing-in even of a few drops of unrelated blood may be sufficient almost to neutralise the injurious effects of long-continued in-breeding. Mr. Huth asserts that though the Ptolemies habitually married their sisters, nieces, and cousins, they were neither sterile nor particularly shortlived. But Mr. Galton, on the contrary, sees in Ptolemaic experience a proof that close intermarriage is followed by diminished fertility; and in an elaborate essay on the subject Ujfalvy has tried to prove that the in-breeding of the Ptolemies led to physical and mental degeneration.

The closest kind of intermarriage we really have opportunities of studying is that between first cousins, and there is a considerable literature on the subject. But the opinions of the different writers often vary greatly. Some believe that such marriages are absolutely harmless unless the parents are afflicted with the same hereditary morbid tendencies; whereas others express the most alarming opinions on the subject. In any case it seems to be proved that consanguineous marriages have a distinct tendency to lead to idiocy, deaf-mutism, and the eye-disease called *Retinitis pigmentosa,* about a fourth or even a third part of all persons suffering from this disease being offspring of parents who are related by blood. In this connection I may direct attention to a book on *Marriage between Blood-relations* by a Danish physician, Dr. Mygge, on account of the trustworthiness of his method and the number of cases considered. He found that in the parishes of Denmark which came under his observation there were among the children of related persons comparatively more idiots, lunatics, epileptics, and deaf-mutes than among others; and he considers it probable, though not proved, that such children die in a higher ratio and are more liable to certain diseases. I may also mention some facts which I gathered during my stay at Foula, the most isolated of the Shetland Islands. The inhabitants, altogether 200–250 individuals, are nearly all related by blood, and marriages between cousins are very frequent among them, although they believe that such marriages are far from harmless. The families are generally small; the children between seven and fourteen years of age formed only 14 per cent. of the whole population, whilst in Burra Isle, another island of the same group, where consanguineous marriages were said to be very rare, the children of the same age amounted to 22 per cent. of the population. The people of Foula seemed to be shorter than on other islands, and Mr. Morrison, who had spent ten years among them, was of opinion that their constitution was somewhat feeble, although diseases were not frequent. There were some cases of idiocy; and I was told that in one family where husband and wife had been cousins no less than three children had been deaf-mute. With reference to habitual in-breeding in non-European communities, there are a good many statements to the effect that it has proved injurious in one way or other, and in spite of their unauthoritative character they at any rate show that the prevalence of narrow endogamous habits is no evidence of their harmlessness.

On the other hand, there are also several isolated communities, in Europe and elsewhere, in which long-continued in-breeding is said to have been accompanied with no discernible disadvantages. In any case it may be said that this local endogamy is generally something different from marriage with near relatives. Dr. Mitchell found that in almost all the isolated communities along the coasts of Scotland which had been given as instances of close in-breeding such marriages were comparatively rare. According to Dr. Mygge, the like is true of Lyø and Strynø in Denmark. And Dr. Andrew Wood states of the fisher-folk of Newhaven that though they keep themselves much segregated, they are very careful regarding intermarriage, and look upon the union of relatives as an infringement of the laws of morality.

At the same time it seems that close intermarrying, even though continued for a considerable time, has in particular cases been harmless or almost so. In some parishes of Denmark Dr. Mygge found no evil effects of consanguineous marriages, whilst in others the effects were very conspicuous. And from the investigations of Darwin it appears that, notwithstanding the injury which most plants suffer from self-fertilisation, a few have almost certainly been propagated in a state of nature for thousands of generations without having been once intercrossed. There is evidence that the bad consequences of self-fertilisation and close inter-breeding may almost fail to appear under favourable conditions of life. In-bred plants, when allowed enough space and good soil, frequently show little or no deterioration; whereas, when placed in competition with another plant, they often perish or are much stunted. Crampe's experiments with brown rats proved that the breeding in-and-in was much less injurious if the offspring of the related parents were well fed and taken care of than it was otherwise. And this is in striking accordance with Dr. Mitchell's observations as to consanguineous marriages in Scotland. We may then perhaps suppose that consanguineous marriages are more injurious in savage regions, where the struggle for existence is often very severe, than they have proved to be in civilised society, especially as it is among the well-to-do classes that such marriages occur most frequently. In England, according to G. H. Darwin, cousin-marriages among the aristocracy are probably 4½ per cent.; among the middle and upper middle class, or among the landed gentry, 3½ per cent.; but in London, comprising all classes, they are probably only 1½ per cent. He thinks that the slightness of the evils which he found to result from first-cousin marriages may depend upon the fact that a large majority of Englishmen live under what are on the whole very favourable circumstances.

Taking, then, into consideration all the facts bearing

on the subject which are known to me, I cannot but think that in-breeding generally is, in some way or other, more or less detrimental to the species. And here I find a quite sufficient explanation of the want of inclination for, and positive aversion to, sexual intercourse between persons who from childhood have lived together in that close intimacy which characterises the mutual relations of the nearest kindred. We may assume that in this, as in other cases, natural selection has operated, and by eliminating destructive tendencies and preserving useful variations has moulded the sexual instinct so as to meet the requirements of the species. It must not be argued that marriages between cousins have proved too slightly injurious to produce such a selection. For if, as I maintain, the family consisting of parents and children prevailed as a social unit among our early human or ape-like progenitors, the peculiarity of the sexual instinct of which I am speaking would have grown up as a consequence of the harmfulness of unions between the very nearest relatives, unless indeed it was an inheritance from a still earlier mammalian species. But once acquired, it would naturally show itself also in the case of more remote relatives or quite unrelated persons who lived in close intimacy from childhood, however harmless the unions between them might be. And through an association of ideas and feelings it might readily lead to prohibition of sexual intercourse between individuals who did not live together at all.

This explanation of the origin of exogamy is, so far as I can see, unaffected by the question *why* in-breeding is injurious to the species. Many writers

on the subject believe that all the evils resulting from
it are due to the combination and consequent increase
of morbid tendencies common to both parents, and
that therefore the presence or absence of such tendencies decides whether consanguineous unions are
harmful or not. Others maintain that the evils of
close interbreeding or self-fertilisation in plants are
in some measure due to consanguinity or self-
fertilisation as such. Darwin, for example, held the
opinion that while the sterility of distinct species
when first crossed, and of their hybrid offspring,
depends on their sexual elements having been differ-
entiated in too great a degree, a certain amount of
differentiation is also necessary or favourable for
the fertilisation or union of two organisms. But, as
already said, my theory of the origin of exogamy does
not stand or fall with any particular explanation of
the injuriousness of in-breeding.

In support of my theory I wish still to emphasise
certain facts. Its assumption that exogamy is rooted
in a peculiarity of the sexual instinct is in full agreement with the general rule that exogamous prohibitions do not apply to marriage alone, but to sexual
intercourse in general; the few exceptions to this rule
have reference to remoter kindred only. It explains
a world-wide institution by a mental characteristic
which may be presumed to be common to all races
of men. It traces the origin of this mental characteristic to the needs of the species. It co-ordinates three
parallel groups of facts which seem intrinsically to
belong together: the exogamous rules, the aversion
to sexual intercourse between persons living together
from childhood, and the injurious consequences of

in-breeding. And it finds the same general law governing analogous phenomena in the two great kingdoms of the organic world: the cross-fertilisation of plants, the various arrangements to prevent in-breeding among animals, and the exogamy in mankind.

CHAPTER V

MARRIAGE BY CAPTURE

WE shall now proceed to a discussion of the various modes of contracting a marriage. One is to take the woman by force both without her own consent and without the consent of her kindred, that is, marriage by capture.

This method of obtaining a wife has been found in many parts of the world. A few instances may be quoted. In Tierra del Fuego marriage by capture sometimes occurs among both the Yahgans and the Onas. Of the latter it is said that when they make war on a neighbouring tribe they kill off the men and marry the women, whereas in times of peace, when they take wives from their own tribe, marriages are arranged by peaceful negotiations between the fathers of the parties. In many Brazilian tribes, also, women are captured from other tribes and married to the captors; and among some of the South American Indians wars seem to be waged solely for this purpose. Among the Luiseño Indians on the coast of California one method of marriage is said to have been "for a man and several of his friends to carry off by force the woman he wished to marry, even from the house of her parents."

Of the Chukchee, inhabiting the north-eastern corner of Asia, we are told that in olden times "a company of young men would seize a young girl in the open, bind her hands and feet, and carry her to the house of one who wanted to have her for a wife. Not only the men of alien families, but even the relatives and the cousins, acted so, after having been refused by the father of the girl. The assault and the ravishing, however, were not considered as a reason for implacable hatred and feuds. The parents would come afterwards and ask for ransom, which was paid, not in reindeer, but one woman for another. . . . Even at present a case of ravishment may happen now and then." Among the Samoyeds, Votyaks, Ostyaks, and various other peoples belonging to the former Russian Empire, bride-stealing is, or has recently been, resorted to if the bridegroom cannot afford to pay the fixed purchase-sum. Among the Kalmucks it sometimes happens that the suitor abducts the girl when neither she nor her parents are willing to yield to his wishes, but if the abducted girl has slept in his hut the parents are compelled to consent to his marrying her. Marriage by capture is occasionally practised among several tribes in India. Among the Bhuiyas of the Orissa States, "if a young man is in love with a girl, and either she or her parents will not consent to a marriage, he gathers together a band of his friends, and, when he gets an opportunity, carries her off, his companions guarding the flight. This method of obtaining a bride often leads to sanguinary conflicts, owing to the girl's friends attempting to prevent the abduction or to rescue her." The Hos in Bengal, also, "practise marriage by capture, the young men carrying off the girl from some dance or market in spite of any resistance, real or feigned, that she may make. In this case the bride-price is settled afterwards." Speaking of the Chittagong hill tribes in general, Lewin states that "those who had few women went with arms in their hands, and took what they wanted from a weaker community."

Cases of marriage by capture are found in the Malay Archipelago and Melanesia, and are reported from all parts of the Australian continent. "Sometimes a surprise party will be organised to attack a camp, slaughter the males and abduct and appropriate the females. This wholesale abduction is paralleled by individual cases of forcible abduction, on which occasions the woman, if resisting, will be cruelly beaten." But, contrary to statements made by some early observers, marriage by capture is usually said to be merely an exceptional or occasional mode of contracting marriage in Australia; it leads to feuds or quarrels, and for this reason the tribes very generally set themselves against the practice. From various parts of Africa, also, we hear of cases in which wives are acquired by force.

Capture of women for wives prevailed among ancient Semites. In Arabia it was common before Muhammad. Among the Hebrews members of the military class were allowed to marry foreign women taken in war, contrary to the law which forbade intermarriage with the Gentiles. Marriage by capture has been found among the Indo-European peoples. According to the *Laws of Manu,* the mythical Hindu legislator, one of the eight legal modes of concluding a marriage was the *rākshasa* mode, that is, "the forcible abduction of a maiden from her home, while she cries out and weeps, after her kinsmen have been

slain or wounded, and their houses broken open."
This mode was permitted to the Kshatriyas, or war-
rior caste, by the sacred tradition. According to
Dionysius of Halicarnassus, marriage by capture at
one time existed throughout Greece; and according to
Sakellarios it occurred there occasionally even in
quite recent times. Reminiscences of it are preserved
in the traditions of the early Romans. The ancient
Teutons evidently captured women for wives. Of
the Scandinavians, Olaus Magnus says that they were
constantly at war with one another "propter raptas
virgines aut arripiendas." In the earliest Teutonic
laws the "rape-marriage" is no doubt a punishable
offence, but still it is a marriage. In the Irish
Nennius we read of a rape of wives by the Picts from
the Gael. Marriage by capture also occurred among
the Slavs in early times. The Cossacks of Little
Russia and the Ukrainia practised it still in the seventeenth century, and many Southern Slavs in the beginning of the nineteenth or later. In High Albania
forcible capture of a girl occasionally takes place
even to this day. The same is the case among the
Caucasian mountain tribes, who consider that a captured girl becomes the wife of her captor by being
deflowered by him.

This list of peoples among whom marriage by
capture has been found might easily be enlarged.
But among no people is it known to have been the
usual or normal mode of contracting a marriage.
As appears from the statements quoted above, it is
chiefly practised either as an incident of war or as a
method of procuring a wife when it is difficult or
inconvenient to get one in the ordinary manner. We

thus notice its occurrence among savages living in small family groups, like the Fuegians, various Brazilian tribes, and the Bushmen; in the Australian tribes, where many young men for various reasons find it extremely hard to get married; and among many peoples of a higher type as a substitute for marriage by purchase, by which a man tries to lower the price of the bride or to avoid payment altogether. Custom may require that the matter shall be settled afterwards with the parents of the captured girl, and in such cases the capture is rather a preliminary to marriage than a mode of contracting it. But Dr. Grosse undoubtedly goes too far when he maintains that marriage by capture has never been a form of marriage recognised by custom or law, though it has been an occasional and punishable act of violence.

On the other hand, the prevalence of marriage by capture has undoubtedly been much exaggerated by some other writers. It has been represented as being at one time the normal mode of contracting a marriage among uncivilised peoples. But there is no evidence whatever that it was so. We have no reason to assume that a man in order to procure a wife was in ordinary circumstances compelled to take her by force from her relatives. Savages do not usually live at odds with all their neighbours; among many of them wars are quite exceptional, and some of them are said to have no wars at all. It is impossible to believe that there ever was a time when friendly relations between families who could intermarry did not exist.

The theory of an early stage of marriage by capture has been supported by reference to some very widespread customs which have been interpreted as survivals of capture in the past. But these customs do not prove what they are meant to prove, because they may be much more readily explained otherwise. First, there are a large number of cases in which sham fighting between the bridegroom or his party and the bride's family, or some other kind of resistance made by the latter, forms part of the wedding ritual. I shall quote a few instances of this class of supposed survivals of marriage by capture.

Among the Akamba, in British East Africa, "in former days on the day of the marriage the bridegroom went with five or six brothers and friends and seized his prospective bride in the fields near the village; the girl would call out and her brothers would assemble and attack the bridegroom's party; they would fight with sticks and even swords, and if the girl's brothers won they would take their sister back to their village. A palaver would then take place between the two families, and the girl's father would demand more dowry; the suitor would then pay up perhaps another ten goats, and the second time the bridegroom would go alone to his father-in-law's village and would receive his bride without any trouble and take her to his father's village." Among the Roro of British New Guinea, according to Professor Seligman, on the wedding day a party of men belonging to the bridegroom's local group, but not including the bridegroom, surround the house of the girl's parents and carry it by mimic assault, with great fury and shouting. "The bride rushes out and runs away as fast as she can, and although she is soon overtaken and caught, she defends herself to the best of her ability, with hands, feet, and teeth.

Meanwhile a sham fight rages between the adherents of the bride and bridegroom. In the midst of the commotion is the bride's mother armed with a wooden club or digging stick, striking at every inanimate object within reach and shouting curses on the ravishers of her daughter. The other women of the village join in the weeping." Among the Mongols, when the bridegroom—conspicuous by the bow-and-arrow case he carries slung from his shoulder—and his party arrive at the bride's tent, her brother plants himself in front of the door and demands of the strangers what brought them there. "We want to enter your tent," they reply. "Then you'll have to fight for it!" is the answer. The strangers and the other party begin to scuffle, pulling each other about a good deal. After a sham fight lasting a few seconds, the defenders give in and invite the assailants to enter the tent. In some parts of Morocco, when the bridegroom's party come to fetch the bride, stones are thrown at them; or the bridegroom and two other men dressed like him are beaten by the men and women of the bride's village; or her brother or uncle, before he carries her into the nuptial chamber, has a sham fight with the bridegroom. In the country villages of Burma it is the custom to tie a string across the road along which the bridegroom must pass to the house of his intended, when he comes in procession with all his friends, carrying the greater portion of the belongings with which he intends to set up house. The people who have put up the string, usually young men intent on a jollification of their own, stop the happy man and threaten to break the string with a curse on the married couple unless some money is given them.

MARRIAGE BY CAPTURE

Among the Teutonic, Slavonic, Romance, and other peoples of Europe it is a common marriage custom to barricade or stop the bridal procession on its way; and this custom has also been regarded by several writers as a survival of marriage by capture. The barricading sometimes consists in throwing logs, or even weapons, before the bridal waggon, but more frequently only a rope or a string of flowers is spread across the way; and the bridegroom has to pay a ransom in order that the waggon shall be allowed to pass. The barring of the wedding procession with a cord is also found in Gloucestershire and in Wales. But in the eighteenth century and, in fact, until recent years a Welsh bridegroom met with more serious resistance. On the morning of the wedding-day the groom with his friends demanded the bride. Her friends gave a positive refusal, upon which a mock scuffle ensued. The bride, mounted behind her nearest kinsman, is carried off and is pursued by the groom and his friends with loud shouts. When they have fatigued themselves and their horses, he is suffered to overtake his bride, and leads her away in triumph. The mock capture of a bride occurred a century ago in some parts of Scotland and Ireland as well.

Some customs of this class may, no doubt, nave been suggested by genuine capture of the bride. But this does not imply that capture was ever the usual mode of contracting a marriage. In a warlike tribe the capture of a woman for wife from an alien tribe may be admired as an act of bravery and therefore playfully imitated by ordinary people at their weddings. In some countries the bridegroom and bride are regarded as king and queen, but who would look upon this as a survival from a time when marriage was contracted only by royal persons? In most cases, however, it seems that the ceremonial resistance of the girl's relatives is a symbolic expression of their unwillingness to give up the girl or of their feeling of sexual modesty, which is particularly felt with regard to the nearest relations. Of the sham fight at a wedding in Pentecost Island, Dr. Codrington observes that it no doubt represents the feelings with which the bride's kinsmen regard the loss of her services; "it cannot be the loss of any rights of intercourse, since she was unapproachable by any of them." But the girl's parents and relatives may not only regret the loss of her services; they may also be sorry to part with her for purely sentimental reasons, and the mother's tears may be as genuine an expression of sorrow as they are among ourselves. The parents' reluctance, real or feigned, to give away their daughter may show itself in various ways. Dr. Jochelson says that among the Yukaghir in Siberia the go-between puts his proposition to the girl's parents in a very disguised form, and that her father, wishing to display all the dignity of his house, usually answers at first with a refusal. The same is done in some Berber tribes of Morocco. Among the Ewhe-speaking peoples of the Slave Coast, on the day of the marriage ceremony the bridegroom sends a messenger with rum to the parents of the bride soon after daybreak and asks for his wife. The parents affect reluctance, and delay the messenger with various excuses till about noon, when the bridegroom despatches a second messenger on the same errand. This messenger also fails, and it is not until the arrival of a third one, who comes about sunset, that the parents overcome their hesitation. Of course, there may also be mercenary motives for refusing too early a settlement, as also for putting obstacles in the way of the bridegroom's party, which can only be overcome by the payment of a ransom. Dr. Samter, again, believes that the stopping of the bridal procession is meant as a measure against evil spirits. I have myself suggested that the sham fights at weddings in Morocco may partly have a purificatory significance, as is the case with similar fights on various other occasions; and in his book on the civilisation of the South American Indians, Dr. Karsten has expressed the belief that the violence to which the young woman is subjected when forcibly abducted is intended to purify her and rid her of supernatural enemies, while the fast movement will further help her to escape them. The great speed at which bride and bridegroom are driven to and from church at German peasant weddings is obviously meant as a safeguard against supernatural dangers.

Very often resistance is made, or grief expressed, principally or exclusively by the bride. And this also has been represented as a survival of earlier marriage by capture.

Of the Araucanians in Chili, for example, we are told that their marriage ceremonies consist in nothing more than carrying off the bride by pretended violence, which is considered an essential prerequisite to the nuptials. "The husband, in concert with the father, conceals himself with some friends near the place where they know the bride is to pass. As soon as she arrives she is seized and put on horseback behind the bridegroom, notwithstanding her pretended resistance and her shrieks, which are far from being serious. In this manner she is conducted with much noise to the house of her husband, where her relations are assembled, and receive the presents agreed upon, after having partaken of the nuptial entertainment." On the east coast of Greenland, according to Dr. Nansen, the only method of contracting a marriage is still for the man to go to the girl's tent, catch her by the hair or anything else which offers a hold, and drag her off to his dwelling without further ado. Violent scenes are often the result, as single women always affect the utmost bashfulness and aversion to any proposal of marriage, lest they should lose their reputation for modesty. But "the woman's relations meanwhile stand quietly looking on, as the struggle is considered a purely private affair, and the natural desire of the Greenlander to stand on a good footing with his neighbour prevents him from attempting any interference with another's business." Among the Turkomans "the young maiden, attired in bridal costume, mounts a high-bred courser, taking on her lap the carcase of a lamb or goat, and setting off at full gallop, is followed by the bridegroom and other young men of the party, also on horseback; but she is always to strive, by adroit turns, etc., to avoid her pursuers, that no one of them approach near enough to snatch from her the burden on her lap." This game is said to be in use amongst all the nomads of Central Asia. Among the Bedouins of Sinai, should the girl get an inkling of her betrothal, "it is considered etiquette for her to make a show of escaping to the mountains"; and in one tribe she actually runs off to hide in the mountains for three days instead of remaining in a tent near her father. In Morocco the bride is expected to cry during the preparation for her departure.

The ceremonial reluctance or crying of the bride is found among all Indo-European peoples. In the Grihyasūtras—"the Folk-Lore Journals of ancient India"—a certain prayer is enjoined for the bride's crying, which proves that this crying was an essential form at an ancient Hindu marriage, as it is still in modern India. The Roman bride fled to the lap of her mother, and was carried off by force by the bridegroom and his friends. The Spartan bridegroom carried off the bride with feigned violence. In modern Greece, when the bridal procession starts for church, the bride bursts into tears, and refuses to follow, and on the bridesman saying, "Leave her alone, as she weeps," she replies, "Take me away from here, but let me weep." In Germany it is a very general belief that the bride's crying is auspicious, that if she weeps during the marriage ceremony she will be happy in her married life. So they say in the Upper Palatinate, "She who cries not before must cry afterwards," or, "Laughing bride, weeping wife; weeping bride, happy wife." Among Slavonic peoples the crying of the bride is most essential. Thus in Russia much importance is attached to the bride's having "a good cry," and the more she cries, the more she gains the admiration of her friends. In Serbia, when the elders had arranged a marriage between a young man and a young woman, it was formerly the custom for the bridegroom to seize the bride by force and carry her off; and it would have been considered highly indelicate for the girl to be a consenting party to the arrangement. Various writers maintain that the official crying of the bride in modern Europe also belongs to the survivals of marriage by capture.

The resistance and weeping of the bride, however, can no more than the opposition made by her relatives be regarded as such a survival. As her relatives are naturally reluctant or sorry to part with her, so she is sorry to be separated from them; and in either case the feeling of sadness or grief is ceremonially expressed and emphasised at the wedding. But, as clearly appears from some of the statements quoted, the behaviour is also largely due to coyness or sexual modesty, real or assumed. This was pointed out by Spencer as one origin of the ceremony of capture; and before him C. O. Müller had explained the Spartan ceremony as an ancient custom founded on the idea "that the young woman could not surrender her freedom and virgin purity, unless compelled by the violence of the stronger sex." Sexual modesty shows itself in various ways in the preliminaries to, or the conclusion of, a marriage not only on the part of the woman but on the part of the man; and the bridegroom, also, may have to be captured. Among the Garos of Assam, on the day fixed for the celebration of the marriage "some relatives of the bride go over to the bridegroom's *machan* (or hut) with a view to bring him in. On seeing them coming, or on being apprised of their coming, the latter takes to his heels and runs into a solitary room or enters a forest. The bride's people make diligent search, and on finding him out, try to bring him by force, at the same time holding out all sorts of temptations in order to induce him to consent to the marriage; and on these means failing to have effect, they throw him down in a pool of water, and when on being ducked two or three times he at length expresses his consent, they take him out of the water and triumphantly lead him captive to the bride's house. The bride, too, on her part flees into a lonely room; but what makes her case somewhat different from that of the bridegroom is that she never goes into a forest." Among the Greeks of southern Macedonia it is the bridegroom and not the bride who is "lifted." On the last day of the week-long celebration an envoy from the bride comes to gird the bridegroom, attempting at the same time to lift him from the ground, and he resists to the best of his ability.

There are yet other sham fights at weddings, which are obviously no survivals of marriage by capture, but accentuate the antagonism between different social groups and the solidarity of the members of each of them. The struggling bride may be assisted by her female friends, and in various cases the struggle is chiefly between them and the bridegroom. In Morocco the bridegroom is sometimes attacked by all the women assembled outside his house, or they curse both his and the bride's father, as if the marriage were an offence against their sex; and the sex antagonism is also conspicuous in the fights which take place between the bachelors and the unmarried women or the women in general, in the young men's attempts to take something from the bride, who is defended by the other women and her bridesmen, and in the robberies which the men of the bridal procession commit on the bridegroom's mother and sisters as well as on the bride. Among the Arabs of Moab, again, the women of the bridegroom's tribe attack the bride when the procession approaches a camp in the tribe; they do not want to receive the stranger, whose arrival they regard as an insult to their own beauty and attractions.

Marriage by capture is supposed to have left behind traces in the language spoken by the women. To such an extent, we are told, did the Caribs capture women from neighbouring tribes that the men and women spoke different languages or, at any rate, had two more or less distinct vocabularies, one of which was used by the men and by the women when speaking to the men, and the other only by the women between themselves. This theory, however, has been justly criticised. Differences between the speech of men and women are found all over America and in many other parts of the world, but nowhere—not even among the Caribs—are these differences so great as to constitute two different languages in the proper sense of the word. They may be due to various causes. Sapper and Lasch have emphasised the social-economic factor of differentiation of occupation and labour. Peculiarities of speech are always apt to arise among people who are closely associated with each other, as the inhabitants of the same district or the members of the same class of society; and the segregation of the sexes naturally leads to a similar result. As Mr. Crawley points out, "in modern Europe sexual separation to some extent still influences popular language, women and men respectively using certain terms peculiar to each sex." As regards the women's dialect among some South American Indians, the suggestion has been made that this dialect, with its fuller tone, represents an older form of the tribal speech, which has been retained by the women; "of a distinct language," says Krause, "which might have arisen through the reception of female captives from foreign tribes, there is no question here." The comparative isolation of the women from the outside world undoubtedly accounts for the fact, noticed by myself among the Berbers of the Great Atlas, that the women use the old Berber numerals in cases where the men invariably use Arabic loan-words. Finally, it should be remembered that, even if certain peculiarities of the women's speech are due to exogamous habits, there may be exogamy without marriage by capture.

Many other practices have been regarded by imaginative writers as survivals of marriage by capture. This is the case with the lifting of the bride over the doorstep, the veiling of the bride, the use of rings at weddings, the throwing of a shoe after the departing bride and bridegroom, the avoidance of parents-in-law, and even our honeymoon, "during which the bridegroom keeps his bride away from her relatives and friends." Several of these customs will be dealt with in our discussion of marriage rites. None of them has the faintest claim to be in any way associated with marriage by capture.

CHAPTER VI

CONSENT AS A CONDITION OF MARRIAGE

A MARRIAGE concerns not only the contracting parties but other individuals as well. Hence the conclusion of it may require the consent of the latter or even be arranged by them; and, on the other hand, the consent of the bride or the bridegroom or both may be dispensed with.

We have seen that infant- or child-betrothals are common among many of the lower races, and in such cases the consent of the parties is out of the question. But often enough the betrothal is not considered binding on either party, or is regarded as binding on the female only, although we may assume that as a rule the marriage is consummated. Among various savage peoples marriage contracts are concluded by the parents of the parties even when these are grown-up. Thus in many of the uncivilised tribes of India marriages are generally planned and arranged by the parents of the young people concerned. In several African tribes, also, the parents, and especially the father, arrange for the son's marriage; among the Xosa Kafirs it is the rule that the young man's father chooses the first, and sometimes even the second, wife for his sons. In Tikopia, one of the Santa Cruz Islands, and in the Banks Islands, according to Dr. Rivers, when a man is old enough to marry, a wife is chosen for him by his father's sister, or if he himself selects one, the choice is ratified by her; "a man would never marry against the will of his father's sister." Among some peoples a marriage is considered to require the consent not only of some near relatives, but of the communities to which the parties belong; in Australian tribes it is often arranged by the camp council or the leading men of the community. Considering that marriage brings together strange families or larger groups of kindred, or constitutes a new tie between friendly ones, it is not surprising that the fathers or parents or other relatives of the parties want to have a voice in the matter. The power of interference depends, of course, upon the authority which the families or their heads possess over the individual members of the family. Among the Xosa Kafirs, for example, the father rules as long as he lives over the whole of his family, including the married sons.

Much more frequently than the young man is the young girl dependent upon somebody else's will in the choice of a partner. Although the subject of family authority among the simpler peoples requires much further investigation, I think we may safely say that among most of them a girl is in her father's power till she marries, while in some instances his authority over her continues even after her marriage. Yet among various peoples the consent of a mother, brother, or maternal uncle is regarded as particularly essential to a girl's marriage, and in such cases the father may even have little or nothing to say in the matter. But the necessity of the father's or somebody else's consent by no means implies that the girl is, or can be, given in marriage against her own will.

A large number of statements relating to savages in different parts of the world show that the consent of the woman to her marriage is very frequently not only asked as a matter of fact, but even required by custom. There are no doubt many instances to the contrary as well. But from my collection of data I have come to the conclusion that these are less numerous than those in which the woman's wishes are, or must be, consulted; and a similar inference may be drawn from the list compiled by Messrs. Hobhouse, Wheeler, and Ginsberg.

As to the circumstances influencing the matter, we may without the slightest hesitation make the negative statement that the woman's liberty of choice among the lower races has not increased in proportion to their advancement in culture. On the contrary, if the Australian natives are excepted, it proves to be decidedly greater among the lowest savages than among the more advanced ones. It is greater among the lower hunters than among the higher hunters, greater among the incipient agriculturists than among the pure and the cattle-keeping agriculturists, greater among the lower pastoral tribes than among the higher pastoral tribes, and greater among the hunters and agriculturists as a whole than among the pastoral peoples. The main reason why progress in economic culture among the lower races has thus been unfavourable to the woman's liberty of choosing her husband is that it has led to marriage by purchase, which naturally tends to restrict her liberty. While marriage by purchase hardly occurs among the lower hunters and is rare among incipient agriculturists, it is more frequently found among higher hunters, and especially among pure and cattle-keeping agriculturists; it is more prevalent among higher pastoral tribes than among lower pastoral tribes, and, though very frequent among the higher agriculturists, it is more prevalent among the pastoral tribes as a whole than among the agricultural tribes. The development of marriage by purchase thus follows the same lines as the restriction of the woman's liberty of choice to an extent which makes it impossible to doubt that there has been a causal connection between them. But it seems that there is also another reason for the unfavourable influence which advancement in economic culture has exercised upon the woman's liberty of choice. By leading to accumulation of property and the distinction between richer and poorer people it naturally increases the interest which the family takes in the marriage of its members, and its head becomes less willing to allow individual inclinations to have their free play.

In this discussion of the circumstances which have interfered with savage women's liberty to choose their husbands we have so far taken no notice of the Australian aborigines, who, contrary to the lower hunters in other parts of the world, generally seem to allow their women no voice at all in the matter. Marriage by ordinary purchase does not exist among them, although the man may have to make small presents of game or weapons to the kindred of his bride, and we must therefore look for some other explanation of the compulsion to which their women are subject. The chief reasons for this compulsion are undoubtedly the exceptionally great prevalence of infant-betrothals, the habit of the old men of appropriating to themselves the comeliest women, and the custom of procuring a

wife by the exchange of a sister or other female relative, which gives the woman no voice in the matter
whether the barter takes place in her infancy or at a
later age. These customs are connected with the extraordinary tyranny exercised by the old men and the great
difficulties the younger men experience in getting
wives, or young wives, in any other peaceful way than
by infant-betrothals or the exchange of related females.
Hence the utter disregard of the woman's wishes
among the Australian natives is due to particular circumstances of an essentially local character, and can
by no means be regarded as a survival from a more
primitive stage than that represented by the other lower
hunters, whose social organisation is certainly of a less
developed type than that of the best known Australian
tribes. It is indeed doubtful whether the whole of the
Australians should be included in the class of lower
hunters. In view of all these facts it is impossible to
agree with M. Letourneau in his sweeping statement
that during a very long period woman was married
without her wishes being at all consulted. There is,
on the contrary, every reason to believe that in primitive ages she was much freer in her choice of partner
than she is now in the Australian tribes and among
many other savages on a higher level of culture.

It should be added that even where custom, strictly
speaking, gives the woman no voice in the matter,
she may nevertheless possess means of preventing a
marriage which is distasteful to her or of breaking
one which has been forced upon her against her
will. She may enlist the sympathy of her mother
or other female relatives, whose intervention would
prevail upon the father to change his mind; or she

may employ superstition as a weapon against an
objectionable proposal. Among the Berbers of the
Aith Sadděn, in the neighbourhood of Fez, when the
young man's mother, accompanied by some other
women, comes to the house or tent of the girl's parents
to let them know that her husband intends to sue for
their daughter on behalf of his son, it lies in the girl's
power to influence the proceedings although she is
not at all consulted in the matter. If she is fond of
the young man she dresses herself in fine clothes and
sits down with the women, trying to be as attractive
as possible; on the other hand, if she dislikes him
she makes use of bad and ominous words which
should not be mentioned on this occasion, or she
behaves like a woman at a funeral, scratching her face
and dirtying herself with cow-dung. The result of
this may be that no further steps are taken, for fear
lest a marriage arranged in such circumstances should
be unlucky. Moreover, it has sometimes happened
in the same tribe that the girl has prevented the proposed marriage by running away on this occasion, or
on the day of the intended wedding. Of various
peoples we learn that it is a common custom for
women to run away from men who have been forced
upon them by their parents; and among the Berbers
inhabiting the mountain regions of Central Morocco
I found the following curious institution. A woman
who does not like to remain with her husband may fly
to another man's house or tent, and embrace the pole
supporting the roof or one of the vertical tent-poles,
or, if there is no such pole, take hold of the handmill
and turn it round as if she were grinding. Then the
owner of the house or tent is obliged to marry her,

whether he be a bachelor or a married man and whatever be the number of his wives; and in addition he has to pay to the abandoned husband a compensation, fixed by custom, which varies considerably in different tribes and even in different divisions of the same tribe —among the Aith Saddĕn it amounts to five hundred dollars. This singular custom is based on the idea that some grave misfortune would befall the man if he did not wed the woman who in the said manner took refuge with him. For by taking hold of the pole of his dwelling or turning round his handmill, she puts ʿār on him, that is, transfers to him a conditional curse.

A very common method by which a woman can obtain the husband she desires without the consent or against the will of her parents is to elope with him. While this practice indicates that the mutual consent of the parties is not always sufficient for the conclusion of a marriage, it also provides a remedy for the insufficiency. It is resorted to if the young man is too poor to pay the price asked for the girl, or otherwise, from no fault of hers, is unable to marry her in the ordinary way. Among many peoples elopement is a veritable institution, recognised by custom as a method of concluding a marriage or at least as a preliminary to it. Frequently the lover may afterwards have to pay for his bride or to conciliate her people with some gift; but the elopement may also by itself be sufficient to make the runaway couple husband and wife. Nowhere is marriage by elopement more frequent, and indeed more needed, than in many Australian tribes. Among the Kurnai in Gippsland, according to Howitt, a man, with rare exceptions, "could acquire a wife in one way only, namely, by running off with her secretly and with her own consent." It was the business of a medicine-man to aid the elopement of young couples, and this gave sanction to the practice, which arose from the difficulty in finding a wife. If the parties are prohibited from intermarrying on account of the relationship in which they stand to each other, the elopement is punished with great severity, whereas otherwise the lover may, at least in certain circumstances, retain the woman with whom he eloped. In many cases he has to fight the man to whom she has been promised or, if she is already married, her husband, or a more general struggle ensues in which kindred are involved; and in either case the issue of the fight decides whether he will be allowed to keep the woman or not. But among some Australian tribes he may retain the woman if they stay away till a child is born or the girl is with child, or even if "the happy couple straightway elope, and remain together in the bush for two nights and one day, in order to elude the pretended search of the tribe to whom the female belonged."

When passing from the savage and barbarous races of men to those next above them in civilisation, we find paternal, or parental, authority and filial reverence at their height. In ancient Mexico necessitous parents were allowed to dispose of any one of their children in order to relieve their poverty, and a youth was seldom permitted to choose a wife for himself, but was expected to abide by the selection of his parents. In ancient Peru there was a law to the effect that sons should obey and serve their fathers until they reached the age of twenty-five, and that none should marry without the consent of his own parents and of those of the girl, a marriage without such consent being invalid and the children illegitimate. But we are told that the preference of the parties was also to be consulted.

The idea that filial piety is the fundamental duty of man has up to our days dominated the Chinese legislation relating to the family. The house-father reigns almost supreme in his household, and not even marriage withdraws the son from his power. No person, of whatever age, can act for himself in matrimonial matters during the lifetime or in the neighbourhood of his parents or near senior kinsfolk. The power of these guardians is so great that they may contract a marriage for a junior who is absent from home, and he is bound to abide by such engagement even though already affianced elsewhere without their privity or consent. The consequence of this system is that in many cases the betrothed couple scarcely know each other before marriage, the wedding being the first occasion on which the man catches a glimpse of his wife's face. In Japan the authority of a house-father was in former times as strong as in China. It was the established principle of Japanese customary law that a member of a house must obtain the consent of the head of the family for his or her marriage, and often the consent of the parties themselves was not required. According to the regulations of the new Civil code of Japan, the free consent of the persons who marry is necessary in addition to that of the parents "who are in the same house"; and when a man has completed his thirtieth year and a woman her twenty-fifth, the consent of the parents is no longer required. But as a matter of fact, marriages are still generally arranged by the parents of the parties.

In ancient Chaldæa the father likewise had great power over his children. We are told that a daughter was given away in marriage by her father without being able to raise any objection to his choice, and that a son also could not conclude a valid marriage without the consent of his father; but it is not known whether the father's right to interfere with the matrimonial affairs of his son lasted till his death. That his power over his son was great appears from the fact that a disobedient son might be sold as a slave.

The importance which the ancient Hebrews attached to the duties of a child to its parents may be at once learned from the placing of the law on the subject among the Ten Commandments, and from its position there in the immediate proximity to the commands relating to the duties of man towards God. A father might sell his child to relieve his own distress, or offer it to a creditor as a pledge. He had unlimited power not only to marry his daughters, but even to sell them as maids into concubinage, though not to a foreign people. He also chose wives for his sons, the selection, however, sometimes being made by the mother; and there is no indication that the subjection of sons ceased after a certain age. According to the later Jewish law, the consent of parents is no legal requirement when the parties to the marriage are of age. But Mielziner states that, in consequence of the high respect and veneration in which father and mother have ever been held among Israelites, "the cases of contracting marriage without the parents' consent fortunately belong to the rarest exceptions."

According to Muhammadan law, the woman's consent is not required if she is still in her father's power. Among the Hanafīs and the Shī'ahs the father's right to marry his daughter without her consent comes to an end when she arrives at puberty, but this is not the case among the Mālikī school of Muhammadans. Among them she ceases to be in his power only by his death, or by her being expressly emancipated by him during his lifetime, or by marriage, or, according to some jurists, when she has reached the age of at least thirty. On the other hand, when marriage is contracted on behalf of a woman who is no longer in her father's power, it is necessary that she should give her consent to it, either in express terms or, if she be a virgin, at least by implication; and in the latter case her silence or laugh is construed to imply consent. In Morocco, Algeria, Tunis, and many parts of Palestine it is the general rule that the parents of a girl marry her without asking for her consent. But the Bedouins of the desert differ from the other Muhammadan natives of Palestine in allowing their girls to accept or reject a proposal; and in Mecca a virgin is seldom forced into marriage, although it is considered proper that she should behave as though she submitted to her father's will only because she has to obey him. According to all the Muhammadan schools, a son is at liberty to contract a marriage without his father's consent when he has attained his puberty, which is mostly presumed on the completion of the fifteenth year. But although the father certainly has the right to impose the status of marriage on his children during their minority, sons and daughters alike, the law takes care that this right shall not be exercised to the prejudice of the infant; any act of the father which is likely to injure the interests of the minor is considered illegal, and entitles the judge to interfere in order to prevent the completion of such act or, if complete, to annul it. As a matter of fact, however, in Morocco and elsewhere parents not infrequently arrange the marriage of their son even though he be grown up, according to their own taste; and custom may require that he should comply with their wishes. Where the separation between the sexes is so strict as it often is in the Muhammadan world, the interference of parents in the matrimonial affairs of their son can hardly be felt as a burden by the young man, especially as he can readily divorce a wife whom he does not like. And for a girl it would be no easy matter to choose between suitors whom she does not know.

Among the ancient Romans, in relation to the house-father, "all in the household were destitute of legal rights—the wife and the child no less than the bullock or the slave." The father not only had judicial authority over his children—implying the right of inflicting capital punishment on them, though not without a just cause—but he could sell them at discretion. Even the grown-up son and his children were subject to the house-father's authority, and in marriage without *conventio in manum* a daughter remained in the power of her father or tutor even after marriage. The consent of the *paterfamilias* was indispensable to the marriage of children, sons and daughters alike; and so strict was this rule that down to the reign of Marcus Aurelius the children of a *mente captus* could not contract a legal marriage while in the power of their father. the latter being incapable of giving his consent.

It has been suggested by Sir Henry Maine and others that the *patria potestas* of the Romans was a survival of the paternal authority which existed among the primitive Aryans. But no clear evidence of the general prevalence of such unlimited authority among other so-called Aryan peoples has been adduced. The ancient jurist observed: "The power which we have over our children is peculiar to Roman citizens; for there are no other nations possessing the same power over their children as we have over ours." Among the Greeks and Teutons the father had the right to expose his children in their infancy, to sell them in case of urgency as long as they remained in his power, and to give away his daughters in marriage without consulting their wishes; but this does not imply the possession of a sovereignty like that which the Roman house-father exercised over his descendants of all ages. It was very frequently the lot of a Greek woman to be given in marriage to a man whom she did not know. In Greece and among all the Teutonic nations the father's authority over his son came to an end when the latter grew up and left his home; and a grown-up son might choose his own wife. But it seems that among the Teutons a man, in doing so, might have been required by custom to take counsel with his kinsfolk.

Nor is there any evidence that the *patria potestas* of the Roman type ever prevailed in full in India, great though the father's or the parents' authority has been, and still is, among the Hindus. In Vedic times the father seems to have been the head of the family only as long as he was able to be its protector and maintainer, decrepit parents being even allowed to die of starvation. Macdonell and Keith maintain that considerable freedom was probably left both to man and woman in selecting a wife or a husband, although no doubt parents often arranged suitable marriages for their children. According to some sacred books from a later age, the father and the mother have power to give, to sell, and to abandon their son, because "man formed of uterine blood and virile seed proceeds from his mother and his father as an effect from its cause"; whereas in other books it is said that "the gift or acceptance of a child and the right to sell or buy a child are not recognised." According to the *Laws of Manu,* a daughter might choose her husband in accordance with her own wish, but the legislator disapproves of such a "voluntary union of a maiden and her lover . . . which springs from desire and has sexual intercourse for its purpose." Whatever be the strict legal rights of a parent, filial piety is a most stringent duty in a child. A man has three Atigurus, or specially venerable superiors: his father, mother, and spiritual teacher; to them he must always pay obedience; he must do what is agreeable and serviceable to them; he must never do anything without their leave. Similar feelings prevail among the modern Hindus; while the duty of daughters is from the day of their marriage transferred entirely to their husbands and their husbands' parents. According to the existing customs of the Hindus, the consent of the parents on the girl's side is essential, and on the boy's it is considered necessary on a first marriage, and is always advisable. A native writer states that "the Hindu youth has to maintain an attitude of utter indifference about every proposal regarding his marriage, and when any arrangement in that respect is made by his parents, grandparents, uncles or elder brothers, he has to go through the ceremony out of his sense of duty to obey or oblige them."

According to ancient Russian laws, fathers had great power over their children; but it is not probable that a son could be sold as a slave. Baron von Haxthausen, who wrote before the Emancipation in 1861, says that "the patriarchal government, feelings, and organisation are in full activity in the life, manners, and customs of the Great Russians. The same unlimited authority which the father exercises over all his children is possessed by the mother over her daughters." Even the adult son was subject to his father's authority until he had himself children arrived to years of discretion, or had in his turn become the head of the family. It was a common custom for a father to marry his young son to a grown-up woman in order to secure an additional female labourer, and he cohabited himself with the wife during the son's minority. According to Professor Bogišić, the power of the father is not so great among the Southern Slavs as among the Russians. But a son is not permitted to make a proposal of marriage to a girl against the will of his parents; and among the Croatians and Serbians it is quite exceptional for the young man himself to look about for his future wife. A daughter, of course, enjoys still less freedom of disposing of her own hand.

In ancient Ireland the son was under the father's

control till formally emancipated; but it is not known at what age the emancipation took place. The Welsh laws refer to the giving of a daughter in marriage by her kindred as well as by her father. She does not seem to have been entirely at the disposal of the latter, nor to have been, in theory, entirely free.

In Europe the paternal authority of the archaic type has gradually yielded to a system under which the father has been divested of the most essential rights he formerly possessed over his children—a system the inmost drift of which is expressed in the words of the French Encyclopedist: "Le pouvoir paternel est plutôt un devoir qu'un pouvoir."

Even in pagan times the Roman *patria potestas* was subject to important restrictions. The life of the child was practically as sacred as that of the parent long before Christianity became the religion of Rome. Alexander Severus limited the father's right of punishing his children to simple correction, and Diocletian and Maximilian took away the power of selling freeborn children as slaves. Under the jurisprudence of Justinian a father could not force his son or daughter in marriage. But at the same time the right of a voice in his children's marriages was stoutly maintained: the consent of the head of the family remained essential to the validity of the marriage of anyone under his power, irrespective of age.

Canon law adopted the principle that no marriage can be concluded without the consent of the persons who marry; but, unlike Justinian's law, as a consequence of its doctrine that marriage is a sacrament, it ruled that, however young the bridegroom and bride may be, the consent of their parents or guardians is not necessary to make the marriage valid. The Church disapproved of marriages contracted without such consent: the lack of it was a "prohibitory impediment" (*impedimentum impediens*), rendering the marriage illicit, but not a "diriment impediment" (*impedimentum dirimens*), rendering it null and void. The stipulations of Canon law influenced secular legislation. An edict of Clothaire I. in 560 prohibited the forcing of women to marry against their will. According to the laws of Cnut, no woman or girl could be compelled to marry a man whom she disliked. In an Anglo-Saxon betrothal formula from the tenth century the girl's consent is unconditionally required. And various early Teutonic law-books in continental countries likewise prohibited the forcing of a woman into marriage against her will. As to the canonical prescription that a marriage is valid without the consent of parents or guardians, it seems that the English temporal law more or less acquiesced in it, although it regarded "wardship and marriage" as a valuable piece of property; and in the later Middle Ages German women were able to marry without parental consent, though at the risk of being disinherited. The feelings of the people seemed to have been opposed to such marriages. Attempts were made to induce the Church to change its law on the subject, but in vain; the matter was definitely settled at the Council of Trent, after a lively discussion.

Luther and other reformers were of a different opinion: they maintained that a marriage contracted without the consent of parents should be regarded as invalid, unless the consent was given afterwards. This principle was gradually accepted by most legislators in Protestant countries, but with the modification that parental consent could be refused for good reasons only and, in case of need, the consent of the authorities could take its place. In Roman Catholic countries, also, the canonical doctrine met with opposition; legislators declared parental consent to be necessary for the validity of a marriage, and no appeal could be made in the case of refusal. Henry II. of France declared, in 1556, that a marriage contracted by a minor without the consent of ascendants was null and void; and the later legislation went further in the same direction. If a marriage was contracted without such consent by a person who was below the age of twenty-five, it was annulled; if contracted by a person between twenty-five and thirty, it was valid, but disinheritance might be the consequence; and if contracted by a person above the age of thirty, it had still to be previously notified to the ascendants by "three respectful acts." Indeed, according to the French "Code Civil," a son under twenty-five and a daughter under twenty-one could not, until 1907, marry without parental consent.

Generally speaking, in France and other Latin countries the Roman notions of paternal rights and filial duties have to some extent survived among the people throughout the Middle Ages and long after. In the literature of the eleventh century, says M. Bernard, the paternal character "is everywhere honoured, and filial piety everywhere praised and rewarded. In the romances of chivalry fathers are never ridiculous, nor sons insolent and mocking. . . . Above the majesty of the feudal baron, that of the paternal power was held still more sacred and inviolable. However powerful the son might be, he would not have dared to outrage his father, whose authority was in his eyes always confounded with the sovereignty of command." Bodin wrote, in the latter part of the sixteenth century, that although the monarch commands his subjects, the master his disciples, the captain his soldiers, there is none to whom nature has given any command except the father, "who is the true image of the great sovereign God, universal father of all things." Du Vair remarked that we ought to regard our fathers as gods on earth. In the Duke of Sully's Memoirs we read that in his days in France children were not permitted to sit in the presence of their parents without being commanded to do so. Speaking of the women among the nobility and upper classes in France during the eighteenth century, Messrs. de Goncourt remark: "Généralement le mariage de la jeune fille se faisait presque immédiatement au sortir du couvent, avec un mari accepté et agréé par la famille. Car le mariage était avant tout une affaire de famille, un arrangement au gré des parents, qui décidaient des considérations de position et d'argent, des convenances de rang et de fortune. Le choix était fait d'avance pour la jeune personne, qui n'était pas consultée."

According to the present law of France, a son and daughter under the age of twenty-one cannot marry without the consent of the father and mother, or of the father only if they disagree, or of the survivor if one be dead. If both father and mother are dead, or in a condition which renders them unable to consent, the grandparents take their place. Between the ages of twenty-one and thirty the parties must still obtain parental consent, but if this be refused it can be regulated by means of an act before a notary, and if the consent is not given within thirty days the marriage can take place without it. In Italy the consent of parents, or of the father, or of the survivor if one of the parents is dead, is required for a son who has not completed his twenty-fifth year and for a daughter who has not completed her twenty-first; but in case of refusal of consent provision is made for an appeal to a court. In Austria minors, that is, individuals under the age of twenty-four, are incapable of contracting a valid marriage without the consent of their father. In Germany a legitimate child requires, before the completion of his twenty-first year of age, the approval of the father for concluding a marriage, whilst an illegitimate child requires before the same age the approval of the mother; if the father is dead, the mother takes his place. In Sweden parental consent is required of persons under the age of twenty-one, in Switzerland of persons under the age of twenty.

In England, by the common law, the marriages of minors who had attained the age of consent—fixed at fourteen years for males and twelve years for females —were valid without the consent of parents until the year 1753, when Lord Hardwicke's Marriage Act (26 Geo. II., c. 33, § 11) declared such marriages void. According to the present law of England, "where a person, not being a widower nor widow, is under the age of twenty-one years, the father, if living, or, if he is dead, the guardian or guardians, or one of them, or if there is no guardian lawfully appointed, then the mother, if she has not remarried, has authority to consent to his or her marriage; and such consent is required except where there is no person having authority to give it." Yet the marriage of a minor without the requisite consent is not invalid, whether it is by banns or licence or superintendent registrar's certificate; but there may be forfeiture of all the rights and interest in any property accruing to the offending party by force of the marriage. In Scotland, on the other hand, no consent of parents or guardian is required even of minors who have attained the age of puberty; and by the common law of the United States, which was not affected by Lord Hardwicke's Marriage Act, the marriage of minors without the parental consent is likewise good. There are "statutes which forbid the celebration of the nuptials of minors without permission from the parent or guardian; but, in the absence of a clause of nullity, which most of them do not contain, a marriage in disobedience is valid, while yet the participators in it may be subject to a penalty or punishment." In many European countries a marriage entered into without the prescribed parental consent is annulled if the parent whose consent is required demands it, whereas in other countries such a marriage is not invalid but may entail disinheritance.

Before leaving our present subject, we must still consider the origin of that authority which has given fathers or parents a right to interfere with the marriage of their children even in cases when such interference cannot be regarded merely as a safeguard of the children's own interests.

In the first place, the parental authority obviously

depends upon the natural superiority of parents over their children when young, and on the helplessness of the latter; and for similar reasons the daughter, though grown-up, still remains in her father's power. Parents are, moreover, considered to possess in some measure proprietary rights over their offspring, being their originators and maintainers; and in various cases, it seems, the father is also regarded as their owner because he is the owner of their mother. Filial duties and parental rights to some extent spring from the children's natural feeling of affection for their parents, particularly for their mother, and from the debt of gratitude which they are considered to owe to those who have brought them into existence and taken care of them while young. The authority of parents is much enhanced and extended by the sentiment of filial reverence, as distinct from mere affection. From their infancy children are used to look up to their parents, especially the father, as to beings superior to themselves; and this feeling, which by itself has a tendency to persist, is all the more likely to last even when the parents get old, as it is based not only on superior strength and bodily skill, but on superior knowledge and wisdom, which remain though the physical power be on the wane. "In the Russian people," says Leroy-Beaulieu, "parental power is supported by religious feeling and reverence for age. . . . 'Where white hairs are, there is good sense, there is right'—such is, with variations, the burden of many popular proverbs." "Long life and wisdom," say the Iroquois, "are always connected together"; and throughout West Africa the aged are "the knowing ones." Among peoples who possess no literature the old men are the sole authorities on religion as well as on custom. In Australia the great deference shown to them is partly due to the superstitious awe of certain mysterious rites which are known to them alone, and to the knowledge of which young persons are only very gradually admitted. Dr. Rivers takes the magical power of the old men to be the original source of their dominance in Melanesia. Among the East African Embe "it is only by means of the rankest superstition that the old men are able to maintain their supremacy over the hot-blooded youths"; they convince the warriors, by presenting them with some magic emblem, that in the hands of the sages alone rest the fate and fortune of those who fight in a battle. And old women, also, are often believed to possess supernatural power, in which case their influence, in spite of the subservient position of their sex in general, is almost as great as that of a medicine-man. Old age itself inspires a feeling of mysterious awe. The Moors say that, when becoming old, a man becomes a saint, and a woman a *jinnîya,* or evil spirit—there is something supernatural in both.

The beliefs held regarding the dead also influence the treatment of the aged whose lives are drawing to an end. Certain Central African tribes are reported to treat their old people with every kindness in order to secure their good-will after death. A missionary in East Africa heard a negro say with reference to an old man, "We will do what he says, because he is soon going to die." In China the doctrine that ghosts may interfere at any moment with human business and fate, either favourably or unfavourably, "enforces respect for human life and a charitable treatment of the infirm, the aged, and the sick, especially if they stand on the brink of the grave." The regard for the aged and the worship of the dead are often mentioned together in a way which suggests that there exists an intrinsic connection between them. In such cases, however, it is impossible accurately to distinguish between cause and effect. While the worship of the dead is, in the first place, due to the mystery of death, it is evident that the regard in which a person is held during his lifetime also influences the veneration which is bestowed on his disembodied soul.

Among the peoples of archaic culture, in particular, there is a close connection between filial submissiveness and religious beliefs. In China and Japan the reverence for parents almost forms a part of the worship of ancestors. As to the Israelites, Philo Judæus remarks that the commandment enjoining obedience to parents occupies its position immediately after those prescribing the duties of man towards God because parents are something between divine and human nature, partaking of both—of human nature inasmuch as it is plain that they have been born and that they will die, and of divine nature because they have engendered other beings, and have brought into existence what did not exist before. What God is to the world, that parents are to their children; they are "the visible gods." The religious character of filial duties is very conspicuous both in Muhammadanism and in Hinduism. Disobedience to parents is considered by Moslems as one of the greatest of sins, and is put, in point of heinousness, on a par with idolatry, murder, and desertion in an expedition against infidels. According to ancient Hindu ideas, a father, mother, and spiritual teacher are equal to the three Vedas, equal to the three gods, Brahman, Vishnu, and Siva. A man who shows no regard for them derives no benefit from any religious observance; whereas, "by honouring his mother he gains the present world; by honouring his father, the world of gods; and by paying strict obedience to his spiritual teacher, the world of Brahman." In the Greek writings there are numerous passages which put filial piety on a par with the duties towards the gods. To the ancient Romans the parents were hardly less sacred beings than the gods. In Russia the father, like the Tsar, "was thought to hold from Heaven a sort of right divine, to rebel against which would have been sacrilege." According to a Slavonic maxim, "a father is like an earthly god to his son."

Among the ancient nations of culture the father was invested with sacerdotal functions. In primitive antiquity, says Fustel de Coulanges, "the father is not only the strong man, the protector who has power to command obedience; he is the priest, he is heir to the hearth, the continuator of the ancestors, the parent stock of the descendants, the depositary of the mysterious rites of worship, and of the sacred formulas of prayer. The whole religion resides in him."

Another very important reason for the connection between filial submissiveness and religious beliefs was no doubt the extreme importance attached to the curses and blessings of parents. The Israelites believed that parents, and especially a father, could by their blessings or curses determine the fate of their children; indeed, we have reason to assume that the reward which in the fifth commandment is held out to respectful children was originally a result of parental blessings. We still meet with the ancient idea in Ecclesiasticus, where it is said: "Honour thy father in word and deed, that a blessing may come upon thee from him. For the blessing of the father establisheth the houses of children; but the curse of the mother rooteth out the foundations." The Moors have a proverb that "if the saints curse you the parents will cure you, but if the parents curse you the saints will not cure you"; in other words, the curse of a parent is even stronger than that of a saint.

The notion that the parents' blessings beget prosperity and that their curses bring ruin prevailed in ancient Greece. Plato says in his *Laws:* "Neither God, nor a man who has understanding, will ever advise anyone to neglect his parents. . . . The curses of parents are, as they ought to be, mighty against their children as no others are. And shall we suppose that the prayers of a father or mother who is specially dishonoured by his or her children are heard by the gods in accordance with nature; and that if a parent is honoured by them, and in the gladness of his heart earnestly entreats the gods in his prayers to do them good, he is not equally heard, and that they do not minister to his request? . . . Therefore, if a man makes a right use of his father and grandfather and other aged relations, he will have images which above all others will win him the favour of the gods." We may assume that originally the efficacy of parents' curses and blessings was ascribed to a magic power immanent in the spoken word itself, and that their Erinyes, like those of guests and suppliants and

beggars, were only personifications of curses pronounced in case of ill-treatment or neglect. But in
this, as in other similar instances, the fulfilment of
the curse or the blessing came afterwards to be looked
upon as an act of divine justice. According to Plato,
"Nemesis, the messenger of justice," watches over
unbecoming words uttered to a parent; and Hesiod
says that if anybody reproaches an aged father or
mother, "Zeus himself is wroth, and at last, in requital
for wrong deeds, lays on him a bitter penalty." It also
seems to be beyond all doubt that the *divi parentum*
of the Romans, like their *dii hospitales,* were nothing
but personified curses. For it is said, "If a son beat
his parent and he cry out, the son shall be devoted
to the parental gods for destruction."

In aristocratic families in Russia children used to
stand in mortal fear of their father's curses; and the
country people still believe that a marriage without
the parents' approval will call down the wrath of
Heaven on the heads of the young couple. Some of
the Southern Slavs maintain that if a son does not
fulfil the last will of his father, the soul of the father
will curse him from the grave. The Serbians say,
"Without reverence for old men there is no salvation."

Various uncivilised peoples, also, ascribe great
efficacy to the curses or blessings of parents. Among
the Mpongwe of Western Africa "there is nothing
which a young person so much deprecates as the curse
of an aged person, and especially that of a revered
father." Among the Nandi in British East Africa,
"if a son refuses to obey his father in any serious
matter, the father solemnly strikes the son with his
fur mantle. This is equivalent to a most serious

curse, and is supposed to be fatal to the son unless he obtains forgiveness, which he can only do by sacrificing a goat before his father." The Barea and Kunáma, in North-East Africa, are convinced that any undertaking which has not the blessing of the old people will fail, that every curse uttered by them must be destructive. Among the Bogos, in the same neighbourhood, nobody takes an employment or gives it up, nobody engages in a business or contracts a marriage, before he has received the blessing of his father or his master.

Why are the blessings and curses of parents supposed to possess such an extraordinary power? One reason is no doubt the mystery of old age and the nearness of death. Not parents only, but to some extent old people generally, are held capable of giving due effect to their good and evil wishes, and this capacity is believed to increase when life is drawing to its close. The Herero, according to Büttner, know really no blessing save that conferred by the father on his death-bed. According to Teutonic ideas, the curse of a dying person was the strongest of all curses. A similar notion prevailed among the ancient Arabs; and among the Israelites the father's mystic privilege of determining the weal or woe of his children was particularly obvious when his days were manifestly numbered. But, at the same time, parental benedictions and imprecations possess a potency of their own owing to the parents' superior position in the family and the respect in which they are naturally held. The influence which such a superiority has upon the efficacy of curses is well brought out by certain facts. According to the Greek notion, the Erinyes avenged wrongs done by younger members of a family to elder ones, even brothers and sisters, but not *vice versâ*. The Moors say that the curse of a husband is as potent as that of a father. The Tonga Islanders believe that curses have no effect "if the party who curses is considerably lower in rank than the party cursed." Moreover, where the father was the priest of the family, his blessings and curses would for that reason also be efficacious in an exceptional degree.

However, the facts which we have hitherto considered are hardly sufficient to account for the extraordinary development of the paternal authority in the archaic State. Great though it be, the influence which magical and religious beliefs exercise upon the paternal authority is largely of a reactive character. A father's blessings would not be so eagerly sought for, nor would his curses be so greatly feared, if he were a less important personage in the family. So, too, as Sir Henry Maine aptly remarks, the father's power is older than the practice of worshipping him. "Why should the dead father be worshipped more than any other member of the household unless he was the most prominent—it may be said, the most awful—figure in it during his life?" We must assume that there exists some connection between the organisation of the family and the political constitution of the society. At the lower stages of civilisation—though hardly at the very lowest—we frequently find that the clan has attained such an overwhelming importance that only a very limited amount of authority could be claimed by the head of each separate family. But this was changed when clans and tribes were united into a State. The new State tended to weaken and destroy the clan system, whereas at the same time the family tie grew in strength. In early society there seems to be an antagonism between the family and the clan. Where the clan bond is very strong, it encroaches upon the family feeling, and where it is loosened the family gains. Hence Dr. Grosse may be right in his assumption that the father became a patriarch, in the true sense of the word, only as the inheritor of the authority which formerly belonged to the clan.

But whilst in its earlier days the State strengthened the family by weakening the clan, its later development had a different tendency. When national life grew more intense, when members of separate families drew nearer to one another in pursuit of a common goal, when along with industrial progress the younger members of a family became economically more independent of their parents, the family again lost in importance. Other factors also, inherent in progressive civilisation, contributed to the downfall of the paternal power—the extinction of ancestor-worship, the decay of certain superstitious beliefs, the declining influence of religion, and last, but not least, the spread of a keener mutual sympathy throughout the State, which could not allow that the liberty of children should be sacrificed to the despotic rule of their fathers.

CHAPTER VII

MARRIAGE BY CONSIDERATION AND BY THE EXCHANGE OF PRESENTS. GIFTS TO THE BRIDE AND TO THE BRIDEGROOM

AMONG the lower races consent to the contraction of a marriage is not generally given for nothing. In most cases some consideration has to be offered to the father or other relatives of the bride, either in the form of the exchange of bride for bride, or of service, or of the giving of property of some kind or other.

With reference to the Australian natives Dr. Howitt observes: "It may be safely laid down as a broad and general proposition that among these savages a wife was obtained by. the exchange of a female relative, with the alternative possibility of obtaining one by inheritance (Levirate), by elopement, or by capture. . . . It seems to me that the most common practice is the exchange of girls by their respective parents as wives for each other's sons, or in some tribes the exchange of sisters, or of some female relatives, by the young men themselves." The prevalence of the exchange of bride for bride among those natives has been attested by many other writers with regard to different tribes, although the custom does not seem to occur in all parts of Australia. It has been said that among the Australian aborigines a wife is a man's most valuable possession on account of their extreme poverty, and that, having no equivalent in property to give for one, a native is generally obliged to get her in exchange for a female relative. But there are many peoples who are equally poor or poorer and yet have never been known to give daughters or sisters in exchange for wives. It seems that an important reason for the remarkable prevalence of this practice in Australia is the unusual difficulty in getting a wife, which must to some extent be due to the rigorous class and clan rules greatly restricting the circle within which a man is allowed to marry. This difficulty does not exist for a man who has a sister to be given in exchange for a wife, because he can thereby get a woman from a class and clan into which he is permitted to marry. If, for example, among the Kamilaroi of New South Wales a Kumbo man can marry a Muri woman, the brother of the latter, who is a Muri man, can also marry the sister of the former, who is a Kumbo woman. The practice of exchanging bride for bride is found in various other parts of the world, but mostly side by side with marriage by ordinary purchase as an economic measure intended to save the bride price. With special reference to the exchange system in the Solomon Group in Melanesia, Dr. Thurnwald expresses the opinion that "mutual exchange of women probably originated as a pledge of good-will in the establishment of friendly relations between two communities"; and he believes that this form of marriage was the original one from which the buying of women with objects of value has been derived.

More widespread than marriage by exchange is the custom of obtaining a wife by services rendered to her father. This practice, with which Hebrew traditions

have familiarised us, is especially found among many
North and South American Indians, among various
Siberian peoples, in a large number of aboriginal
tribes in China, Indo-China, and India, in many
islands of the Malay Archipelago, and among several
African peoples. The man generally has to go and
live with the family of his future spouse for a certain
time, during which he works as a servant. The period
of service varies greatly among different peoples: it
seldom lasts less than a year, and may even last as many
as ten or twelve or fifteen years. During this time he
may or may not have access to the girl. He may have
to serve after his marriage as well, until a child is born
or longer, and he may have to remain with his wife's
family for ever. But, as has been justly pointed out,
a form of marriage under which a man is permanently
transferred to his wife's family is to be distinguished
from the form of marriage under which he serves his
father-in-law for a limited time for the wife whom he
will afterwards take away with him to his own home;
and I can find no sufficient ground for the suggestion
that the custom of serving for a wife is the relic of an
earlier custom by which a man went to live permanently
in his father-in-law's house. Of several peoples we
are told that the first wife only is obtained by service.

Among various tribes service is the regular, if not
exclusive, method of acquiring a wife. In other cases
marriage by service occurs, not as the regular form of
marriage, but as a substitute for marriage by purchase,
when the suitor is too poor to pay the ordinary bride
price. And among various peoples a man cannot obtain a wife by service alone, but, besides serving for
her, has to pay a price for her. The practice of serving

for a wife is obviously, in a large measure, due to the unwillingness of a father to give his daughter in marriage for nothing, as is proved by the many cases in which service is a substitute for ordinary purchase. But from various statements it appears that it also has another meaning: the period of service is intended to test the young man's ability to work and to show whether he is an acceptable husband and son-in-law. This has been strongly emphasised by Dr. Jochelson, who writes with reference to the Koryaks in Siberia: "A serving bridegroom is not an ordinary workman. The principal thought is not his usefulness, but the hard and humiliating trials to which he is subjected. The bridegroom is given a poor bed, he is ill-fed, he is not allowed to sleep late, he is sent on exhausting errands. As a herdsman he must pass his nights without sleep, while the proprietor of the herd and the bride's brothers are resting. In a word, during his term of service, his endurance, patience, and meekness, his adroitness as a hunter, and his zeal and frugality as a herdsman, are tested. The bride's father gives his assent to the marriage only after the bridegroom has stood the probation well. This view of the trial of a bridegroom, who must perform tests dangerous to his life, and win contests, is also found in Koryak tales." In Cambodia the period of service is likewise a period of probation, in which it is the youth's business to render himself agreeable to the young lady as well as her parents. Speaking of the service of the bridegroom among the Naudowessies, in the region of the North American great lakes, Carver observes that by this means "the father has an opportunity of seeing whether he is able to provide for the support of his daughter and the children that might be the consequence of their union." Among the South American Indians the services which a man has to render his intended father-in-law are obviously, to a large extent, meant to be a test of his ability.

Spencer believed that the obtaining of wives by services rendered, instead of property paid, constitutes a higher form of marriage, and is developed along with the industrial type of society. But this view is not borne out by facts. Marriage by service is found, nay flourishes, among hunting tribes; and in other cases also the services required of a suitor are not such as presuppose any higher development of economic culture. On the other hand, where there is marriage by purchase there must be some accumulation of property. Hence service as a substitute for the normal form of purchase may be said to be found among more advanced savages alone.

Most frequently the consideration given for a wife consists of property of some kind or other. The amount varies greatly among different peoples. In the lowest tribes it is very inconsiderable, and among many tribes of a more advanced type the consideration is likewise of small value. It is often represented as a gift only, the offering and acceptance of which constitute no act of purchase; whereas in other cases it is of a considerable amount and makes the conclusion of a marriage a genuine business transaction. Among North American Indians the bride price is often paid in horses, among African peoples in cattle or goats. Among some tribes it is uniformly fixed by custom, but more frequently it varies according to the circumstances. It is greatly influenced by the rank and wealth of the families of the parties, or by the personal qualities of the girl—her beauty, strength, or ability; and a virgin or a girl generally commands a better price than a widow or a repudiated wife. In most cases the consideration for a bride is given to her father, but he may have to share it with other members of the family or relatives of the girl, or special presents are given to them; her mother, in particular, is a frequent recipient. Sometimes the consideration, or a large part of it, is given to the maternal uncle of the bride, and her brothers may also play a prominent part in the transactions. Among some North American and African tribes the bride price gives the husband no claim over the children born, for whom a special payment has to be made; but among other African peoples he is entitled to reclaim the bride price in case his wife dies before bearing a child, or to demand another woman, generally her sister, as a substitute.

Where the paying of a bride price is a regular custom it would be considered highly disgraceful to a girl and her family if she were given in marriage for nothing. According to Yakut ideas, "it would mean that she was not worth any price, was friendless, was an outcast. It can be understood, therefore, that the Yakut women look down upon the Russian women, who, as they say, pay somebody to take them." The Kafir women pour scorn and contempt on one who has not been duly bought by cattle; they call such a woman an old cat, because the cat is the only animal that the natives consider unworthy of being sold. But she is a proud woman for whom a larger sum than usual is paid.

Like other forms of marriage by consideration, the

giving of material objects for a bride is in the first place due to the unwillingness of the person or persons who have a right to dispose of a girl's hand to part with her for nothing, and to the readiness of a man to give something in order to obtain a wife. This form of marriage has generally been called "marriage by purchase"; but in many cases there is no justification at all for such a term, and in others it may be used only if it is understood that girls are not sold by their relatives like chattels. The gift may be an expression of good-will or respect on the part of the bridegroom. It may be a proof of his ability to keep a wife. It may serve as a protection to the wife against ill-usage and to the husband against misbehaviour on the side of the wife. In many cases the price is said to be a compensation for the loss sustained in the giving up of the girl or a remuneration for the expenses incurred in her maintenance till the time of her marriage; and the gift to her mother is regarded as a reward for nursing her, as a "price of the mother's milk," or sometimes, it seems, as a reward for guarding her virginity, as "the price of the virgin." Mercenary motives may be prominent: daughters may be bartered away to the highest bidders and be trained for the purpose of fetching a high price. But whatever be the reason for claiming a consideration for a bride and whether the consideration be large or small, it does not confer on the husband the right to do with the wife whatever he may please. He can only "buy" the rights which custom grants to a husband; and however great these rights may be, I think we may safely say that they never are quite absolute, and that among no people a married woman is completely at the mercy of her husband. Among many African peoples the parents may in certain circumstances take back their daughter on restoration of the bride price.

It has been suggested that marriage by purchase arose out of marriage by capture. We are told that abduction in spite of parents was the primary form; then there came the offering of compensation to escape vengeance; and this grew eventually into the making of presents beforehand. In support of this view instances have been quoted of peoples among whom a man who carries off or elopes with a woman afterwards has to pay compensation if she is to become his wife. But these cases merely show that marriage by consideration is the recognised form of marriage, although forcible abduction or elopement may be a preliminary measure leading up to it. They by no means imply that the bride price was originally a ransom. Marriage by consideration prevails among a large number of peoples who have never been known to be in the habit of capturing women for wives; and, as I said in the preceding chapter, marriage by capture cannot be proved to have been the useful form of marriage among any people.

While the rendering of some consideration for the bride undoubtedly is the normal mode of securing marriage at all grades in the uncivilised world, it has, generally speaking, assumed increasing importance with the advance of economic culture. Messrs. Hobhouse, Wheeler, and Ginsberg observe that the increase is sharper in the pastoral as compared with the agricultural stages, and that "the same relations are even more strongly marked when we distinguish purchase proper from other forms of consideration." Among pastoral peoples marriage by consideration seems to be very nearly universal. Of some uncivilised peoples we are told that the commercial view of marriage is one of comparatively modern growth.

That the giving of a consideration for a bride is not an act of ordinary purchase is also obvious in cases where the bride's people have to present the bridegroom or his people with a return gift. The exchange of presents at a marriage is, in fact, a very widespread practice, and frequently the amount of the return gift is fixed by custom. Among many tribes it is the rule that the consideration given for a wife shall be returned in a present of equal value, and sometimes the return gifts even exceed the original gifts. Speaking of the marriage customs of the Yukaghir of the Siberian *tundra,* Dr. Jochelson remarks that the exchange of gifts "is designed to bring the members of both families into close contact"; and Professor Hobhouse rightly suggests that this practice may, generally, be "a method of cementing the union of the two families. In some cases the exchange is obviously connected with a feeling of shame at the idea of making a daughter an article of traffic. In Florida, of the Solomon Group, when fifty coils of native money are offered by the bridegroom's party, the bride's party give in return five pigs, and when a hundred coils are offered they give ten pigs; "and they say that the money buys the pigs and not the damsel." Again, among the Western Islanders of Torres Straits, according to Dr. Haddon, "the return of presents on the father-in-law's part appears to be the result of a feeling that a wife costs too much, and that the husband should not be impoverished." But sometimes the return gift depends on the behaviour of the husband, and thus serves as a protection for the wife.

The return gift may take the shape of a dowry given to the bride by her father or parents or other relatives but also directly or indirectly benefiting her husband. The practice of giving a dowry to a daughter prevails among many simple peoples, although among others nothing of the kind is said to be found. The dowry often consists of some food, clothes, ornaments, household goods, or other objects, but it may also include or consist of a certain number of domestic animals. Sometimes the dowry given to the bride by her father is represented as a return gift to her husband; and where, as among the Marea of North-Eastern Africa, it becomes the exclusive property of the husband, it is really nothing else. In other instances the wife gets back her dowry in case of separation or divorce though the husband may have the usufruct of it so long as the marriage lasts. Among various peoples there is an interesting connection between the bride price and the dowry in so far that the bride price, or a part of it, is given to the bride by her father as a dowry or is looked upon as a settlement or provision for the wife. In many tribes the suitor gives a present to his prospective wife, or a bridegroom to his bride either before or immediately after the marriage.

Marriage by consideration not only is prevalent among most uncivilised races, but is also found among peoples who have reached a higher degree of culture. In China a present is given by the father of the suitor, the amount of which is not left to the good-will of the parties, as the term "present" would suggest, but is exactly stipulated for by the negotiators of the marriage. The people will not hear of the marriage presents being called a "price" for the girl; but Mr. Jamieson thinks that they are a survival from a time when the transaction was one of ordinary bargain. Among the poor, parents may actually purchase a young girl and bring her up as a daughter until she is marriageable, thus securing her services in the household and reducing the expenses of a wedding. In Japan marriage by sale and marriage by capture are said to have been common in ancient days; but from the time of the Taiho-ryo (701–1192) customs gradually became more refined.

Marriage by consideration has prevailed in all branches of the Semitic race. In Babylonia a suitor had to give to the father of his intended wife a bride price or present, the amount of which varied according to the rank of the parties; and if the young man did not himself possess the sum which was required, his parents were expected to provide him with it. But from the Laws of Hammurabi we learn that although it was the general custom for a man to pay a bride price to his father-in-law, this payment was not universal, and also that the bride price reverted to the husband if the wife died without having granted him children. In Genesis we read that Jacob served Laban, his mother's brother, for seven years for each of his cousins Leah and Rachel; but the usual method of obtaining a wife in ancient Israel was by paying a bride price, called *mohar* or *mahr*. According to Talmudic law the mutual consent of the parties to marry each other has to be legally manifested by a special formality, which gives validity to the marriage

contract The usual formality is that called *kaseph,*
or "money." In the presence of two witnesses the
man gave to his chosen bride a piece of money—even
a *peruta,* the smallest copper coin used in Palestine,
was sufficient for the purpose—or any object of equal
value, with the words, "Be thou consecrated to me";
but during the Middle Ages it became customary for
the act of betrothal by *kaseph* to be performed by
means of a plain ring instead of a piece of money, and
this custom has ever since prevailed up to our time.
The betrothal by *kaseph* may be a survival of the old
marriage by purchase, but it has also been supposed
to be an imitation of the Roman *coëmtio.*

Among the ancient Arabs a bride price, *mahr,* was
given by the bridegroom to the father or guardian of
the bride; and this bride price has survived in Muhammadan law, where it has been confounded with
the *ṣadāq,* which was a gift offered to the bride by the
bridegroom. Although the Koranic law presumes that
the *mahr,* or *ṣadāq,* shall be the property of the bride,
this rule is not always followed in practice. In the
rural districts of Palestine, for instance, the marriage
contract is avowedly an act of purchase, most part—
or at least one-half—of the *ṣadāq* going to the girl's
father. In Morocco the latter in some places spends
the whole of the sum paid down on the trousseau
of his daughter, whereas in other cases he so spends
only a part of it, keeping the rest for himself; then the
ṣadāq is hardly, as Sīdī Ḥalīl puts it, merely "similar"
to a selling price. But even when the woman has
the full benefit of the *ṣadāq,* the marriage may
nevertheless be an act of purchase. Besides the *ṣadāq*
another payment, often of a much higher amount,

is in many tribes given to the girl's father to be retained by him; this custom is found particularly
among Berber-speaking tribes or their Arabic-speaking neighbours, and is no doubt the old Berber marriage by purchase. Moreover, in many tribes a
payment is also made to other members of the girl's
family than her father, particularly her eldest brother,
who in case her father is dead is her recognised
guardian. This payment is sometimes represented as
a "bribe," the object of which is to induce the other
relatives of the girl to try to influence the father.

It has been supposed that wife purchase was the
basis of Aryan marriage before the separation of
peoples took place. In Vedic times brides were won
by rich presents to their fathers, though a certain
discredit would seem to have attached to the sale of
daughters. One of the eight forms of marriage mentioned by Manu—the *āsura* form—was marriage by
purchase, and he admits that some allowed the two
lower castes, the Vaiśyas and the Śūdras, to practise
it. Manu himself, however, forbade it altogether.
"No father who knows the law," he says, "must
take even the smallest gratuity for his daughter; for
a man who, through avarice, takes a gratuity, is a
seller of his offspring." But the so-called *ārsha* form,
which implied that the bridegroom sent a cow and a
bull or two pairs to the bride's father, was counted
by Manu and other lawgivers as one of the legitimate
modes of marriage. It was expressly denied that this
gift was a gratuity, but there can be little doubt that
the *ārsha* form was the survival of a transaction which
might be called a purchase. Notwithstanding the
prohibition in the *Laws of Manu,* marriage by pur-

chase is found to this day even among high castes, and is frequently practised among the Śūdras.

Aristotle tells us that in the primitive ages of Greece men bought their wives. In heroic times a suitor gave ἕδνα, consisting of cattle, to the father of the bride elect, and a maid was called ἀλφεσίβοια, that is, one who yields her parents many oxen as presents from her suitor, or by some other name compounded from the Greek word for an ox, the gold currency of the time. Contrary to other writers, Hruza maintains that the ἕδνα were not a bride price, but merely a *douceur* intended to prevail upon the father; but he admits that in a yet earlier age marriage by purchase existed in Greece, although, as he rightly points out, the transaction could not have been the purchase of a chattel but only of the rights of a husband.

Marriage by purchase cannot with equal certainty be established as a form of marriage on Roman soil; but a reminiscence of it is supposed to have been preserved in the symbolical process of *coëmtio,* which was the ordinary form in which any Roman citizen, whether patrician or plebeian, might contract a marriage. It was a traditional ceremony representing a purchase of the bride, the intending husband "purchasing" the bride from the person in whose power she was, with a view to thereby acquiring that marital power without which marriage as a legal relationship was considered impossible. On the other hand, there are also writers who deny that *coëmtio* can be regarded as a survival of ancient bride purchase. Marquardt maintains that it was an artificial and comparatively late form of marriage, whilst *confarreatio,* the specifically patrician kind of marriage which suggested no idea of

[169]

purchase, was the oldest form of marriage in Rome. Karlowa thinks that if marriage by purchase prevailed at ancient Rome or among the ancestors of the Romans, a survival of it remained, not in the *coëmtio,* but in the *arrha sponsalitia,* which in historical times was given to the bride.

Marriage by consideration was a custom of all Teutonic peoples. There is a trace of marriage by service in the *Eyrbyggja Saga:* Vîgstyr says to the berserk Halli, who asked for the hand of his daughter Âsdî, "As you are a poor man, I shall do as the ancients did and let you deserve your marriage by hard work." But the general consideration given for a bride was money paid down by the bridegroom. Originally, we may presume, the amount of it depended on agreement, but during the period of the lawbooks, both in England and on the Continent, it was generally fixed by custom or by statute. The Kentish law of king Aethelbirht speaks of a man buying a maiden with cattle, and the transaction is called a "bargain." In Germany the expression "to purchase a wife" was in use till the end of the Middle Ages, and we find the same term in Christian IV.'s Norwegian law of 1604. In Holland the bride is still, in the language of the common people, represented as *verkocht,* that is "sold." But here again we should notice that marriage by purchase did not imply the purchase of a piece of property: the ancient Teutons bought the *mund,* or protectorship over the woman and other rights which marriage conferred on the husband.

Marriage by purchase prevailed among the early Slavs. In old Russian a marriageable girl was called a *kunka,* from *kuna,* "marten," because her parents might exchange her for marten-skins, the usual medium of payment in ancient Russia. "To this day among the Russian peasantry," says Schrader, "the first act of the nuptials is the suit or proposal, which is a purely commercial transaction. The father of the suitor, usually accompanied by a relative, visits the girl's parents and says, 'We have a purchaser; you a commodity: will you sell your ware?' Then follows the bargaining, which, as our informants state, differs in no respect from a negotiation about the sale of a cow." Among the Southern Slavs the marriage by purchase still partially prevails, or did so recently. In Serbia, at the beginning of the nineteenth century, the price of girls reached such a height that Black George limited it to one ducat. In High Albania "marriage is entirely by purchase, except for the occasional forcible capture of a girl."

The ancient Celts paid a price for their brides. In Ireland it consisted of various objects, such as articles of gold, silver, or bronze, clothes or horse-bridles, cattle or swine, land or houses. It often had the form of a yearly payment from the husband after marriage, and we find it laid down in the Brehon law that the woman's father was entitled to the whole of the first year's bride price.

Among all these peoples, however, marriage by consideration has in the course of time been subjected to modifications, which are very similar to certain customs already noticed among some uncivilised tribes; and it has led to institutions totally different from the original practice. The general trend of this process is that the parents of the woman more or less lose the economic advantages they derived from her marriage, and that greater regard is paid to the interests of the contracting parties.

Here, also, we meet with the practice of offering a return gift; and although this practice, as we have seen, may serve different purposes, it seems in some cases at least to be a mitigation of marriage by purchase. In China the parents of the bride, or her guardians, accept only a part of the proffered presents, returning the balance, to which they add some articles for the parents of the bridegroom. The exchange of presents forms, in fact, the subject of a long section in the old penal code; for "the marriage articles and betrothal presents once exchanged, the parties are considered irrevocably engaged." In India, besides the *ārsha* form of marriage, another mode of preserving the symbol of sale, while rejecting the reality, appears to have been the receipt of a gift of real value, such as a chariot and a hundred cows, which was immediately returned to the giver. This arrangement is said by Āpastamba to have been prescribed by the Vedas "in order to fulfil the law"—that is, apparently, the ancient law by which the binding form of marriage was a sale. In ancient Greece there were at the conclusion of a marriage not only the ἕδνα given for the bride, but also the μείλια or presents given by her father to the bridegroom. Tacitus, after speaking of the gifts for which a German obtains his wife, says that the wife "in her turn brings her husband some gift of arms. This," he adds, "represents to them our marriage bond, the mystic celebrations, and all the gods of matrimony." The Welsh *agweddi* was, strictly speaking, a payment made by the kindred or parent of the bride to the bridegroom, although the word sometimes seems to have been used to include the marriage portion of the bride as well. The dowry which the bride brought with her may also be partly regarded as a return gift to the husband.

In this group of peoples we also meet with gifts offered to the bride by the bridegroom; and although these gifts no doubt may have an independent origin, they may also be a survival of the old bride price. And we know that in many cases the price paid for the bride, instead of being appropriated by her parents or guardian, became wholly or in part her own property.

In China special presents are sent for the bride, and the money given to her parents is generally spent in outfitting her. In Japan the proposed husband sends certain prescribed presents to his future bride, and this sending of gifts forms one of the most important parts of the marriage ceremony; in fact, when once the presents have been sent and accepted, the contract is completed and neither party can retract. Considering that marriage by purchase once prevailed in Japan, it is reasonable to suppose that the sending of presents is a relic of that custom. There is, however, an exchange of gifts: the bride also gives certain conventional presents to her future husband and his parents and relatives, and as to the value of these presents she should always be guided by the value of those brought by the bridegroom.

In the Laws of Hammurabi we read not only of a bride price, but also of presents which the bridegroom gave to the bride. Similar gifts were offered to the bride in ancient Israel. Abraham's servant "brought forth jewels of silver, and jewels of gold, and raiment, and gave them to Rebekah: he gave also to her brother and to her mother precious things." In ancient Arabia the bridegroom offered to the bride a gift, called *sadāq,* at their wedding. But over and above these gifts the bride price, or a part of it, became in the course of time the property of the Semitic bride. Herodotus was probably well informed when he wrote that among the Babylonians "the marriage portions were furnished by the money paid for the beautiful damsels." Dr. Koschaker believes that in Sumerian law the old bride price survived as a present, called *nig-mussa,* which the bridegroom gave to the bride. Among the Israelites the *mohar* was sooner or later, wholly or partly, given to the bride; Laban's daughters complained that their father had sold them as slaves and wasted their *mohar.* In Arabia the *mahr* was even in pre-Muhammadan times, at least occasionally, given to the wife as her property; and under Islam the distinction between *mahr* and *ṣadāq* disappeared altogether.

To this day the custom of the husband providing the wife with a dowry is found among both Jews and Muhammadans. In order to protect the wife in the event of her becoming widowed or divorced, it was established by the Jewish law that before the nuptials the husband was to make out an obligation in writing, which entitled her to receive a certain sum from his estate in the case of his death or in the case of her divorcement. This obligation was termed *kethūbhāh* (the marriage deed). As minimum of this obligation was fixed the sum of two hundred silver *denarii* at the marriage of a virgin and one hundred at the marriage of a widow. For the security of the wife's claim to

the amount fixed in the *kethūbhāh* all the property of
the husband, both real and personal, was mortgaged.
The *kethūbhāh* is still retained in most Jewish marriages, though it has little legal significance in many
countries. It is said that the institution in question
was originated or regulated by Simon ben Shatach,
about 100 B.C. But it seems very probable that it is
in some way connected with the old custom of marriage by consideration.

This is undoubtedly the case with the Muhammadan *mahr* or *ṣadāq,* which, though handed over to the
father of the bride, is presumed by the Koranic law to
become the property of the bride herself. Islam
requires the giving of a *ṣadāq* for the contraction of a
valid marriage. It is true that a man may legally
marry a woman without mentioning a *ṣadāq,* but in
such a case the law presumes a consideration in her
favour by virtue of the contract itself. In some parts
of Morocco the *ṣadāq* is fixed once for all by custom,
although the amount may vary greatly even inside the
same tribe; but as a rule it varies according to circumstances. At Fez people who are not considered
well off pay seventy to a hundred dollars for a virgin
and thirty to forty for a widow or a divorced woman,
while the *ṣadāq* may be as much as six hundred dollars
if the parents of the parties are wealthy. In Mecca
the *mahr* varies between a couple of dollars and some
hundred. The *ṣadāq* is commonly smaller if the
woman is a widow or a divorced wife; but in
Morocco, at least, it is not invariably so. There is
nothing in the Koran or in the traditions tending to
show that the whole of the *ṣadāq* must be paid prior
to the consummation of the marriage; hence later

jurists have held that only a portion of it should be considered payable at once or on demand, and the remainder within a certain stipulated period or on the dissolution of the contract, whether by divorce or the death of either of the parties.

Among the Indo-European peoples the transformation of the bride price is indicated in their languages by the fact that the words used for it subsequently assumed the meaning of dowry. In India the price originally due to the parents or guardian of the bride who surrendered her to the bridegroom became in after times a wedding present, which the bride received from the bridegroom either directly or through her parents. Among the Greeks of the heroic age the father did not always keep the ἕδνα for his own use, but bestowed them wholly or in part on the daughter; and we are also told that the bridegroom himself gave presents to his wife, when he saw her unveiled for the first time or after the "mystic night." In Rome the bridegroom gave to the bride a betrothal present, called *arrha sponsalitia,* which may, or may not, have been the survival of an earlier bride price.

Among the Teutonic peoples a similar process of development took place. In the time of the folk-laws, from the sixth to the ninth century, the bride price is no longer paid to the father or guardian of the bride, but to the bride herself, the right of the guardian being practically limited to the receipt of the *handgeld,* that is, to a merely formal fulfilment, a *solidus* and a *denarius* according to Salic law. This, however, does not mean that the former bride price was actually paid to the bride at the conclusion of the marriage: since the wife's property was subject to the husband's control during his lifetime, the bride price was really transformed into a provision for the widow, payable only after death from the husband's goods. "When light begins to fall upon the Anglo-Saxon betrothal," say Pollock and Maitland, "it is not a cash transaction by which the bride's kinsmen receive a price in return for rights over their kinswoman; rather we must say that the bridegroom covenants with them that he will make a settlement upon his future wife. He declares, and he gives security for, the morning-gift which she shall receive if she 'chooses his will' and the dower that she shall enjoy if she outlives him. Though no doubt her kinsmen may make a profit out of the bargain, as fathers and feudal lords will in much later times, the more essential matter is that they should stipulate on her behalf for an honourable treatment as wife and widow." As to the morning gift—which has survived very long in Europe, indeed in Germany and Switzerland up to our own time—various writers have expressed the opinion that it originated in the bride price or formed a part of it. It has, further, been regarded as a *pretium virginitatis;* but against this view the argument has been adduced that the morning gift was also sometimes given to widows. The very name of this gift, however, certainly suggests that it has something to do with the consummation of the marriage. But it is quite possible that some other idea than that of mere compensation was connected with it. In Morocco and other Muhammadan countries a present of money is given by the bridegroom to the bride immediately before, or sometimes after, the consummation of the marriage; and I have found reasons to believe that its original object was to serve as a safeguard against evil influences.

Among the Great Russians, according to Professor Kobalewsky, the father, as a rule, disposes of the money received from the bridegroom in favour of his daughter, giving her as dowry a larger or smaller sum, according to what he has himself received. In the Brehon law it is stipulated that the woman's father, though entitled to the whole of the first year's bride price, gets only two-thirds of the second year's, one-half of the third year's, and so on; whilst in each case what is left of the price belongs to the wife. In ancient Wales the husband had to give to his wife a present "for her maidenhood" on the morning after the consummation of the marriage. Its amount, which was fixed by the law, depended on the status of her father.

From marriage by consideration we have thus reached the practice of providing the bride with a marriage portion, which in part consists of the price paid for the bride. The marriage portion serves different ends, often indissolubly mixed up together. It may have the meaning of a return gift. It may imply that the wife as well as the husband is expected to contribute to the expenses of the joint household. It is very often intended to be a settlement for the wife in case the marriage is dissolved through the husband's death or otherwise. But as in such cases the husband generally has the usufruct of the portion as long as the marriage lasts, it may be a return gift to the man at the same time as it is a settlement for the woman. And it may also be, practically, a means of buying a husband.

GIFTS TO THE BRIDE

In ancient Babylonia the bride usually brought a dowry from her father's house, which remained her property, although the husband had the usufruct of it. Among Muhammadans the father of the bride often gives her something in addition to the ṣadāq or *mahr* provided by the bridegroom. In Egypt not only the dowry paid by the bridegroom but an additional sum supplied by the bride's family, which is often more than the dowry itself, is expended in purchasing the articles of furniture, dress, and ornaments for the bride; and at Fez custom requires the father of the bride to spend on her trousseau from his own money at least the same amount as the ṣadāq.

Among the Vedic people dowries were not infrequently given by fathers or brothers in order to secure the marriage of daughters or sisters. It may be assumed that in such cases the husband appropriated the dowry, as well as her earnings, if any; for even in later times in India the rise of the recognition of women's property as their own (*strīdhana*) is only slow. The Hindu law recognises the dominion of a married woman over this property, but the husband has nevertheless power to use and consume it in case of distress. In ancient Gaul, according to Cæsar, the wife brought a dowry, but the husband also added an equal amount taken from his own property; and on the death of either party the survivor received both portions, along with the revenues accumulated after marriage. Among the Irish the fact that the husband paid the bride price did not prevent the bride bringing goods or valuables of her own, if she had them; very frequently, in fact, she brought with her jewels or gold or herds or lands, which continued to be her own special property. Moreover, in many cases the friends of the young couple made a collection for them, of which two-thirds belonged by law to the man and one-third to the woman. In ancient Wales the daughter seems to have been entitled to a marriage portion or settlement from her father or kindred, which usually included not only things of utility for a new household but also articles for her own use. At Athens it was the general rule that a woman at her marriage brought with her a dowry, usually consisting of money and often also of movable objects, rarely of real estate. It was the wife's contribution towards the expenses of the marriage, and at the same time served as an obstacle to the dissolution of the union for frivolous reasons. The amount of the dowry was left to the discretion of her father, and there is no evidence that it was a legal obligation for him to provide his daughter with any dowry at all. At the same time the dowry became almost a criterion of honourable marriage as distinguished from concubinage; Isæus says that no decent man would give his legitimate daughter less than a tenth of his property. The husband enjoyed the usufruct of the dowry; hence Euripides, transferring to the heroic age the practice of his own time, makes Medea complain that her sex had to purchase husbands with great sums of money. But the dowry remained the wife's property; and as the husband might have to pay it back some day, he was generally required to mortgage real estate as security. In the time of Aristotle nearly two-fifths of the whole territory of Sparta were supposed to belong to women as their dowers.

In Rome, even more than in Greece, the marriage

portion became a mark of distinction for a legitimate wife. A woman had a legal right to demand a *dos,* or dower, from her father, but it was to be given to her husband, not to herself, as a contribution towards the defrayal of the expenses of the joint household, although it was also intended as a provision in the interests of the wife. According to the ancient law of the Republic the husband had all the rights and remedies incident to ownership as such, including amongst others the right to alienate and mortgage; and he was recognised as the sole owner of the *dos* not only during the marriage but also after its dissolution. But in the course of time the husband's rights were subjected to important restrictions. The *Lex Julia de adulteriis* of the year 18 B.C. prohibited him from alienating or mortgaging any *fundus Italicus* comprised in the *dos;* and Justinian extended this prohibition to any dotal land whatever. The husband's right to the use and the fruits of the *dos* was restricted to the time during which the marriage lasted. In the law prior to Justinian his obligation to restore the *dos* was still a very limited one: he continued to be acknowledged as the true owner of it even after the dissolution of the marriage, and it was only within certain limits that the law allowed the wife, or the person who provided the *dos,* to maintain an obligatory claim for a return of it side by side with the ownership of the husband. But Justinian's law imposed upon the husband the duty to return the *dos* in all circumstances, except when the dissolution of the marriage was caused by the misconduct of the wife. These restrictions in the husband's right to dispose of his wife's marriage portion were probably, to some extent, connected with the loosening of the marriage tie; the confusion of the *dos* with the husband's patrimony was of comparatively little moment as long as marriage was contracted for life, but must have become intolerable when divorces grew frequent. But it seems that the lines upon which the development of the Roman law of *dos* proceeded were also largely determined by the influence of Greek law, according to which the wife was the owner of her marriage portion.

The general tradition of the Roman *dos* was carried on by the Church, the practical object of the marriage portion being to secure for the wife a provision of which the husband could not wantonly deprive her and which would remain to her after his death. The Justinian principle that the wife's dotation remains her property, although the husband administers and has the use of it, underlies the later legislation on the subject, though it has been more or less modified in the laws of the different countries. Justinian declared, in several constitutions, that the giving of a *dos* is obligatory for persons of high rank only; but the old custom did not fall into desuetude. According to many later laws a daughter is entitled to demand a dowry at her marriage. The Prussian "Landrecht" of 1794 still prescribes that the father, or eventually the mother, shall arrange about the wedding and fit up the house of the couple. According to the "Code Napoléon," on the other hand, parents are not bound to provide their daughter with a marriage portion; and the same principle has generally been adopted by modern legislation. Yet there is still a strong feeling, especially in the so-called Latin countries, in favour of dotation. This feeling, as Sir Henry Maine remarks, is the principal source of those habits of saving and hoarding which characterise the French people, and is probably descended, by a long chain of succession, from the obligatory provisions of the Roman law.

In our days there is particularly one factor that tends to preserve the marriage portion as a social institution of some importance. In a society where monogamy is prescribed by law, where the adult women outnumber the adult men, where many men never marry, and where married women too often lead an indolent life—in such a society the marriage portion not infrequently becomes a purchase-sum by means of which a father buys a husband for his daughter, as formerly a man bought a wife from her father.

In India the difficulty of finding a husband for a daughter has led to undisguised purchase of bride-grooms. Whilst the low castes ordinarily pay for the bride, the high castes pay for the bridegroom; and in some cases very large sums are paid, especially where hypergamy prevails, that is, where girls must marry in a caste equal or superior to their own, or where there is a great shortage of women. In recent times the bridegroom price has been affected very largely by the educational qualifications of the bride-groom. A Kāyastha graduate in Bengal usually fetches from Rs. 500 to Rs. 1,000, and in some instances even Rs.10,000 have been recorded.

CHAPTER VIII

MARRIAGE RITES

EVEN when the consent which is necessary for the conclusion of a marriage has been given and other conditions mentioned above have been fulfilled, something may still be required to make the union valid or the marriage, from the legal point of view, complete. Moreover, though not indispensable for the conclusion of a marriage, certain ceremonies are often observed in accordance with old-established custom.

The rites connected with the conclusion of a marriage often form a long sequence of practices and taboos, which may commence at the moment when the marriage is first thought of and last till after it has been concluded. They are particularly prominent at the betrothal and the wedding and during the period lying between these events. The length of this period, or of the interval between the celebration of the betrothal and the wedding, varies indefinitely—it may last for years or months or days or only a few hours; or there may be no such period at all. In the West of Ireland only a day or two intervenes between the festive betrothal and the nuptial ceremony. Among the Jews it became in the Middle Ages customary to solemnise both the betrothal and the marriage proper on the same day either contemporaneously or with an interval of a few hours, during which the bridal party feasted merrily at the new husband's cost. In ancient Rome the betrothal, or *sponsalia,* although the proper and usual preliminary to marriage, was not legally necessary; and in the ritual of the Christian Church, which is largely derived from the Roman *sponsalia* and *nuptiæ,* the betrothal and nuptials were from early times combined in practice. But in popular customs they still remain separate, though the introduction of the ecclesiastic ceremony has led to a great confusion of the rites practised on those occasions.

In a monograph on the marriage rites of a single people or group of related peoples it is natural to deal with them in the order in which they follow upon one another. This is what I have done in my book on *Marriage Ceremonies in Morocco.* But in the present treatise I shall adopt another method. Similar rites will be grouped together even though found at different stages of the ritual. This, of course, does not imply that no notice is taken of their place in the sequence; the occasion when a rite occurs is often of the greatest importance for its interpretation. But the same rite may occupy a different place in different cases; sometimes, for instance, it may be practised at the betrothal and at other times at the wedding, or it may occur on both occasions among the same people. My chief aim will be to discuss the meaning of the rites.

The most general social object of marriage rites is to give publicity to the union. "Publicity," says Miss Burne, "is everywhere the element which distinguishes a recognised marriage from an illicit connection." In order to be recognised as valid, the union may have to be sanctioned by an official. This is the case not only in modern civilised countries; there are savage tribes in which the chief formally declares the parties married.

Publicity may be achieved in other ways as well. Under the Muhammadan Sunnī law it is required that there should be at least two witnesses present to attest the conclusion of the contract of marriage. The Roman *confarreatio,* the patrician form of marriage, needed the presence of the Pontifex Maximus, the Flamen Dialis, and ten other witnesses. In Teutonic countries the betrothal has up to modern times taken place in the presence of witnesses.

Publicity may have to be given to the sexual consummation of the marriage. Among the Bantu Kavirondo in East Africa the bridegroom consummates it in the presence of a large number of girls and women. In Teutonic countries, where a marriage was formerly regarded as legally valid only when it could be proved that the couple had been together under the same blanket, the bride and bridegroom went to bed in the presence of witnesses; and this custom has survived up to quite modern times. It is also found among the Slavonic peoples.

An extremely frequent method of giving publicity to the union is to celebrate it with feasting, the guests being, in a way, regarded as witnesses. Sometimes the wedding takes place in the house of the bride's parents, sometimes in that of the bridegroom; but feasts may also be held in both places. At the same time the wedding does not merely serve the object of making the marriage public, it brings together the families of the bride and the bridegroom and strengthens the ties of friendship. In this respect its social importance must be particularly great in countries where a common meal is looked upon almost as an act of covenanting.

MARRIAGE RITES

The various marriage rites are performed for many different purposes. Some of them have direct reference to the separation of the bride from her old home. To these *rites de séparation,* as they are called by Professor van Gennep, belong, for example, the ceremonial resistance made by her relatives or herself and the official crying of the bride, which have been discussed in a previous chapter. Other rites have been called *rites d'agrégation,* or "rites of aggregation." But a large number of marriage ceremonies may be classed under neither of those headings.

Some of the most frequent marriage rites symbolise the union between the parties or, rather, are originally intended to strengthen the marriage tie. First, there is the joining of hands, which is found among many savage tribes and has of old been one of the most important marriage rites among all Indo-European peoples. It may undoubtedly be an expression of several different ideas. By the Roman *dextrarum junctio* the bride came under the *manus* of the husband, or was "handed over" to him. The joining of hands is also from early times the outward sign of a troth that two persons give to each other; *Handschlag, Hand in Hand geloben, Handgelübde,* are familiar legal phrases in Germany. But it is obvious that the rite in question, very frequently at least, is a symbolic act of union. In some European countries, such as Poland, Bulgaria, and Portugal, and in many parts of India, the hands of the bridal pair are not only joined but tied together.

The union between the bride and bridegroom may also be represented by the tying of something to each of them separately. Among the Nandi, in British

East Africa, they bind a sprig of a certain grass on to each other's wrists; and among the Basuto, a Bechuana tribe, a strip of the dewlap of a slaughtered ox is tied round the girl's wrist and another round the bridegroom's, which signifies that they are now bound to each other. It seems that betrothal and wedding rings, partly at least, serve a similar purpose. The wedding ring was in use among the ancient Hindus, and the betrothal ring in ancient Rome, where the man presented it to his fiancée. The same custom prevailed in Christian Europe throughout the Middle Ages and later, but was subsequently mostly succeeded by an exchange of rings. The ring, however, was only slowly introduced in the northern countries, replacing the old Teutonic customs of tying a knot or breaking a gold or silver coin, one half of which was kept by the woman and the other half by the man; and the exchange of rings is not known to have existed in Scandinavia until the end of the seventeenth century. Various superstitions connected with the marriage ring indicate that it is regarded as a symbolic tie between the couple. To lose it or break it means death or the dissolution of the union or some other misfortune. In the north-east of Scotland people say that if a woman loses her marriage ring "she will lose her man."

An extremely frequent and widespread marriage rite, which prevails among both savage and civilised peoples, is the eating together of bride and bridegroom. Among Hindus of every rank and caste it is the custom for them to take food together from the same leaf or the same plate. In ancient Greece they partook together of a sesame-cake. In Rome a cake made of the old Italian grain called *far,* from which the patrician

[188]

marriage received its name of *confarreatio,* was offered to Jupiter Farreus and partaken of by bride and bridegroom in the presence of witnesses. And at the present day the custom of eating together—usually from the same plate or dish, or of the same loaf of bread, or with the same spoon—at the betrothal or, more often, at the wedding is found in many parts of Europe. As for the meaning of this rite, there can be no doubt that it was originally something more than a mere symbol. In Sweden there was a popular belief that if a girl and a youth ate off one morsel, they would fall in love with each other. In Germany, it is supposed that if the couple eat the "morning soup" with the same spoon, they will have a peaceful married life. In one of the Arabic-speaking mountain tribes of Morocco it is the custom for bride and bridegroom to eat together the liver of the sheep which was slaughtered for the occasion when the bridegroom was for the first time painted with henna, for the purpose, I was told, "of making them dear to one another." But the rite of eating together may also lay a mutual constraint on the couple by sealing the union through an act of covenanting, which has naturally been suggested by one of the most prominent features of married life, the husband's sharing of food with his wife.

Besides, and sometimes combined with, the rite of eating together there is the rite of drinking together, which is likewise in the first place a symbol of, or a means of strengthening, the union of the couple. Among some South American Indians they drink from the same bowl or drink brandy together. In China the couple, before the consummation of the marriage, drink wine or a mixture of wine and honey alternately from two goblets, which are sometimes tied together with a red string, the bridegroom, after having sipped from his goblet, handing it over to the bride, and the bride handing hers over to the bridegroom, and so repeatedly. In Japan, also, they drink wine together, exchanging cups nine times, and this constitutes the entire ceremony. The rite of drinking together is found in Europe from Italy to Norway, from Brittany to Russia, and there are traces of it in Scotland too. It forms part of the nuptial ceremony among the Jews of all countries.

There are various rites that are intended to ensure or facilitate the consummation of the marriage. Eggs, earthenware vessels, or objects of glass are often ceremonially broken at weddings in Europe, Morocco, and elsewhere. In Argyllshire, "when the health of bride and bridegroom is drunk, someone must throw a glass over their shoulder and break it 'for luck.'" At Newburgh, after the marriage ceremony and just as the newly-married couple are leaving the bride's house, a plate containing salt is at some marriages stealthily broken over the head of the bridegroom. At Guisborough in Cleveland the bridegroom took the plate which, with a small cake upon it, had been presented to the bride on the arrival at the door of her home, and threw it over his left shoulder, "their hope of future happiness depending upon it being broken on falling to the ground." In the Saalfeld country, after the wedding, one of the bridesmaids hurries home first, gets beer or brandy, and offers a glass to the bridegroom who empties it and tosses it behind his back. If the glass breaks, it is good; if not, not. At the German *Polterabend*—which is celebrated on the eve of the wedding day—all sorts of old pottery are broken outside the bride's house, and the North Germans say, "The more shards the more luck." In the Upper Palatinate, on the same night, a window is broken in her house, and many shards are said to indicate wealth. Up to the present day the breaking of a glass has remained one of the most characteristic features of Jewish weddings; the bridegroom breaks it with his foot, or it is broken by the Rabbi. Various fanciful explanations have been suggested for this ceremony, but its true meaning, as I understand it, has to my knowledge never been recognised. Many facts strongly suggest that both this and other rites consisting in the breaking of some fragile object were intended, in accordance with the principle of homœopathic magic, to ensure the consummation of the marriage, which in Europe and elsewhere has been supposed to be impeded by the sorcery of rivals or other malign influences. That this intention has generally been more or less disguised is not to be wondered at considering the nature of the subject; but among some of the Southern Slavs it is stated with a frankness which leaves no room for doubt. Among the Serbs of Syrmia the head of the family, about midnight, conducts the bride into the bridegroom's room and closes the door. "He now takes a glass filled with wine, drinks its contents to the health of the young couple, and throws it then at the door so that it is shattered to pieces; this is regarded as a symbol of the imminent loss of virginity." While the bride and bridegroom are together, the guests are making an uproar, breaking glasses and pots, and they are also trying to break an egg which has been put into a sack, "as a sign of the marriage having been consummated."

Among various peoples a staff or rod or tree is broken, presumably with a similar object in view. Among the Aith Yusi in Central Morocco, when the bride is taken to her new home on the back of a mare, she holds in front of her a cane, with or without a flag, which is fired at by the men of the procession; and I was expressly told that they want to blow it to pieces so that the bridegroom shall be able to break the hymen of the bride that night. It also seems probable that the red colour, which is so frequently used in marriage rites, is regarded as a means of ensuring defloration, and not only as a sign of virginity, as is sometimes said. The Chinese of Canton suspend from the top of the nuptial bed three long strips of red paper containing good wishes, such as, "A hundred sons and a thousand grandsons be your portion!" In Greece and Rome the nuptial bed was covered with red cloths; and at Ekenäs, in Finland, the bridal blanket must be red "in order that the bride shall be happy."

Many rites are practised with a view to making the wife fruitful or the mother of male offspring. In Morocco the bridegroom's mother carries a sieve or a bundle of her son's old clothes on her back, as if it were a baby; or the bride's mother is put into a net by the bachelors and swung to and fro in the same manner as a child is rocked to sleep. When the bride is taken to the bridegroom's place the animal on which she rides must sometimes be a mare, on account of its fruitfulness, and sometimes a stallion, that she may give birth to male offspring; and it is, in certain cases at least, for the same purpose that a little boy rides behind her on the mare. Very similar customs are found in other countries. In some parts of Sweden there is a belief among the country-folk that the bride should have a boy-baby to sleep with her on the night preceding the wedding day in order that her first-born shall be a son; and among many or all Slavonic peoples a boy is offered to the bride or is put to sit on her lap. This custom may have belonged to the primitive Indo-European marriage ritual; for we learn from the Grihyasūtras that in ancient India, on the bride's entering her new home, a little boy was placed on her lap as an omen of male progeny.

Another marriage rite, to be mentioned in the present connection, which has been traced to the primitive Indo-Europeans is the custom of throwing some kind of cereals or fruit on the bride. This practice, or the custom of throwing grain or fruit on the bridal pair or on the bridegroom separately or even on the wedding company, has been found to prevail from India, Indo-China, and the Malay Archipelago in the East to the Atlantic Ocean in the West. In India we can trace it from the Grihyasūtras through the classical Sanskrit literature down to the present day. In ancient Greece the bride, on entering the bridegroom's house, was taken by him to the hearth and was there showered with dates, figs, nuts, little coins, and so forth. In Rome the bridegroom scattered nuts for the boys in the crowd. In Slavonic countries corn and hops are thrown over bride and bridegroom or over the nuptial procession. In some parts of France hemp-seed or wheat is showered over the couple, or the bride is reecived with three loaves of bread. In England other things than rice were formerly, or are still in some places, thrown upon the bride, apart from the modern adoption of confetti. We are told that in the seventeenth century wheat was cast on her head when she came from church. In the north of England one of the oldest inhabitants of the neighbourhood, who has been stationed on the threshold of the bride's new home, throws a plateful of short-bread over her head, so that it falls outside; and a scramble ensues for the pieces, as it is deemed very fortunate to get a piece of the short-bread. At Siston, in Gloucestershire, at the beginning of the eighteenth century, a large cake was broken over the heads of the couple. In Rosehearty, in Aberdeenshire, barley is thrown over the bridal pair as they come to the feasting-place. In the west of Ireland the bridegroom's mother breaks an oaten cake on the head of the bride as the young woman passes the doorway of her future home.

Mannhardt suggests that the custom of throwing grain or seeds or dried fruit over the bride undeniably takes its rise "from the feeling of a sympathetic connection between mankind and seed-bearing grasses and the comparison between the fruit of the body and of corn"; and some later writers likewise assume that it was intended to promote fecundity. It is evident that in certain cases this or kindred customs are looked upon in such a light by the people who practise them; but we also find other ideas attached to these rites. They are often said to be means of ensuring prosperity as well as offspring, or prosperity or abundance only; and in Morocco I found yet other beliefs connected with them, though never the idea of ensuring fertility. The raisins, figs, or dates which are thrown over the bride are said to make everything sweet or to make the bride sweet to the bridegroom's family, or to avert the evil eye from her; and the wheat, flour, or other things which she throws over her head is represented as a means by which she rids herself of evil influences. In other countries, also, customs of this sort are not infrequently regarded as prophylactics or means of purification. Considering how many different explanations of them are given by the people practising them, even in the same country, there can be no doubt that, in certain cases at least, their real origin has been forgotten and a new interpretation substituted for the idea from which they rose. But at the same time we should be on our guard against the assumption, only too common in Anthropology, that similar ceremonies necessarily have their roots in similar ideas, even though practised by different peoples. Objects like corn and dried fruit may certainly be used for a variety of purposes. And if similar ceremonies may have sprung from different motives in different cases, it is obvious that the same ceremony in a given case may also be intended to serve more than one purpose; nay, there is no reason to deny the possibility of mixed motives from the beginning. It is an unwarranted assumption, then, that the custom of throwing grain, seeds, or dried fruit at weddings, wherever it is found, originated in a rite the exclusive object which was to promote fecundity. To ensure prosperity and abundance and to avert evil may have been equally primitive motives for it.

Fish are frequently used for reproductive purposes, and figure, partly at least, on that account in marriage rites. Among oriental Jews the newly-wedded couple immediately after the religious ceremony jump three times over a large platter filled with fresh fish or over a vessel containing a live fish, or step seven times backwards and forwards over a fish; and the ceremony is expounded to be the symbol of a prayer for children. So also it was as a symbol of fertility that fish was formerly eaten on the second day of the wedding week among German Jews. But at Fez I was told that on the ninth day after the actual wedding day the husband buys some fish, which he gives to his wife to prepare, as a means of ensuring prosperity. It would seem that the roe of the fish might suggest not only fertility but abundance. To make the couple prosperous is the object of various marriage rites, both in Morocco and in other countries.

Eggs are frequently used as means of promoting fecundity, and in some marriage rites they are expressly said to hint at offspring. But in Morocco, where they figure at weddings as prominently as anywhere, I have never heard of them being represented as fertility charms on such occasions. They are usually, like other white things, said to make the couple's or the bridegroom's future bright and happy, and sometimes to make the weather fine during the wedding or to give a good year to the community. Among the Jews of Morocco, again, according to an old writer, the bridegroom on the marriage day "takes a raw Egg, which he casts at the Bride; intimating thereby his desire that she may have both an easie and joyful Child-birth." And some West Russian Jews have the custom of setting a raw egg before a bride as a symbol of fruitfulness and that she may bear as easily as a hen lays an egg. There are other ceremonies which are likewise meant to facilitate the delivery of the young wife. In some parts of Sweden a bride must leave the laces of her shoes untied, "so that she may bear children as easily as she removes the shoe," and on returning from church she should dismount quickly from her horse, snatch off the bridle, hit the animal on the nose, and loosen the saddle-girths in order to have an easy labour.

There are many marriage rites through which one of the partners tries to gain mastery over the other. In Morocco the bridegroom, in order to become the ruler, taps the bride three or seven times on her head or shoulder with his sword, or beats her three times between her shoulders with the cord of his dagger, or smacks or kicks her gently, or drinks first from a bowl which he then holds for her to drink from. In Croatia the bridegroom boxes the bride's ears in order to indicate that henceforth he is her master. In Russia, as part of the marriage ceremony, the father took a new whip, and after striking his daughter gently with it, told her that he did so for the last time, and then presented the whip to the bridegroom. Among many Slavonic peoples the bridegroom gently beats the bride three times, "as a sign that she owes him obedience," or in order that she shall forget her earlier sweethearts and be afraid of her husband. It is also the custom for the bride to pull off the bridegroom's boots, and in Russia the bridegroom formerly used to beat the bride on the head with the boot-leg to show that she now was in his power and had to obey him; but among the Slovenes the bride nowadays beats the bridegroom with the boot-leg, so as to make him understand that she is not always going to pull off his boots.

On the other hand, there are also rites that are intended to make the husband considerate or subject to his wife. Among the Brahmans of Eastern Bengal the bride lays upon the bridegroom's lips a padlock and turns the key, "so showing that the door of unkind speech has been closed." In many parts of Germany, when the priest joins the hands of the couple, the bride tries, in a literal sense, to get the upper hand, the bridegroom trying to do the same, and often a struggle of hands ensues, which is sometimes settled by the priest placing the man's hand uppermost; and one of the pair, generally the bride, also tries, for the same purpose, to put the foot on the top of the foot of the other party. In Wärmland, in Sweden, the bride endeavours to see the bridegroom before he sees her, and to sit down first in the bridal chair, so as to have the mastery. Among the Great Russians, when a glass of brandy has been offered to the bridegroom and another glass to the bride, each of them tries to pour a little of the brandy into the other's glass, and it is believed that the one who first succeeds in doing so will have more influence and power in the married life. In Wales the bride should always buy something as soon as she is married, and before the bridegroom can make a purchase; "Then she'll be master for life," say the old women. In Morocco, too, the bride in various ways tries to make herself the ruler. She mounts the ram which is to be slaughtered for the occasion when she is painted with henna and boxes its ears, the ram representing the husband; she hangs on it a necklace to make him weak and harmless like a woman; and when its stomach has been removed she puts her right foot on it. She also waves her right slipper seven times towards the door of the nuptial chamber when ʳhe hears the bridegroom's steps outside; or she throws at him one of her slippers when he enters; or she beats him three times on his body with her slipper, though in this case it is said that she will become the ruler of the house only if he cries out, whereas otherwise he will rule over her. We must not presume, however, that all these and similar rites are practised for the purpose, or the sole purpose, of gaining mastery; and even when a rite is so now, it may very well have originated in a different idea. We shall see that bride and bridegroom are also beaten for purificatory purposes; and this may be the case even when the bride is beaten by the bridegroom, or the bridegroom by the bride. In the Hiáina in Morocco the bridegroom, being alone with the bride, gently slaps her on her forehead and shoulders with the flat of his sword, "so as to expel evil spirits." At Demnat, in the Great Atlas, again, the bride beats the bridegroom sometimes with a piece of rock-salt, which is much feared by the spirits, and sometimes with her slipper; and this certainly suggests that the slipper ceremonies mentioned above as means of getting power over the other partner may at the same time be, or have been, methods of purification.

Besides marriage rites which are supposed to confer positive benefits upon bride or bridegroom or both, there are others that are intended to protect them from evil influences or to rid them of such influences, that is, prophylactic or cathartic rites. There is a very general feeling or idea that bride and bridegroom are in a state of danger, being particularly exposed to other

persons' magical tricks or evil looks, or to the attacks
of evil spirits, or to some impersonal mysterious cause
of evil, and therefore stand in particular need of protection or purification. Moreover, the bride is considered to be not only herself in danger but also a
source of danger to others. Customs that have direct
reference to her may therefore at the same time be
looked upon as safeguards against evils which threaten
the bridegroom—as is evidently the case with various
rites which immediately precede the consummation of
the marriage—and also other persons less intimately
connected with her. Purificatory ceremonies are thus
of frequent occurrence on the bride's arrival at the
bridegroom's home.

Sometimes care is taken to shut out evil influences
from the place where the marriage is celebrated. Thus
in Russia all doors, windows, and even the chimney
are closed at a wedding, to prevent malicious witches
from flying in and hurting the bride and bridegroom.
Very frequently guns are fired off at a wedding, and in
many cases at least the object of this is, or has been, to
dispel evil spirits or other evil influences; and the same
may be said of the terrific noise or loud music which so
often forms a part of the marriage ritual. In Morocco,
when the bride is taken to her new home, guns are
frequently fired off in front of the animal on which she
rides, and there are loud music and the peculiar
trilling noise called *zghârît* produced by the women,
and the same is repeated on her arrival; on the latter
occasion the purificatory or protective character of
the firing of guns is particularly obvious when it is
done so close to the bride that she is enwrapped in the
smoke, or when a shot is fired inside the room which

she is going to occupy. Gun-fire is a frequent practice
at country weddings in Europe, and sometimes it is
expressly said to drive away evil spirits. In rural parts
of the county of Durham the bridal party is escorted to
church by men armed with guns, which they fire again
and again close to the ears of bride and bridesmaids;
and at Guisborough in Cleveland guns are fired over
the heads of the newly-married couple all the way
from church. In Germany there is much shooting
and noise-making on the night before the wedding
(*Polterabend*) and on the way to church. Among
Slavonic peoples the wedding guests make a terrific
uproar outside the bridal chamber while the marriage
is being consummated.

Among high-caste Hindus of the Punjab "the bridegroom always carries an iron weapon with him to drive
away the evil spirits which haunt him, especially at
the marriage ceremony." In Morocco it is the custom
for the bridegroom to carry a sword, dagger, or pistol,
and on the occasion when he is painted with henna
swords are crossed over his head or in front of him to
ward off evil spirits, who are afraid of steel and, especially, of weapons made of this metal. So also swords
are sometimes crossed over the head of the bride at her
henna-ceremony, and she, too, may carry a dagger.
And in order to drive away evil spirits or other evil
influences, the bridegroom sends his sword in advance
to be put on the bridal bed, or puts it there himself, or
hangs it on the wall, or lays a pistol underneath the
pillow. In other Muhammadan countries there are
in the bridal procession two men with drawn swords
escorting the bride; and from the Song of Solomon it
appears that the bridal procession of a Hebrew wed-

ding also contained armed men, holding their swords upon their thighs "because of fear in the night." In various parts of Germany the bridesmen protect the bride with drawn swords; and in France, in the seventeenth century, the couple had on the wedding day to pass under two swords forming an Andrew's cross. In Normandy, when the bridegroom joined the bride in the marriage chamber, one of his friends cracked a whip in order to drive away the evil spirits who might otherwise molest the couple.

The most important of all prophylactic or cathartic rites at Moorish weddings is the custom of painting the bride and bridegroom with henna, a colouring matter produced from the leaves of the *Lawsonia inermis,* or Egyptian privet, which is considered to contain much *baraka,* or benign virtue, and is therefore used as a means of purification or protection on occasions when people think they are exposed to supernatural dangers. The henna is applied to the bride's hands and feet, and occasionally also to her legs below the knees, her arms, face, and hair; while the bridegroom sometimes has it smeared on the palm or fingers or little finger of his right hand, sometimes on both hands, and sometimes on his feet as well. These rites are extremely prevalent in the Muhammadan world, particularly the custom of painting the bride.

It is likewise a widespread custom among Muhammadans that the bridegroom has a bath before meeting the bride; and the bride also is purified by bathing or water-pouring. So too, among the ancient and modern Hindus and among other Indo-European peoples it has been or still is considered an essential preparation for a wedding that the bride, or frequently the bridegroom also, should have a bath. In ancient Greece they bathed in water drawn from a particular fountain of running water, which at Athens was the fountain of Callirrhoë; and in modern Greece the bride's bath still forms part of the nuptials. In Cromarty the bride has her feet washed on the day before the wedding, money is put into the water and when she sits with her feet in the basin or tub, her girl friends scramble for the coin. In the north-east of Scotland, on the evening before the marriage, there was the ceremony of "feet-washing": a few of the bridegroom's most intimate friends assembled at his house, a large tub was brought forward and nearly filled with water, and the groom was stripped of shoes and stockings and his feet and legs were plunged in the water. The same custom prevailed in Northumberland, and there the bride, too, had her feet washed though in a more private way. There may, no doubt, be other than superstitious reasons for the bathing or washing of bride and bridegroom, but the ceremonial character of the act certainly suggests a purificatory object. And so do other water ceremonies so frequently connected with weddings. It is a common custom in Morocco that when the bride arrives at the bridegroom's place, purifying substances, like milk, water, and henna, are offered her or sprinkled on her. The Shī'ahs have a tradition that the Prophet, before he gave his daughter in marriage to 'Alī, commanded her to fetch water and then sprinkled both her and 'Alī with it, invoking God to protect them and their offspring against the devil. In ancient Rome it was the custom to receive a bride "with water and fire"—*aqua et igni accipere;* and water ceremonies of some sort or other have been, or still are, practised at weddings in many other European countries, as also in ancient and modern India and among various savage tribes.

Besides water, fire is a frequent means of dispelling evil influences at weddings. In Morocco burning candles play a prominent part on such occasions, and partly, no doubt, for superstitious reasons; for the spirits love darkness and are terrified by light. In ancient Greece and Rome the bride was always taken to her new home with torches, and in Rome one of these torches was made of whitethorn, which was believed to keep away evil influences. Brand thinks it doubtful whether the custom of carrying torches in the bridal procession ever prevailed in England, although there are indications that it did; but among the Scandinavian peoples torches have been in frequent use at their weddings up to recent times, and, as Troels-Lund observes, their object was undoubtedly to keep away the powers of darkness. At Hindu weddings lights and other objects are waved round the heads of the bride and bridegroom as a protection against evil spirits. But fire is used at weddings as a means of dispelling evil influences not only on account of its light but because it burns. In Swatow, in China, when the bride arrives at the bridegroom's home, she steps over a flare-up fire on the ground, made by burning a few wisps of dry grass, to be purified from "the contamination of any devils or other dangers that she may have come across on the road." Among the White Russians, before a wedding, straw is burned inside the houses of both bride and bridegroom to drive away evil spirits; the bridegroom, when fetching the bride from her home, must ride or drive over a burning fire, and so also the bride, when arriving at the house of her parents-in-law, must pass a fire, in which she throws coins. In North Germany, when a bridal pair are going to church, it is the custom, before they leave the house, to throw a firebrand on the threshold over which they must pass.

In many parts of Europe and in India the bride, on her arrival at her new home, is, or formerly was, taken three times round the fire of the hearth. In ancient Rome, after the ceremony of the joining of hands, a sacrifice was made, and bride and bridegroom walked round the sacrificial altar. In Germany the bride is led three times round the fire by the bridegroom or his mother. These rites have been interpreted as aggregation rites; but I doubt that this explanation discloses their original meaning, at least in full. They seem too similar to other fire rites, which obviously serve a purificatory purpose, to be disassociated from them. In some places in Germany, while the bride is taken round the hearth fire is thrown after her, or she is placed on a chair and live coals are shovelled underneath it. And in certain cases the circumambulation of the hearth already takes place in the bride's old home. How could it in such cases be regarded as an aggregation rite?

The circumambulation is not always performed round the hearth. Among some Southern Slavs the bride is taken three times round the church before she is allowed to enter it. In the Isle of Man, according to Waldron (who wrote in 1726), when the bridal company arrived at the churchyard, they walked three times round the church before entering; and in Perthshire, according to Sinclair (who wrote at the end of the same century), they walked round the church after leaving it, keeping the church walls upon the right hand. Dr. Winternitz has no doubt that the circumambulation of the church is a survival of an older custom of leading the bride round the sacrificial fire; and the great antiquity of this rite, together with its prevalence among so many Indo-European peoples, certainly speaks in favour of his suggestion. In any case the circumambulation of a holy place, like a church or something connected with it, decidedly has the appearance of a cathartic or prophylactic rite.

Circumambulation may by itself be regarded as a safeguard against evil influences, apart from the purifying nature of the place or object round which it is performed. It may serve as a protection for the inhabitants of the place by allowing such influences to evaporate from a dangerous person who is about to enter it, and it may also be a safeguard for the latter by neutralising the danger of entering a strange place. In Morocco the bride, on her arrival at the bridegroom's village, is in some cases taken three or seven times round the mosque of the place, but in other cases round the whole village or, more often, round the bridegroom's house or tent. Certain circumstances connected with this rite obviously show that it is supposed to have the effect of ridding the bride of the evil influences which she may carry with her; and the same is suggested by the fact that the circumambulation is combined with other purificatory rites. In some places the bride, after her tour round the bridegroom's tent or village or the mosque in it, beats the tent three times with a cane, as I was told, in order that the evil shall go away from it, or to remove any evil which may be

in the bridegroom's family and to expel death from
the domestic animals; it would be very unpleasant for
the young wife if a child or animal should die shortly
after her marriage, as its death would naturally be associated with her presence. But in Morocco bride and
bridegroom are also themselves beaten or tapped for
purificatory purposes. At Amzmiz, in the Great
Atlas, the bride's brother after he has placed a silver
coin in one of his sister's slippers and then put them on
her feet, taps her three times with his own slipper,
presumably to drive away evil influences. In ancient
India the bridegroom was chaffed or beaten. In some
parts of Germany he is beaten by the wedding-guests,
especially the unmarried ones. In France both bride
and bridegroom were formerly ceremonially struck
with the hand or with a stick in church after the nuptial ceremony, and this was supposed to do them good.
Mannhardt, who gives many instances of the custom of
beating a bridegroom or bride, suggests that its object
is to expel evil spirits which might otherwise prevent
fecundity; but there is no reason to think that the rite
is intended to expel evil influences merely for the
purposes of making the union fruitful.

Besides marriage rites which are meant to drive off
evil spirits or other evil influences, there are rites
that are intended to safeguard bride or bridegroom by
deception. Disguises at marriages are widespread, and
many writers have suggested that their object is to
deceive malignant spirits who lie in wait for the young
couple.

Thus, among some sections of the Brahmans of
South India, especially the Tamil sections, the bride
is on the fourth day dressed up as a boy and pretends

to be the bridegroom, and another girl is dressed up to represent the bride. In ancient Cos, according to Plutarch, the bridegroom was dressed in woman's clothes when he received his bride; whilst in Sparta, after the bride had been carried off by her husband, "the bridesmaid received her, cut her hair close to her head, dressed her in a man's cloak and shoes, and placed her upon a couch in a dark chamber, where she had to wait for the entrance of the bridegroom." Among the Egyptian Jews in the Middle Ages the bridegroom donned feminine attire, whilst the bride wore a helmet and, sword in hand, led the procession and the dance. At Fez, when the betrothal of a young man is celebrated in his parents' house, some negresses whose profession is to assist women on festive occasions dress him up as a bride with garments which they have brought with them. He is then placed on cushions on a mattress opposite the door, and sits there with his eyes closed as if he were a bride. On the other hand, in some country places in Morocco the bride imitates the appearance of a man by having designs resembling whiskers painted on her face, or by wearing her shawl thrown over her left shoulder and a dagger slung over her right, or by leaving her old home clad in a man's cloak. At Klovborg, in Denmark, on the first day of the wedding the bride and bridegroom dress themselves in old clothes, she in man's and he in woman's, and then they hide themselves from each other. It is also the custom in Denmark, and in Esthonia and Russia as well, to put the bridegroom's hat or cap on the bride. Among the people of Southern Celebes the bridegroom at one stage of the proceedings puts on the garments which have just been put off by the bride.

I doubt, however, whether all these practices can be explained as attempts to deceive evil spirits. The fiancé or bridegroom can hardly be protected against such spirits by being dressed up as a bride, as he is at Fez, or by putting on the garments which have been worn by his bride, since the bride is supposed to be haunted by evil spirits as much as, or even more than, the bridegroom himself; nor does the bride seem to be particularly well protected by pretending to be the bridegroom, as in South India, or by wearing his cap or hat. Facts of this sort seem better to agree with Mr. Crawley's theory of "inoculation," according to which the bride or bridegroom assumes the dress of the opposite sex in order to lessen the sexual danger by wearing the same kind of clothes as "the loved and dreaded person," and the greatest possible assimilation between them would best serve the purpose of neutralising that danger. In some parts of Esthonia the bride is on the wedding day girded with a man's girdle and the bridegroom has a woman's girdle tied round his hat. Similar customs may, as already said, spring from different motives, or there may be mixed motives for the same custom. It should be added that when the bride imitates the appearance of a man, she may do so to be protected not only against evil spirits but against the evil eye.

In many cases some other person or persons than the bride or bridegroom imitate his or her costume or in some way or other personate one of them; and it has been said that persons so disguised may be supposed to serve as dummies to attract the attention of the demons or to divert to themselves the envious glance of the evil eye and so allow the real bride or bridegroom

[209]

to escape unhurt. It is a common custom among Slavonic, Teutonic, and Romance peoples that when the bridgegroom or his representative comes to fetch the bride from her home, a false bride is substituted for the real one, another woman, frequently an ugly old one, or a little girl, or even a man, being palmed off on him as the bride. In Brittany the substitutes are first a little girl, then the mistress of the house, and lastly the grandmother. In the Samerberg district of Bavaria a bearded man in woman's clothes personates the bride; in Esthonia the bride's brother or some other young man. Sometimes the substitution takes place at the betrothal, and sometimes only at the wedding-feast. As for the meaning of the custom, I think it must be admitted that it allows of more than one explanation. The attempt to palm off a mock bride on the bridegroom may be another of those rites, already mentioned in connection with marriage by capture, by which the girl and her relatives show opposition to her marriage and till the last put obstacles in the bridegroom's way.

In India mock marriages with things or trees or animals are often resorted to for the purpose of averting some dreaded evil from the bride or bridegroom or both. Tree-marriages, in particular, prevail widely throughout Northern India; and, as Dr. Crooke observes, the idea that the tree itself is supposed to die soon after the ceremony "seems to point to the fact that the marriage may be intended to divert to the tree some evil influence, which would otherwise attach to the wedded pair." In the Punjab mock marriages, owing to fear of ill luck, take place either when a widower wishes to marry a third wife, or when the horoscope of a girl shows that the influence of certain stars is likely to lead to early widowhood. In cases of the former kind the mock marriage is celebrated sometimes with a certain tree or bush and sometimes with a sheep, which is dressed up as a bride and is led by the bridegroom round the sacrificial fire while the real bride sits by. And the fear of ill luck is due partly to the suspicion, caused by the death of the two former wives, that the wife of the man is destined to die, and particularly the wife taken by the third marriage, which is considered to be peculiarly inauspicious; but partly also to the belief that the jealousy of the spirit of the first wife is instrumental in causing the death of subsequent wives, although in the case of a fourth marriage the evil influence of the first wife is supposed to have spent itself and therefore no mock marriage is usually deemed necessary. In mock marriages of the second kind, again, a pitcher full of water is dressed like a boy, and the girl is taken through the ceremonies of marriage with this pseudo-bridegroom. The ceremonies are then repeated with the real bridegroom by way of an informal marriage; and it is supposed that the effect of the evil star will befall the pitcher and not the bridegroom, thus averting the disaster of early widowhood.

There are, further, cases in which the bridegroom or the bride, instead of assuming the appearance of somebody else or being represented by a substitute, is sheltered by some person or persons who are dressed up to resemble him or her, so that there apparently are two or more bridegrooms or brides. Thus at Fez, when the bride is taken to her future home, she is accompanied not only by the bridegroom's people who have come to fetch her, some men of her own family, and a

crowd of boys, but by some—perhaps six or eight—
women relatives, who are dressed exactly like herself
so that no one can distinguish between them; this was
said to protect her from magic and the evil eye. In
Egypt, again, when the bridegroom goes to the mosque
before meeting the bride, he walks between two friends
dressed like himself. Among the Livonians two
bridesmaids are dressed exactly as the bride. So also
in Belford "the bride and her maids are dressed alike";
and I am told that this has been the custom also elsewhere in England. The functions of bridesmaids,
bridesmen, and groomsmen have been not only to
attend upon bride and bridegroom but to protect them
from evil influences, even when no attempt is made
to imitate their dress; people always feel safer in company. In Shetland the best-man must sleep with the
bridegroom during the night before the wedding.
Among the White Russians he lies down on the nuptial
bed before the bride and bridegroom. Among other
peoples he or some bridesmen are present when
the marriage is consummated, or bridesmen and
bridesmaids have to prevent the speedy consummation of it.

An effective method of protecting the bride against
external influences, particularly the evil eye, is to shut
her up in a box when she is taken to her new home.
This is done in the north of Morocco, where the bride
is transported to the bridegroom's house in a so-called
'ammarîya on the back of a mule or a horse; and in
one tribe this box is made of oleander branches, which
are supposed to afford particularly good protection
against the evil eye. In other parts of that country,
and in the Muhammadan world in general, she is

taken to the bridegroom's home with her face well covered, and the same is the case elsewhere, also in many uncivilised tribes. The veiling of the bride is referred to in Genesis. It has been common in Europe; and the importance which the ancient Romans attached to this custom appears from the ordinary use of the word *nubere* or *obnubere* to denote a woman's marrying. Its primary object was in all probability to protect the bride, particularly against the evil eye; the veil of the Esthonian bride is expressly said to serve this purpose. But in Morocco I have also found another idea connected with the veiling or covering of the bride: her own glance is considered dangerous to others. Misfortune would befall any person or animal she looked at before she has seen her husband on her arrival at his house; or if she looked at anybody on her way to it, there would be fighting and manslaughter at the wedding that very day. In ancient India the bridegroom had to guard himself against the evil eye of his bride.

It seems that particular care is often taken to protect bride or bridegroom against dangers from above. In China, "when the bride ascends the bridal sedan she wears a hat of paper, and an old woman who has sons and grandsons holds an umbrella over her." The *chuppah,* or canopy, under which Jewish marriages are still celebrated, seems to have been derived from the canopied litter which in ancient time was occupied by the bride during the procession. In the Scandinavian countries, England, and France a square piece of cloth (in French called *carré* and in English "care cloth") was held over the bride and bridegroom at the benediction. In some parts of Germany the bridegroom wears on the wedding day a tall hat, which he only removes in church. Among various Slavonic peoples he keeps his head covered at the table. In Bohemia and among some Ugro-Finnic peoples he wears a fur cap even though the marriage is celebrated in the summer; and a Syryenian bride has her head covered with a cap made of sheepskin until the nuptial ceremony and does not remove it even at night.

Bride and bridegroom must be protected against dangers not only from above but from below. In Morocco the bridegroom must avoid sitting on the ground, so as not to be affected by evil influences; on certain occasions he is carried by his best-man or other bachelor friends; and throughout the wedding he has the backs of his slippers pulled up so as to prevent their falling off. Similar and still greater precautions are taken with regard to the bride, who would be unlucky if her foot came in contact with the ground. Bride and bridegroom have *baraka,* or "holiness," and persons or objects possessed of this delicate quality are in many cases not allowed to touch the ground; moreover, the real native country of the spirits is under the ground and they are therefore always liable to haunt its surface. Very similar marriage customs are found in other countries. The bride is frequently carried to her future home—on an animal or a litter or a man's back or in some other manner; and although this, of course, may be done for the sake of convenience, or may be a ceremonial expression of the reluctance which a virgin bride pretends to feel against being given away in marriage, there can be no doubt that the fear of her touching the ground also has something to do with it. Among the Cheremiss the custom of carrying the bride to the carriage by which she is to be conveyed to the bridegroom's house, and of carrying her into the house on her arrival, is expressly said to be connected with the idea that a bride must not put her foot on the bare ground.

At Foochow in China, again, the floor of the reception-room in the bridegroom's house is covered with red carpeting from the place where the sedan stops to the door of the bride's room, in order to prevent her feet from touching the floor; and it is presumably for a similar reason that a Chinese bride on leaving her own home walks all the way from her room to the sedan chair in her father's shoes, which are then left behind before she steps into the chair. In England, according to Brand, there was "a custom at marriages of strewing herbs and flowers, and also rushes, from the house or houses where persons betrothed resided to the church." In Sunderland the footpath of the street in which the bride lives, and along which she must pass in order to be married at the church, is sprinkled with sawdust. Formerly sea-sand was used; and if the custom was to be fully carried out in its integrity, the sand or sawdust should stretch all the way from the bride's house to the church gates. In Newcastle-on-Tyne sand is strewn on the pavement before a bridal pair tread on it. At Cranbrook in Kent, when a newly wedded pair leave the church, the path is strewed with emblems of the bridegroom's calling; thus carpenters walk on shavings, butchers on sheepskins, shoemakers on leather parings, and blacksmiths on scraps of old iron. The red carpet at weddings is familiar to all of us.

That these customs are, at least in part, due to superstitious fear of too close a contact with the ground is the more probable because there are other practices apparently intended to protect bride and bridegroom against supposed danger from below. In Morocco a needle or some salt is put into the right slipper of the bride, or of the bridegroom as well, as a charm against spirits or other evil influences. In many places a coin or coins are put into their shoes; and although this practice, which is particularly common among the Scandinavian peasantry, is often supposed to prevent poverty or to produce wealth, it is not infrequently expressly said to be regarded as a safeguard against evil. In some parts of Scotland, according to Dalyell, "the bridegroom has sought protection by standing with the latchet of his shoe loose and a coin under his foot, probably for interception from the earth."

To carry a bride over the threshold is a very widespread practice; it occurs or has occurred, for example, in China, Palestine, Cairo, Morocco, ancient Rome, and many modern European countries, including Great Britain. In Wales the bride, on her return from the marriage ceremony, was always carefully lifted over the threshold because "it was considered very unlucky for a bride to place her feet on or near the threshold," and "trouble was in store for the maiden who preferred walking into the house." In some parts of Scotland, in the beginning of the last century, when the wedding party arrived at the bridegroom's house, "the young wife was lifted over the threshold, or first step of the door, lest any withcraft or *ill e'e* should be cast upon and influence her." Side by side with the carrying or lifting of the bride over the threshold there is a custom which simply requires her to avoid

stepping on it—a rule which prevailed in ancient
India. And the threshold may be considered dangerous to the bridegroom also; in Salsette, an island near
Bombay, he is carried into the house by his maternal
uncle, and afterwards he himself lifts his bride over the
threshold. As for the fear of the threshold, I venture
to believe that it is chiefly due to that uncanny feeling
which superstitious people are apt to experience when
they first enter a dwelling, passing through the doorway from daylight into dimness. This feeling easily
gives rise to the idea that the threshold is haunted by
mysterious beings, whether the souls of dead people
or spirits like the *jinn,* or is, generally, a seat of supernatural danger.

Fear of dangers threatening bride and bridegroom
from below may also be the origin of the familiar custom of throwing an old shoe or old shoes after them,
which is found not only in England and Scotland, but
in Denmark, on the Rhine, and among the gypsies of
Transylvania, and evidently occurred in ancient
Greece, as appears from the representation of a wedding on a vase in the museum of Athens. In most
cases the shoe is thrown after the bridal pair when
they leave for church or return from church or after
the wedding breakfast; but a shoe may also be thrown
after the bride and the bridegroom separately, as was
the case in the Isle of Man. Various explanations have
been given of the origin of this custom; to say that
it is considered to bring good luck is, of course, not
to explain it. It has been interpreted as a relic of
marriage by capture, being "a sham assault on the
person carrying off the lady"; as a method of ensuring
fecundity; as a means of averting evil influences,

because spirits may be afraid of leather; or as an offering to dangerous spirits. All these theories seem to me unsatisfactory for various reasons. It should be noticed that a shoe is thrown after a bride and a bridegroom when they go somewhere; that the throwing of it occurs side by side with practices apparently intended to protect them against evil influences from below; and that it is also a custom found in England, Denmark, Germany, and elsewhere to throw a shoe or a slipper after a person who goes on a journey or to do business or a shooting. Brand says that in England it is accounted lucky by the vulgar to throw an old shoe after a person when they wish him to succeed in what he is going about. These facts suggest that the old shoe was meant to serve the persons in question as an extra magical protection on their way, in addition to the shoes or boots they wore. They remind us of the extreme care taken by Moorish brides and bridegrooms to prevent their slippers from falling off their feet and of the Chinese bride wearing her father's shoes for fear of contact with the ground. In Scotland it was the custom to wish brides and bridegrooms "a happy foot."

Evils are averted from bride and bridegroom not only by positive rites but by abstinences of various kinds. Being in a dangerous state or a source of danger to others, they must observe the utmost caution in all their doings and do as little as possible. On certain occasions they must not look round. There are taboos prohibiting them from eating or drinking in public, from eating much, from eating certain victuals, or from eating at all. Silence is imposed on brides, and the bridegroom may have to refrain from speaking

aloud. Some peoples consider it necessary for them
to keep awake. And very frequently continence has
to be observed for a shorter or longer time after
marriage. Instances of this may be quoted from all
parts of the world.

So far as Indo-European peoples are concerned the
hypothesis has been set forth that the custom of practising continence for some time after marriage may
be traced back to the primitive period of their race.
It was incorporated into ancient Indian law and exists,
or has recently existed, in many European countries.
In various parts of Germany and Switzerland continence is observed for three nights after marriage,
which are frequently known as the "Tobias nights";
it is believed that otherwise the wedded life of the
couple would be unlucky, whereas if they abstain from
intercourse the devil will not be able to do any harm.
In some districts of France also continence is or
recently was practised for three or two nights after
marriage or on the first night, and in several places in
Brittany the bride is during this night entrusted to the
supervision of the best-man and the bridesmaid. In the
latter part of the eighteenth century Lord Hailes was
informed that abstinence on the wedding night was
"still observed by the vulgar in some parts of Scotland." Now it may be argued that the continence
observed after marriage in so many countries of Europe
is not a survival of an ancient pagan custom, but is
due to the teaching of the Christian Church. A decree
of the alleged fourth Council of Carthage, said to have
been held in the year 398, enacted that when the bridegroom and bride have received the benediction, they
shall remain that same night in a state of virginity out

of reverence for that benediction. This enactment was received into the Canon Law; and by subsequent enactments the period of chastity which married couples were required or recommended to observe was extended from one to two or three nights, often with special reference to the example set by Tobias, who (according to the version of the Vulgate) by advice of the archangel Raphael abstained from carnal intercourse with his wife Sarah for three nights. It is conceivable that the same horror of sexual defilement as induced the Church to prescribe continence in connection with various other religious acts also might independently have led to the decree imposing continence in connection with the sacrament of marriage; but it seems more probable that this decree and the subsequent appeal to the archangel's advice to Tobias only gave religious sanction and scriptural support to an old pagan custom which was highly congenial to the ascetic tendencies of the Church. A similar view has recently been advocated by Sir James Frazer with much fullness of detail. This view derives support, first, from the fact that the rule of continence after marriage is not only found among pagan peoples in all parts of the world but existed among the Vedic Aryans; and, secondly, from its persistence in European folk-custom, which suggests a deeper foundation than ecclesiastical injunction alone.

At the same time it must be admitted that the custom of deferring the consummation of the marriage for a time may have a different origin in different cases. Sometimes it is attributed to resistance on the part of the bride, and there may be some truth in this. More frequently, however, the custom in question is ascribed to sexual bashfulness in the bridegroom or in both parties; and when intercourse is said to be postponed till the guests have gone away and in some other cases, this seems a very natural explanation of the postponement. Yet it can hardly be doubted that the rule of continence to which bride and bridegroom are subject, like other taboos imposed upon them, is mainly the outcome of superstitious fear. If it is considered dangerous for them to speak or eat or sleep, it is not surprising if sexual intercourse between them is supposed to be fraught with danger. In most cases of compulsory continence we are not told of any such reason for it; but sometimes it is said that the observance of it is essential for a happy wedded life, or that it will make the offspring good, or that it will prevent the devil from doing harm, while we read in the Book of Tobit that a wicked demon, named Asmodæus, out of spite and jealousy slew the woman's seven bridegrooms as soon as they had gone in to her on the wedding night.

With reference to the Vedic practice Oldenberg says that its original meaning, though it was obviously no longer understood by the people, must be sought in the fear of spirits who, in the act of copulation, might slip into the woman and endanger her offspring or might even themselves impregnate her, but were supposed to be misled by a pretence of omitting the consummation of marriage. The idea that evil spirits may slip into women when they have sexual intercourse is familiar to Muhammadans even at the present day. I was told in Morocco that it is always necessary for the husband before having intercourse with his wife to say the *bismillāh,* "In the name of God," lest the devil should enter the woman and make the child a villain; and this belief has the support of the Muhammadan traditions. Sir James G. Frazer, again, observes that "the intention of the custom is perhaps not so much to deceive the demons by pretending that the marriage is not to be consummated, as to leave them free scope for making love to the bride in the absence of the bridegroom." This conjecture is, so far as I know, directly supported only by one statement, recently made by Dr. Karsten with reference to the Canelos Indians of Ecuador. I am of opinion that anthropologists are often apt to look for too much reasoning at the bottom of primitive customs. Many of these are based on vague feelings rather than on definite ideas. Sexual intercourse, which in many cases is regarded as a mysterious cause of evil, is held particularly dangerous to bride and bridegroom, who are much exposed and very sensitive to all sorts of evil influences, and is therefore abstained from while the danger lasts. But to speculate on the specific nature of the danger and of the evil influences causing it, or on the way in which continence is supposed to avert that danger, is, in the absence of direct evidence, the more precarious, as it is very doubtful whether the people themselves have any clear theory on the subject.

The prophylactic observances which play such an important part at marriages in all parts of the world raise the interesting question, Why are bride and bridegroom supposed to be in a dangerous condition, and why is the bride considered dangerous to others? In order to answer these questions, I have compared the rites practised in Morocco at weddings where the bridegroom is a bachelor and the bride a maiden with those practised in cases where either bride or bridegroom or both have been married before. This comparison showed that the rites of a purificatory or protective kind to which the bride or bridegroom is subjected depend on the circumstance whether she or he, but not both parties, has been married before or not. A bridegroom who is a bachelor has to undergo the same ceremonies whether the bride be a maiden, a widow, or a divorced wife, whereas these ceremonies are omitted in the case of a bridegroom who has or has had another wife, quite independently of the state of the bride; and a bride who has not been married before is subjected to the same ceremonies whether the bridegroom be a bachelor, a widower, or a polygamist, whereas these ceremonies are, if not altogether done away with, at all events much reduced in the case of a bride who is a widow or a divorced wife, quite independently of the state of the bridegroom. From all this I conclude that, even though some of the purificatory and protective marriage rites have sprung from fear of hymeneal blood or from the idea that the bride may carry evil with her both as a new-comer into the bridegroom's household and in her capacity of being a woman, the bulk of these rites are due to the fact that the person who is subjected to them is bride or bridegroom for the first time. She or he enters into a new state, the wedding is, to use a phrase coined by M. van Gennep, a *rite de passage;* and to pass into a new condition or to do a thing for the first time is not only in this, but in many other cases, considered to be attended with danger. But it must in addition be noticed that in the present instance the nature of the act itself which is sanctioned by the wedding is apt to increase the supposed peril. I venture to believe that this explanation in the main holds true not only of the Moors but of other peoples as well. Evidence from a detailed comparison between the prophylactic and cathartic rites practised at first and those practised at second marriages is unfortunately wanting. But we often hear that widows or divorced wives are married with less formality than girls.

Besides marriage rites which are purely magical, there are others of a religious or semi-religious nature, often performed by a priest. In some cases these rites are intended to serve some specific purpose, such as the securing of offspring, but most frequently their object is to promote the welfare of the couple in general either by bestowing on them positive benefits or by protecting them against evil. They are found among both savage and civilised peoples. In some African tribes sacrifices are offered to ancestral spirits or to a fetish. Among the Maori of New Zealand an aristocratic marriage was accompanied with a great feast at which a priest recited certain prayers or invocations over the couple. Among the Igorot of Luzon a priestess performs the marriage ceremony, praying to the spirits of the deceased in the presence of all the kinsfolk of the couple. In ancient India various deities were invoked at the weddings; and modern Hindus, except the very lowest, consider it essential for the validity of a marriage that a Brahman, acting as priest, should be present at its celebration. Religious marriage rites occurred in ancient Greece; thus the bride dedicated to various deities that superintended the union of the sexes her girlish toys and other gifts, and more especially her maiden tresses, now shorn. At the Roman *confarreatio,*

as noticed above, a cake of *far* was offered to Jupiter
Farreus, and in the historic period an animal sacrifice
was made at a wedding in Rome; but we do not know
to what deity it was offered or, indeed, if it was offered
to any deity at all. Generally speaking, the religious
side of ancient Indo-European marriage rituals has
been exaggerated by earlier writers, who have put a
religious interpretation upon many purely magical
ceremonies by associating them with the worship of
divine beings.

The founder of Christianity did not prescribe any
particular ceremonies in connection with marriage, but
it has been assumed that the celebration of it among
Christians was from the very first accompanied with
suitable acts of religious worship. The testimony of
the Fathers, from the middle of the third century onwards, shows that marriages contracted without any
formal benediction did occur, but they were dis-
countenanced by the Church. Yet, though the dogma
that marriage is a sacrament gradually developed from
St. Paul's words, τὸ μυστήριον τοῦτο μέγα ἐστίν—in the
Vulgate translated, "Sacramentum hoc magnum est"
—and was fully recognised in the twelfth century,
marriage without benediction was nevertheless regarded as valid in the Church till the year 1563, when
the Council of Trent decreed that thenceforth no marriage should be considered valid unless celebrated by
a priest in the presence of two or three witnesses.

Luther's opinion that all matrimonial affairs belong
not to the Church, but to the jurists, was not accepted
by the legislators of the Protestant countries. Marriage
certainly ceased to be thought of as a sacrament, but
continued to be regarded as a divine institution. And

sacerdotal nuptials became no less obligatory on Protestants than on Roman Catholics.

It was the French Revolution that first gave rise to an alteration in this respect. The Constitution of the 3rd September, 1791, declares that the law regards marriage only as a civil contract to be established by means of a civil act. To this obligatory act a sacerdotal benediction may be added, if the parties think proper. Since then civil marriage has gradually obtained a footing in the legislation of most European countries, although in many of them, as in England, the parties may choose the religious or the civil rite, just as they like, both making the marriage equally valid by law.

The legal importance which has been attached to the religious ceremony in Christian countries has no counterpart in either Jewish or Muhammadan law. Although the former regards marriage as a divine institution, the omission of the benediction would not invalidate a marriage. The priestly benediction is mentioned neither in the Bible nor in the Talmud; and the regular presence of a Rabbi at a wedding is not earlier than the fourteenth century. Nor does Muhammadan law require religious rites for the contraction of a valid marriage. In all cases the religious ceremony is left entirely to the discretion of the *qāẓī* or person who performs the ceremony, and consequently there is no uniformity of ritual.

From this survey of marriage rites prevalent among many different peoples it appears that they are not empty formalities, but are supposed to be of great practical importance. Some of them may no doubt be regarded as survivals of earlier, either occasional or regular, methods of concluding a marriage. Certain rites, as we have noticed before, may have been suggested by genuine bride-capture, and in other cases marriage by consideration may have left traces in the wedding ritual after it has ceased to exist as a reality; but, generally speaking, the importance of marriage rites as means of studying earlier forms of marriage or relations between the sexes has been greatly exaggerated. Various rites are partly or exclusively fossilised expressions of such emotional states as sexual bashfulness, sorrow, or anger, whilst others are expressions of joy or erotic feelings. To the latter class belong dancing, which forms a regular feature of wedding feasts in many parts of the world, and the sexual licence in which the guests are often allowed to indulge. But dancing as a marriage rite may also, in particular cases, have a symbolic or magical significance, and, generally, be a method of attaining tumescence. And the sexual indulgence of the wedding guests may, on the principle of homœopathic magic, be a means of assisting bride and bridegroom in achieving the reproductive aims of their union.

In spite of the great value which is so frequently ascribed to marriage rites there are many peoples who are said to have no such rites. This is particularly the case with American and Australian tribes, but also with various South Sea Islanders and several Asiatic and African peoples. Statements to this effect, however, need not indicate the complete absence of marriage rites. It will often be found, as Mr. Crawley points out, that "there is some act performed which is too slight or too practical to be marked by an observer as a 'ceremony,' but which when analysed turns out to be a real marriage rite"; and even when positive rites are wanting, there may be abstinences of some kind or other connected with the conclusion of a marriage. The marriage ritual is particularly profuse among peoples who have reached a higher degree of culture and among tribes that have been in close contact with such peoples. It is nowhere richer than among the peasantry of Indo-European nations and among peoples of Semitic culture; but among the latter it seems largely to be of comparatively recent origin and distinctly suggests that Indo-European influence has been at work. On the other hand, modern civilisation has proved destructive to the old rituals and has had practically nothing new to add to them. This is a natural consequence of the fact that the large bulk of marriage rites have originated in magical ideas which have vanished along with the progress in intellectual culture.

CHAPTER IX

MONOGAMY AND POLYGYNY

AMONG the lower animals certain species are by instinct monogamous and other species polygynous. In mankind, on the other hand, we find marriages of one man with one woman (monogamy), of one man with several women (polygyny), of several men with one woman (polyandry), and of several men with several women (group-marriage). In the present chapter I shall deal with monogamy and polygyny, which are by far the most frequent forms of marriage.

Among the uncivilised races, to judge by my collection of facts, polygyny has not been practised on a large scale by any of the lower hunters and food-collectors, except some Australian and Bushman tribes, nor by any incipient agriculturists, at least among those of the lower type. On the other hand, a considerable number of these low hunting and slightly agricultural tribes are strictly monogamous. To this class belong some of the South American Indians, the aboriginal tribes of the Malay Peninsula, the Andaman Islanders, the Veddas of Ceylon, certain tribes in the Malay Archipelago, the monogamous Negritos of the Philippine Islands, and some at least of the Central African Pygmies. Among the higher hunters, most of whom are found in North America, polygyny is more frequent, although in the majority of their tribes it is practised only occasionally; and exclusive monogamy is very rare, though perhaps not unknown. Among pastoral peoples I have found none that can be regarded as strictly monogamous; and both among them and among the higher agriculturists polygyny is undoubtedly more frequent than among the hunters and incipient agriculturists, although cases of regular monogamy are more frequent among the higher agriculturists than among the higher hunters. This has also been pointed out by Messrs. Hobhouse, Wheeler, and Ginsberg, who say that "the *extent* of polygamy as distinct from the recognition of it as good custom increases almost continuously, only being more marked among the pastoral peoples." According to their tables polygyny is more frequent among the cattle-keeping agriculturists than among the pure agriculturists, and more frequent among the higher pastoral tribes (who have taken to agriculture as a secondary employment) than among the lower ones. It should, however, be noticed that the cases in which polygyny is represented as "general" are comparatively much more numerous among African than among non-African pastoral peoples and higher (that is, pure and cattle-keeping) agriculturists. This fact should serve as a warning not to assume that the frequency of polygyny at the higher grades of economic culture among the simpler peoples is merely due to economic causes.

It is in Africa that we find polygyny at its height, both in point of frequency and so far as the number of wives is concerned, although we also hear that among many African peoples monogamy is the predominant and among a few the exclusive form of marriage. In Unyoro, according to Emin Pasha, it would be absolutely improper for even a small chief to have fewer than ten or fifteen wives, and poor men have three or four each. The number of wives possessed by the King of Benin has been estimated by different writers at 600, 1,000, over 3,000, and 4,000; but he gave some away to men who had rendered him a service. In Ashanti the law limited the king to 3,333 wives, but whether it required him to reach this number is not known. King Mtēssa of Uganda is said to have had 7,000 wives, and the same is the case with the king of Loango. This is, to my knowledge, the high-water mark of polygyny anywhere.

Where polygyny occurs it may be modified in a monogamous direction from both the social and the sexual point of view. The general rule is that one of the wives holds a higher social position than the rest or is regarded as the principal wife; and in most cases it is the first married wife to whom such a distinction is assigned, presumably because monogamy is, or formerly was, the rule among the people and polygyny either a novelty or an exception. The difference between the position of the first wife and that of subsequent ones is not infrequently so great that our authorities represent the former as the only real or legitimate wife and the others as concubines, and speak of monogamy combined with concubinage; but in many or most of these cases we are probably justified in regarding the marriage as polygynous and the concubines as inferior wives, if the term concubinage is restricted to relations that only imply sexual licence. In some cases the higher position of the first wife implies certain sexual privileges; but more often we are told that it is the custom for the husband to cohabit with his wives in turn, or that this is actually required of him. Another matter is how far theory and practice coincide. We have reason to suspect that in polygynous marriages one of the wives is for the time being the favourite.

Polygyny, or a sort of concubinage hardly distinguishable from genuine polygyny, is found among most peoples of archaic civilisation. In China there are, besides the legal principal wife, so-called wives "by courtesy" or lawful concubines; whereas the law forbids the taking of a wife, in the full sense of the term, during the lifetime of the first. The wife is invested with a certain amount of power over the concubines. She addresses her partner with a term corresponding to our "husband," while the concubines call him master. A wife cannot be degraded to the position of a concubine, nor can a concubine be raised to the position of a wife so long as the wife is alive. But the question upon which legitimacy of the offspring depends is not whether the woman is wife or concubine, but whether she has been received into the house of the man or not. In Japan concubinage of the Chinese type existed as a legal institution until it was abolished with the promulgation of the Criminal code of 1880; but the long-established custom still lingers to some extent.

In ancient Egypt polygyny seems to have been permitted but to have been unusual; indeed, Dr. Alan Gardiner points out to me that evidence of non-royal polygyny in Egypt is very hard to find, though not absolutely unknown. The Babylonian Code of Ḥammurabi assumes that marriage shall be monogamous. Yet "if a man has married a wife and a sickness has seized her," he may take a second wife; and if she remained childless he might take a concubine, who, however, could not be put on an equality with the wife. Slave-concubinage was frequently practised in the days of Ḥammurabi, and a female slave who had borne her master children could not be sold. Among the Hebrews, on the other hand, a man could in any circumstances take a plurality of wives, and there was no difference in the legal status of different wives, although a distinction was made between a wife and a slave-concubine. In the case of the levirate marriage the Pentateuch actually ordains a second marriage, a man being compelled to marry his childless brother's widow whether he be married before or not. It is probable, however, that among the ancient Israelites, as among most other peoples practising polygyny, the bulk of the population lived in monogamy, and that in post-exilic times polygyny was a rare exception. There was no limit to the number of wives a man might take; we read of Solomon who had "seven hundred wives, princesses, and three hundred concubines." But in the Talmud it is said that "the wise men have given good advice, that a man should not marry more than four wives." Among European Jews polygyny was still practised in the Middle Ages, and among Jews living in Muhammadan countries it is found even to this day. In Arabia Muhammad set a limit to the number of wives a man might possess, by ordaining that his legal wives should be not more than four; but he might enjoy as concubines any number of slaves he was able to possess. The Prophet himself, however, was allowed as many wives as he wished. Where two or more wives belong to one man, the first married generally enjoys the highest rank and is called "the great lady." But, as a matter of fact, the large majority of men in Muhammadan countries live in monogamy.

Polygyny has been permitted among most of the Indo-European peoples. That it was practised among the Vedic Indians is clearly proved, but it was probably as a rule confined to kings and wealthy lords. None of the Hindu law-books restricts the number of wives a man is permitted to marry; yet some preference is often shown for monogamy, and a peculiar sanctity seems always to have been attributed to the first marriage, as being that which was contracted from a sense of duty and not merely for personal gratification. At the present day, although the Hindu law places no restriction upon polygyny, most castes object to their members having more than one wife, except for special reasons, such as the failure of the first wife to bear a son, or her affliction with some incurable disease or infirmity.

Polygyny occurred among the ancient Slavs, but generally, it seems, only chiefs and nobles were addicted to it. Among some Southern Slavs bigamy is even now allowed in case the wife is unfruitful or becomes insane. In ancient Scandinavia the kings indulged in polygynous practices, and not they alone; a man could not only have as many concubines as he chose, but also more than one legitimate wife. Among the West Germans, according to Tacitus, only a few persons of noble birth had a plurality of wives. There is no direct evidence of polygyny among the Anglo-Saxons, but it cannot have been entirely unknown to them, as it is prohibited in some of their law-books.

[234]

MONOGAMY AND POLYGYNY

Among the ancient Irish we sometimes find a king or chief with two wives. In the Homeric poems genuine polygyny appears to be ascribed to Priamus alone, but he was a Trojan. There can be little doubt that monogamy was the only recognised form of marriage in Greece. Concubinage existed in Athens at all times and was hardly censured by public opinion, but it was well distinguished from marriage; it conferred no rights on the concubine, and the children were bastards. Roman marriage was strictly monogamous. A second marriage concluded by a married person was invalid, although it was not subject to punishment before the days of the Emperor Diocletian. Liaisons between married men and mistresses were not uncommon by the close of the Republic; but such a relation was not considered lawful concubinage in after-time. According to the jurist Paulus a man who had an *uxor* could not have a *concubina* at the same time.

Considering that monogamy prevailed as the only legitimate form of marriage in Greece and Rome, it cannot be said that Christianity introduced obligatory monogamy into the Western world. Indeed, although the New Testament assumes monogamy as the normal or ideal form of marriage, it does not expressly prohibit polygyny, except in the case of a bishop and a deacon. It has been argued that it was not necessary for the first Christian teachers to condemn polygyny because monogamy was the universal rule among the peoples in whose midst it was preached; but this is certainly not true of the Jews, who still both permitted and practised polygyny at the beginning of the Christian era. Some of the Fathers accused the Jewish

[235]

Rabbis of sensuality; but no Council of the Church in the earliest centuries opposed polygyny, and no obstacle was put in the way of its practice by kings in countries where it had occurred in the times of paganism. In the middle of the sixth century Diarmait, king of Ireland, had two queens and two concubines. Polygyny was frequently practised by the Merovingian kings. Charlemagne had two wives and many concubines; and one of his laws seems to imply that polygyny was not unknown even among priests. In later times Philip of Hesse and Frederick William II. of Prussia contracted bigamous marriages with the sanction of the Lutheran clergy. Luther himself approved of the bigamy of the former, and so did Melanchthon. On various occasions Luther speaks of polygyny with considerable toleration. It had not been forbidden by God; even Abraham, who was a perfect Christian, had two wives. It is true that God had allowed such marriages to certain men of the Old Testament only in particular circumstances, and if a Christian wanted to follow their example he had to show that the circumstances were similar in his case; but polygyny was undoubtedly preferable to divorce. In 1650, soon after the Peace of Westphalia, when the population had been greatly reduced by the Thirty Years' War, the Frankish *Kreistag* at Nuremberg passed the resolution that thenceforth every man should be allowed to marry two women. Certain Christian sects have even advocated polygyny with much fervour. In 1531 the Anabaptists openly preached at Munster that he who wants to be a true Christian must have several wives. And the Mormons, as all the world knows, regard polygyny as a divine institution.

MONOGAMY AND POLYGYNY

From the survey of facts we now come to the question how to explain them. Why are some peoples polygynous and others strictly monogamous; and why is polygyny more frequent, or the number of wives in polygynous marriages larger, among some polygynous peoples than among others? These questions cannot be answered in every detail; but it is easy to show that there are certain circumstances that have a tendency to produce polygyny and others that make for monogamy. One factor which has undoubtedly exercised much influence upon the form of marriage is the numerical proportion of the sexes.

It has been asserted that monogamy is the natural form of marriage, because there is an almost equal number of men and women. But this is a fallacious argument. The proportion of the sexes varies, and in some cases varies greatly, among different peoples. Sometimes they are about equal in number, sometimes there are more men than women, sometimes there are more women than men. Now there can be no doubt that a frequent cause of polygyny is an excess of marriageable women and a frequent cause of monogamy a comparative scarcity of them. Although our knowledge of the proportion of the sexes among the lower races is very defective, I think we may safely say that whenever there is a marked and more or less permanent majority of women in a savage tribe polygyny is allowed. I have found no reliable statement to the contrary, and cannot believe that savage custom would make monogamy obligatory if any considerable number of women were thereby doomed to celibacy. On the other hand, there may very well be polygyny where the sexes are equal in number or the males form the majority; we find polygyny, for instance, among Australian tribes in spite of their surplus of men. In such cases some men have to live unmarried at least for part of their life, and unmarried men are found even where there are more females than males. But although an excess of females leads to polygyny, it is never the sole or complete cause of polygyny, indeed it is only an indirect cause of it. While the existence of available women facilitates polygyny or makes it possible, the direct cause of it is generally the men's desire to have more than one wife. There are various reasons for this desire.

First, monogamy requires of a man periodical continence. He has to live apart from his wife for a certain time every month; at the lower stages of civilisation a menstruous woman is an object of superstitious fear. Among many of the simpler peoples the husband must also abstain from his wife during her pregnancy, or at least during the latter stage of it; a pregnant woman is often regarded as unclean, and sexual intercourse with her is sometimes held to injure or kill the child. In a still higher degree than the obligatory abstinence from conjugal intercourse during pregnancy is the necessity to refrain from it after child-birth a cause of polygynous practices. Of a great number of simple peoples we are told that the husband must not cohabit with his wife until the child is weaned; and this prohibition is severe enough, since the suckling-time lasts sometimes for a year, but more often for two or three, and occasionally even for five or six years. This long suckling-time is chiefly due to want of soft food and animal milk. But even when the people have domesticated animals able to supply them with milk, this kind of food may be avoided; the Dravidian aborigines of Central India, for example, regard it as an excrement, and to the Chinese milk is insupportably odious. There is also the fear that intercourse during the period of suckling would harm the child.

One of the chief causes of polygyny is the attraction which female youth and beauty exercise upon the men; a fresh wife is often taken when the first grows old. Even when a man soon after he has attained manhood marries a woman of his own age, he may still be in the prime of life when the youthful beauty of his wife has passed away for ever; and this is especially the case at the lower stages of civilisation, where the women seem to grow old much sooner than among ourselves. A further cause of polygyny is man's taste for variety. The sexual instinct is dulled by long familiarity and stimulated by novelty. A shereef from Morocco was once in my presence asked by some English ladies why the Moors did not content themselves with a single wife like the Europeans. His answer was, "Why, one cannot always eat fish."

It is not, however, from sexual motives alone that a man may wish to have more than one wife. He may do so also because he is desirous of offspring, wealth, and authority. The barrenness of a wife, or the birth of female offspring only, is a very frequent reason for the choice of another partner in addition to the former one. The desire for offspring is certainly one of the principal causes of polygyny in the East. The legal recognition of concubinage in Japan found its justification in the paramount importance of having an issue to perpetuate the ancestral cult. The polygyny of the ancient Hindus seems to have been chiefly due to the dread of dying childless; and the same motive persists among their modern descendants. Many a Persian takes a fresh wife only when the first one fails to give him offspring; and in Egypt, according to Lane, a man having a wife who has the misfortune to be barren, and being too much attached to her to divorce her, is sometimes induced to take a second wife, merely in the hope of obtaining progeny. Among various peoples polygyny is practised or permitted only when the first wife is sterile or does not give birth to male offspring.

Polygyny, however, is practised as a means not only of obtaining offspring but of obtaining a *large* progeny. We have previously discussed the reasons why men like to have children; but there are also reasons why they may like to have many children. Man in a savage or barbarous state of society is proud of a large family, and he who has most kinsfolk is most honoured and most feared. Speaking of African polygyny, Burton observes that the "culture of the marriage tie is necessary among savages and barbarians, where, unlike Europe, a man's relations and connections are his only friends." In some Berber tribes in Morocco polygyny is much practised owing to the prevalence of the blood-feud, which makes it highly desirable for a man to have many sons. Sons work for their parents until they marry, daughters may be a source of income through the bride price paid for them. The desire for children must be a particularly potent cause of polygyny in countries where families are small. Among savage tribes the birth rate is often low, and the mortality of children is very great. With reference to Equatorial Africans,

Winwood Reade observes: "Propagation is a perfect struggle; polygamy becomes a law of nature; and even with the aid of this institution, so favourable to reproduction, there are fewer children than wives." Among African races in particular the desire for large families seems to be an important cause for polygyny.

Polygyny contributes to a man's material comfort or increases his wealth through the labour of his wives. "If I have but one wife, who will cook for me when she is ill?" is a question often asked by the wife-loving Zulu when arguing in support of his darling custom. The more wives an Eastern Central African has the richer he is: "It is his wives that maintain him. They do all his ploughing, milling, cooking, etc. They may be viewed as superior servants who combine all the capacities of male servants and female servants in Britain—who do all his work and ask no wages." Mr. Weeks observes that "a woman on the Congo is the best gilt-edged security in which a man can invest his surplus wealth."

The usefulness of wives as labourers accounts no doubt in part for the increasing practice of polygyny at the higher grades of economic culture, which has been noticed above. But it is certainly not the only cause, nor even the only economic cause, of this increase. Economic progress leads to a more unequal distribution of wealth, and this, combined with the necessity of paying a bride price the amount of which is more or less influenced by the economic conditions, makes it possible for certain men to acquire several wives while others can acquire none at all Speaking of the Iroquois, Colden long ago remarked that "in any nation where all are on a par as to riches and power, plurality of wives cannot well be introduced"; and Morgan observed that "in its highest and regulated form it presupposes a considerable advance of society, together with the development of superior and inferior classes, and of some kinds of wealth."

A multitude of wives, however, may increase not only a man's wealth but also his social importance, reputation, and authority, apart from the influence of the number of his children. We often hear that it makes a man able to be liberal and keep open doors for foreigners and guests. It increases his influence by connecting him with other families. It is a sign of valour, skill, or wealth. Statements such as "polygamy is held to be the test of a man's wealth and consequence," or "a man's greatness is ever proportionate to the number of his wives," are frequently met with in books of travels. When a Congo native "wants to impress you with the greatness of his chief or the importance of the head of his family, he tells you the number of his wives, and he does not mind adding a dozen to the sum total." Polygyny, as associated with greatness, is thus regarded as honourable or praiseworthy, whereas monogamy, as associated with poverty, is thought mean. The former has tended to become a more or less definite class distinction, and among some peoples it is not even permitted to others than chiefs or nobles.

Among polygynous peoples, as elsewhere, social influence or authority is frequently associated with wealth. But even when it is not so, it may be a cause of polygyny. This is the case in the Australian tribes, where the old men possess exceptional power, and in consequence can indulge in polygyny while many of the younger men have to live unmarried. Among the other tribes at the lowest stages of civilisation, whether they be lower hunters or incipient agriculturists, there is no class of people invested with much authority; and among nearly all of them polygyny is either unknown or very rare.

From circumstances that lead to polygyny we shall now turn our attention to such as make for monogamy. Where the sexes are about equal in number, or there is an excess of men, and a woman consequently has a fair chance of getting a husband for herself, she will hardly care to become the second wife of a man who is already married, or her parents will hardly compel her to marry such a man, unless some particular advantages, economic or social, are gained by it. Hence the absence of disparity in wealth or rank in a society tends to make monogamy general. Again, where there is inequality of wealth or otherwise considerable social differentiation, the poor or low class people may have to be satisfied with one wife even though there be an excess of females. We often read that a man must live in monogamy owing to the price he has to pay for a bride or the expenses connected with a wedding. The difficulty of maintaining several wives is also frequently said to be a cause of monogamy. Such a difficulty easily arises where life is supported by hunting and the amount of female labour is limited, or where the produce of agriculture is insufficient to feed a larger family owing to the poverty of the soil, the primitive methods of cultivation, or the small size of the landed property. Among various peoples polygyny is more or less checked by the man's obligation to serve for his wife a certain number of years, or by his having to settle down with his father-in-law for the rest of his life.

The expenses of having several wives are very frequently increased by the necessity of providing each of them with a separate dwelling, a custom intended to prevent quarrels and fights. We may thus say that even when this aim is achieved—which is not always the case—female jealousy is an obstacle to the practice of polygyny. In many cases we are told that no jealousy or rivalry disturbs the peace in polygynous families or that the women put up with or approve of polygyny—because it implies a division of labour, or because it increases the reputation of the family or the authority of the first wife, or because it gives greater liberty to the married women, or for some other reason. The leading wife of a Kikúyu chief, in British East Africa, asked Mrs. Routledge to tell the English ladies that in her country the women like their husbands to have as many wives as possible. Speaking of the Makololo women, Livingstone observes: "On hearing that a man in England could marry but one wife, several ladies exclaimed that they would not like to live in such a country: they could not imagine how English ladies could relish our custom, for, in their way of thinking, every man of respectability should have a number of wives, as a proof of his wealth. Similar ideas prevail all down the Zambesi." But more frequently we hear that polygyny is a cause of quarrels and domestic misery. When the missionary Williams asked a woman in Fiji how it was that she and so many other women there were without a nose, the answer was, "It is due to plurality

of wives; jealousy causes hatred, and then the stronger
tries to cut or bite off the nose of the one she hates."
The Malagasy word for polygyny means "that which
engenders enmity." In Hebrew the popular term for
the second wife was *haṣṣārāh,* meaning "female
enemy." In Muhammadan countries polygyny is
the cause of strife and unhappiness; in Persia, says
Dr. Polak, a married woman cannot feel a greater
pain than if her husband takes a fresh wife whom he
prefers to her. And in India, among both Muhammadans and Hindus, there is much intriguing and
disquiet in polygynous families. The practice of
marrying women who are sisters, which is particularly
widespread among American Indians but also found
among various other peoples, is often said to serve the
purpose of securing more domestic peace, although
this is not the only motive for it.

Female jealousy may be an obstacle to polygyny
either because the husband for his own sake dreads
its consequences or because his wife simply prevents
him from taking another wife or because he has too
much regard for her feelings to do so. Even in the
savage world a married woman often occupies a
respected and influential position, and the relations
between man and wife may be of a very tender character. This is said to be the case among many monogamous or almost monogamous savages, and I am not
aware of a single case in which any such people is
reported to treat its women badly. It is true that the
position of women may be comparatively good also
among peoples who are addicted, and even much
addicted, to polygyny, like the highly polygamous
Warega in Belgian Congo; but the case is different

with many other peoples who practise polygyny on a large scale. Hence I think we may assume that consideration for the woman's feelings is one cause of monogamy among the lower races, although this consideration itself may be due to circumstances which also in other respects lead to monogamy, such as scarcity of women or economic conditions unfavourable to polygyny. And there can be no doubt that the same cause has operated among civilised nations among whom polygyny is forbidden.

Apart from the general regard for the feelings of women, there are in sexual love itself certain elements that tend to make men inclined to restrict themselves to one wife, at least for some time. "The sociable interest," says Bain, "is by its nature diffused: even the maternal feeling admits of plurality of objects; revenge does not desire to have but one victim; the love of domination needs many subjects; but the greatest intensity of love limits the regards to one." The beloved person acquires, in the imagination of the lover, an immeasurable superiority over all others. "The beginnings of a special affection," the same psychologist continues, "turn upon a small difference of liking; but such differences are easily exaggerated; the feeling and the estimate acting and re-acting, till the distinction becomes altogether transcendent." This absorbing passion for one is not confined to the human race. Herman Müller, Brehm, and other good observers have shown that it is experienced by birds; and Darwin found it among certain domesticated mammals. The love-bird rarely survives the death of its companion, even if supplied with a fresh and suitable mate. In mankind the absorbing passion for one is found not only among civilised but also among savage men and women. Suicide from unsuccessful or disappointed love is by no means infrequent among simple peoples, and although apparently more common among women it also occurs in the case of men. With regard to the natives of the Gold Coast, Cruickshank writes: "The African rushes into battle, shouting the name of his lady-love to inspire him to deeds of daring; the canoe-man gives additional vigour to the stroke of his paddle at the mention of her name; the weary hammock-bearer plucks up a new spirit through the same all-powerful spell, and the solitary wayfarer beguiles the tediousness of his journey by a song in her praise." We are told of a negro who after vain attempts to redeem his sweetheart from slavery became a slave himself rather than be separated from her. And the rude Australian girl sings in a strain of romantic affection, "I never shall see my darling again." But although the absorbing character of his love prevents a man for some time from taking another wife, it does not necessarily prevent his doing so for long. Sensual love is fickle; it is influenced by the desire for change. On the other hand, when love implies sympathy and affection arising from mental qualities there is a tie between husband and wife which lasts long after youth and beauty are gone. This leads to a monogamy that is enduring.

Monogamy is the only form of marriage which is permitted among every people; wherever we find polygyny, polyandry, or group-marriage, we find monogamy side by side with it. Moreover, it is in many cases the only form of marriage which is permitted by custom or law. This may be due to the mere force of habit; or, possibly, to the notion that some men must not appropriate a plurality of wives when others in consequence can get none at all; or to the feeling that polygyny is an offence against the female sex; or to the condemnation of lust. As regards the obligatory monogamy of Christian nations, we have to remember not only that monogamy was the exclusive form of marriage recognised in the European societies on which Christianity was first engrafted, but that polygyny was hardly compatible with the spirit of a religion which regarded every gratification of the sexual impulse with suspicion and incontinence as the gravest sin. In its early days the Church showed little respect for women, but its horror of sensuality was immense.

Our examination into the causes of monogamy and polygyny makes it possible for us to explain why progress in civilisation up to a certain point has proved favourable to polygyny, whilst in its highest forms it leads to monogamy. The first tendency is, as we have seen, largely due to economic and social circumstances—the accumulation and unequal distribution of wealth and increasing social differentiation; but it should also be noticed that the considerable surplus of females which among many of the higher savages is caused by their wars is not found at the lowest stages of civilisation, where war does not seriously disturb the proportion of the sexes. The retrograde tendency towards monogamy in the highest grades of culture, again, may be traced to a variety of causes. No superstitious beliefs keep civilised men apart from their wives during pregnancy and for a long time after child-birth. The desire for offspring has become less intense. A large family, instead of being a help in the struggle for existence, is often considered an insufferable burden. A man's kinsfolk are no longer his only friends, and his wealth and influence do not depend upon the number of his wives and children. A wife ceases to be a mere labourer, and manual labour is to a large extent replaced by the work of domesticated animals and the use of implements and machines. The sentiment of love has become more refined and, in consequence, more enduring. To a cultivated mind youth and beauty are by no means the only attractions of a woman, and besides, civilisation has given female beauty a new lease of life. The feelings of the weaker sex are held in higher regard, and the causes which may make polygyny desired by the women themselves no longer exist. The better education bestowed on them, and other factors in modern civilisation, enable them to live comfortably without the support of a husband.

Will monogamy be the only recognised form of marriage in the future? This question has been answered in different ways. According to Spencer, "the monogamic form of the sexual relation is manifestly the ultimate form; and any changes to be anticipated must be in the direction of completion and extension of it." Dr. Le Bon, on the other hand, thinks that European laws will in the future legalise polygyny; and Professor v. Ehrenfels even regards the adoption of polygyny as necessary for the preservation of the Aryan race. Yet I think we may without hesitation assert that if mankind will advance in the same direction as hitherto, if consequently the causes to which monogamy in the most progressive societies owes its origin will continue to operate with constantly growing force, if especially the regard for the feelings of women, and the women's influence on legislation, will increase, the laws of monogamy are not likely to be changed. It is certainly difficult to imagine a time when Western civilisation would legalise the marriage of one man with several women simultaneously.

CHAPTER X

POLYANDRY AND GROUP-MARRIAGE

POLYANDRY is a much rarer form of marriage than polygyny. Cases of it have been noticed among certain South American Indians, and in North America among some Eskimo, the Tlingit, the Aleut, and the Kaniagmiut on the Alaskan coast. In an old description of the conquest and conversion of the Guanches in the Canary Islands in 1402 we read that in the island of Lancerote most of the women have three husbands, "who wait upon them alternately by months; the husband that is to live with the wife the following month waits upon her and upon her other husband the whole of the month that the latter has her, and so each takes her in turn." Sporadic cases of polyandry have been found in Madagascar, among a few peoples on the African continent, in some places in the Malay Archipelago, and among certain South Sea Islanders. But in the Marshall Islands polyandry has been practised on a much larger scale, and it is or has recently been one of the fixed customs of the natives of the Marquesas. According to Dr. Tautain's description of the marriage customs of the latter, all the brothers of a man became from the moment of his marriage secondary husbands to his wife, and all her sisters became secondary wives to him, which, however, did not prevent them from marrying other men if they were not married

[251]

already. But the husbands of one woman were not always brothers. In the Hawaiian Islands it is said to have been usual in the families of chiefs that a woman had two husbands.

In Tibet polyandry has prevailed from time immemorial; and it is still very common there. The husbands are as a rule brothers. The choice of the wife is the right of the elder brother, and the contract he makes is understood to involve a marital contract with all the other brothers as well, if they choose to avail themselves of it; but in many parts of the country the husbands are sometimes other relatives than brothers or, in rare cases, even unrelated persons. All the husbands live together with their common wife as members of the same household. Fraternal polyandry is more or less frequent in vast districts of the Himalayan region from Assam to the dependencies of Kashmir, chiefly among people of Tibetan affinities; and it is also found, though more or less concealed, among various communities of the North Indian plains. An interesting form of polyandry prevails in Ladakh, now politically a division of the Kashmir State, with a population of the Tibetan stock. As soon as the eldest son of a family marries he enters into possession of the family estate, and is then obliged to support the two sons next to himself in age; and these two are not allowed to contract independent marriages but share the wife of their eldest brother, becoming the minor husbands of the lady. But besides being married to the three brothers, a wife can, if she prefers it, enter into another marriage contract with a man from a different family.

Besides the Himalayan region, South India is a great

centre for polyandry. Its prevalence among the Todas of the Nilgiri Hills has attracted special attention. When a boy is married to a girl she usually becomes the wife of his brothers at the same time, and any brother born later will similarly be regarded as sharing his older brothers' rights; but, according to Dr. Rivers, there are a few cases in which the husbands, instead of being brothers, simply belong to the same clan and are of the same generation. If they are brothers they all live together in one village, but if they are not, they may also live at different villages; and if they do so it is the rule that the wife shall live with each husband in turn, generally for a month at a time. In addition to the regular marriage there is among the Todas another recognised mode of union by which a woman becomes the formal mistress of another man; a woman may even have more than one of these lovers, and a man may have more than one mistress. Polyandry prevailed throughout the interior of Ceylon until it was prohibited by the British Governor about the year 1860; and it is recorded to have been at one time universal throughout the island, except among the Veddas. One woman had in many cases three or four or even more husbands, who were most usually brothers, especially in the highest caste. But brothers had not always a wife in common, nor were the husbands always brothers.

Among the Nayars or Nairs of Cochin, Malabar, and Travancore we meet with polyandrous unions of a different, non-fraternal type, the prevalence of which has been testified by a large number of travellers from the beginning of the fifteenth century onwards.

According to Nayar usage every girl, before she attains puberty, goes through a marriage ceremony, the essential incident of which consists in the tying of a *tāli,* or tiny plate of gold, round her neck by the nominal husband, who then, after receiving the customary fee, goes his way; he has no conjugal rights over the girl. Subsequently she was allowed to cohabit with any Brahman or Nayar she chose, and usually she had several lovers, who cohabited with her by agreement among themselves. All the lovers contributed to maintain the woman, but she lived apart from them. I call them lovers rather than husbands; for the polyandrous unions of the Nayars can hardly be called marriages even from a non-legal point of view, considering that they were of the loosest and most fugitive character, that the male partners never lived with the woman, and that according to some accounts the duties of fatherhood were entirely ignored. In these respects there was a vast difference between the Nayars and the other polyandrous peoples of India who have come under our notice. It is true that among the latter, also, men who have access to the woman are not in every case husbands in the full sense of the term, but she is legally married to some or at least to one of them. And there is another difference to be noted. Nothing indicates that the Nayars who regularly had intercourse with the same woman were brothers. Non-fraternal polyandry has been attributed to a few other castes or tribes in South India, which are closely connected with the Nayars.

Generally speaking, polyandry in modern India is restricted to non-Aryan—Tibetan or Dravidian—

tribes or castes. Yet it is often supposed to have existed among the early Aryans. We read in the Mahabharata, of Draupadī, who was won at an archery match by the eldest of the five Pāndava princes and then became the wife of all. This, however, does not prove that polyandry was a genuine Aryan custom. It was not Vedic. Oppert maintains that the occurrence of the polyandry of the five Pāndavas and other peculiar customs closely connects them with the non-Aryan inhabitants of India; and it has also been argued that those princes were warriors, to whom greater licence was allowed in their dealings with women, and that the conquerors would the more readily adopt polyandrous practices existing among the aborigines whom they conquered, since they obviously brought with them as few women as possible. On the other hand, it seems to have been an ancient Aryan custom that an old or impotent married man could engage a substitute for the production of a legitimate heir.

Strabo asserts that polyandry prevailed in Arabia Felix. "All the kindred," he says, "have their property in common, the eldest being lord; all have one wife, and it is first come first served, . . . but the night she spends with the eldest." Some modern scholars think that they have found confirmation of this statement in Sabian and Minæan inscriptions. According to al-Bukhārī it was a custom of the pagan Arabs that several men cohabited with one wife, and that the latter nominated the father of any child to which she gave birth; but Nöldeke observes that a Muhammadan theologian can hardly be regarded as a reliable witness as to the customs of Arabic paganism, and he sees in the pretended polyandry in Central Arabia merely a kind of prostitution. According to Robertson Smith, the former prevalence of "the very grossest forms of polyandry . . . over all the Semitic area seems to be proved by the fact that absolute licence continued to be a feature of certain religious rites among the Canaanites, the Aramæans, and the heathen Hebrews." But I can see no reason whatever to look upon these rites as survivals of earlier marriage customs.

Generally speaking, so far as direct evidence goes, it is only in a few areas that polyandry is, or has been, practised by a considerable number of the population, while among various peoples it has been restricted to more or less exceptional cases. In a single instance, that of the Massagetæ of Turkestan, it is represented as the only recognised form of marriage, but this statement, made by a Chinese writer of the thirteenth century with reference to a foreign people, must be looked upon with suspicion. Very frequently polyandry, like polygyny, is modified in a monogamous direction: as one, usually the first married, wife in polygynous families is the chief wife, so one, usually the first, husband in polyandrous families is often or mostly the chief husband. Any other man with whom he shares his wife is in various cases spoken of as a secondary husband, or as a deputy or assistant who acts as husband and master of the house during the absence of the true lord but on the latter's return becomes his servant, or merely as a recognised paramour or "half-partner." Very frequently the husbands are brothers, although among various peoples whose polyandry is as a rule fraternal the husbands or paramours may also be otherwise related to one another or even unrelated. Where fraternal polyandry prevails the eldest brother is commonly regarded as the principal husband. He chooses the wife, and the contract he makes may implicitly confer matrimonial rights on all the other brothers, although it may also be that each of them has to undergo a special ceremony in order to be recognised as husband. It is sometimes said that the younger brothers can claim the wife as theirs only as long as they continue to live with the eldest one; that if the latter dies she can rid herself of the other brothers by a simple ceremony, at least if she has no children; that the minor husbands often are little better than servants to the eldest brother and can be turned out of doors at his pleasure. Several statements seem to imply, or even expressly affirm, that the younger brothers are not really regarded as husbands of the eldest brother's wife although they have access to her, especially in his absence. In some cases all the children are regarded as the children of the eldest brother; he is called "father," the other husbands being called "uncles," or a distinction is made between "elder" and "younger" or "great" and "little" fathers. In other cases of polyandry—fraternal or non-fraternal—all the husbands are equally regarded as fathers; or the children are divided between them according to seniority, or belong to those whom the mother designates to be their fathers. Among many polyandrous peoples the various husbands live or cohabit with their common wife in turn; if they are brothers, the eldest one is sometimes expressly said to take the lead, or when she is with child she remains with him until the child is born.

Polyandry may be traced to various causes. One of them is a numerical disproportion between the sexes. Among many polyandrous peoples there are said to be more men than women, and their polyandry has in several cases been directly attributed to this fact; and even if some of these statements, in the absence of statistical data, are more or less hypothetical, there are others the accuracy of which is past all doubt. The old statement that there are more men than women in Tibet is supported by some recent writers. In many parts of the Himalayan region in which polyandry is practised the women are distinctly said to be in a minority. Speaking of the polyandry in the Jounsar district, Mr. Dunlop observes: "It is remarkable that wherever the practice of polyandry exists, there is a striking discrepancy in the proportions of the sexes among young children as well as adults; thus, in a village where I have found upwards of four hundred boys, there were only one hundred and twenty girls. . . . In the Gurhwal Hills, moreover, where polygamy is prevalent, there is a surplus of female children." All the records which we have of the Todas from different years show an excess of men over women. In 1871 there were 140.6 men for every 100 women; in 1891, 135.9; according to the census of 1901, 127.4; while Dr. Rivers' figures from his genealogical record give, for 1902, 132.2 men for every 100 women. There has thus been a progressive decrease in the excess of males over females; and at the same time it seems that polyandry also has been somewhat decreasing. This undoubtedly gives support to the common view that the polyandry of the Todas always has been connected with their scarcity

POLYANDRY

of women. In Ceylon, too, a considerable disparity between the sexes has been exhibited by the returns. In the middle of the last century it was found in the greatest degree among the Sinhalese, among whom the surplus of men averaged 12 per cent.; while according to the census of 1901 there were among them 108.8 males to every 100 women. In various islands of the Pacific we likewise find, side by side with polyandry, an excess of men. The Malagasy of Antangenă, who settled down in another province, took to fraternal polyandry because only a small number of their women accompanied them in their exile; but the equilibrium between the sexes was soon re-established, and polyandry disappeared.

Among various peoples polyandry has been traced to economic motives. It has been said that in Tibet it obtains "as a necessary institution. Every spot of ground within the hills which can be cultivated, has been under the plough for ages; the number of mouths must remain adapted to the number of acres, and the proportion is preserved by limiting each proprietary family to one giver of children." And not only does polyandry serve the end of checking the increase of population in regions from which emigration is difficult, but it also keeps the family property together where the husbands are brothers, as they usually are in Tibet. Similar reasons have been assigned for polyandry in Ladakh, Bhutan, South India, and Ceylon. Although economic considerations may lead to polyandry both among the rich and among the poor, it appears from various statements that it is often principally or exclusively practised by the latter, while those who can afford it take a wife for themselves

alone or even indulge in polygyny. Sometimes polyandry is said to be due to the difficulty of raising the
sum to be paid for a wife, which induces brothers or
other men to club together and buy a common wife.
It is obvious that poverty and paucity of women easily
may be a combined cause of polyandry; where
women are scarce the difficulty in procuring a single
wife must be particularly great for the poor. The
polyandry of the Tibetans, the Himalayans, and some
peoples in the south of India has also been said to be
partly due to the dangers or difficulties which would
surround a woman left alone in her home during the
prolonged absence of her husband, when he attends
the cattle or is engaged in traffic or the chase or
military pursuits, or is going from place to place to
earn his livelihood. Sometimes polyandry springs
from a desire for offspring, a married man who has no
offspring sharing his wife with another man to have a
child by her.

It is easy to see that polyandry tends to assume a
fraternal character where it is a result of a disproportion between the sexes or of poverty or of the frequent
absence of the men from their homes, even though it
does not do so in every case; and if it is intended
to keep property together it is necessary that the
husbands should be brothers or at all events near
relatives. When it is impossible for every man to get
a wife for himself owing to the paucity of women,
fraternal feelings may induce a man to give his younger
brothers a share in his wife. When a man is too poor
to take or to maintain a wife for himself alone, he
would by preference choose his brother as his partner,
owing to the economic interests they have in common;

and when a plurality of husbands is desirable in order
that the family and homestead shall not be left without a male supporter and protector for any length of
time, a brother would generally be the most suitable
substitute for the absent husband. Brothers generally
live at the same spot, there is a feeling of solidarity
and fellowship between them, and no stranger is
brought into the world through intercourse with the
same woman. But these circumstances would have
little force if the wife lives apart from her husbands
and the children belong to their mother's kin, as is
the case among the Nayars. These circumstances
are, in my opinion, the immediate causes of the
essential difference between the polyandry of the
Nayars and that of other polyandrists of India as well
as those of Tibet, whose system of fraternal polyandry
seems to be intimately connected just with those conditions which are lacking among the Nayars. If the
men live apart from the woman to whom they are
attached and their property is not inherited by their
children, there is no strong reason on their part why
they should be brothers; and if the woman enjoys a
great deal of independence, as she does among the
Nayars, she is likely to select by preference men
belonging to different families to be her husbands or
paramours.[1] But why did the Nayars not live with
their wives or mistresses and the children borne by
them?

The answer to this question most probably lies in
the military organisation of the Nayars, which pre-

[1] An English lady, to whom I spoke about different kinds of
polyandry, emphatically declared that she would not like to be
married to *brothers*.

vented them from living the ordinary life of a husband and father of a family. Lopez de Castanheda, whose account of them appeared in a work published in the middle of the sixteenth century, wrote that the law interdicting them to marry was established by their kings that they might have neither wives nor children on whom to fix their love and attachment, and that, being free from all family cares, they might the more willingly devote themselves to warlike service. A similar opinion has been expressed by several other writers, although in recent days it has met with little approval. Montesquieu, who shared Castanheda's view, observed that in Europe soldiers are not encouraged to marry. In Rome they were even forbidden to do so, although they were allowed to live in concubinage; and similar rules have been found elsewhere, for example among the Zaporog Cossacks, who occupied themselves with nothing but war and brigandage and whose sexual relations have been represented as polyandrous. But although the military organisation of the Nayars gives us the most probable explanation of the unusual character of their polyandrous habits, it hardly accounts for those habits in full. We must also take into consideration the strong polyandrous tendencies, the laxity of sexual morals, and the freedom enjoyed by the women among the Dravidian peoples; to some extent, I believe, the great demand for Nayar women among the younger Brahmans; and possibly economic circumstances as well. One of our authorities observes that the advantage the Nayars derive from the custom in question is "that one who hath not means himself to maintain a wife, may have a third part of one, and

the cost of her maintenance is only in this proportion."
Whether the Nayar rule of inheritance through the
mother, as has been generally supposed, is a consequence of their non-fraternal polyandry is difficult to
say. According to some accounts the relations between
the men and the children of their mistress were of
such a nature as to make any other rule impossible;
but, on the other hand, there are castes in the same
tract who follow the uterine system of descent and
yet have never been known to practise polyandry of
the Nayar type.

I have dealt so fully with the polyandry of the
Nayars because it has played an important part in the
study of early marriage customs. McLennan and his
followers looked upon polyandry of "the ruder sort,"
in which the husbands are not kinsmen, as a modification of and an advance from promiscuity, and
considered fraternal polyandry to have developed out
of the ruder form; and in a recent essay dealing with
South Indian polyandry Dr. Herbert Müller has
likewise expressed the belief that the polyandry of the
Nayars can be explained only as a late survival of an
ancient marriage system, which was perhaps the earliest in the whole history of marriage. Theories of this
sort explain nothing and are of no value at all. To
explain polyandry is to trace it to its causes, and
when this is done it is found that certain circumstances lead to unions in which the husbands are
brothers and other circumstances to unions in which
they are not so; but I see no reason whatever to
assume that the former kind of union has developed
out of the latter. It would indeed be rather surprising if a people so cultivated as the Nayars had

preserved the primitive form, while lower castes living in the same neighbourhood had grown out of it and changed their polyandry to fraternal.

I certainly do not maintain that my discussion of the causes from which polyandry has sprung gives a full solution of the problem. There are many peoples among whom the males outnumber the females or to whom polyandry would be useful on account of poverty or as a method of keeping property together or for other reasons, and who all the same never practise it. A paucity of marriageable women, for example, may lead to celibacy, prostitution, or homosexual practices, as well as to polyandry. To explain in full why certain factors in some cases give rise to polyandry and in other cases not, is as impossible as it often is to say exactly why one people is monogamous and another people polygynous. But, generally speaking, there can be little doubt that the main reason why polyandry is not more commonly practised is the natural desire in most men to be in exclusive possession of their wives. Among many polyandrous peoples the men are expressly stated to be remarkably little addicted to jealousy.

Although the number of peoples who are known to practise or to have practised polyandry as a regular custom is not large, it has been suggested by several writers that in early times polyandry was the rule and monogamy and polygyny exceptions. In support of this view it has been said to be impossible not to believe that the levirate, or practice of marrying a dead brother's widow, which is a very widespread custom, is derived from polyandry. But the levirate is so easily explained by existing conditions that we have no right to look upon it as a survival at all. Wives may be inherited like other belongings; and even when a son inherits the other property of his father it is easy to understand why he does not inherit the widow, apart from any consideration of age. To inherit her is, generally speaking, to marry her. But nowhere is a son allowed to marry his own mother; hence it is natural, at least where monogamy prevails, that the right of succession in this case should belong to the brother, and even marriage with a step-mother may be looked upon as incestuous. The levirate, however, is not only regarded as a right belonging to the deceased husband's brother, but in many cases as a duty incumbent upon him. The widow and her children are in need of a protector and supporter; and if the man died childless, it may be the duty of his brother to marry his widow in order to "raise up seed" to him, as among the ancient Hebrews.

Group-marriage has been found among peoples who practise polyandry. In his description of polyandry in Sikkim, Tibet, and Bhutan, Mr. White, late Political Agent in Sikkim, states that "three brothers can marry three sisters, and all the wives be in common, but this is not very often met with. In such a case the children of the eldest girl belong to the eldest brother, of the second to the second, and of the third to the third, if they each bear children. Should one or more not bear children, then the children are apportioned by arrangement." In 1869, Dr. Shortt wrote of the Todas: "If there be four or five brothers, and one of them, being old enough, gets married, his wife claims all the other brothers as her husbands, and, as they successively attain manhood, she consorts with them; or, if the wife has one or more younger sisters, they in turn, on attaining a marriageable age, become the wives of their sister's husband or husbands. . . . Owing, however, to the great scarcity of women in this tribe, it more frequently happens that a single woman is wife to several husbands, sometimes as many as six." In a more recent account, Dr. Rivers speaks of the "tendency for the polyandry of the Todas to become combined with polygyny. Two brothers, who in former times would have had one wife between them, may now take two wives, but as a general rule the two men have the two wives in common. . . . When a man or a group of men have more than one wife, the two wives usually live together at the same village, but sometimes they live at different villages, the husband or husbands moving about from one village to the other." Of various other polyandrous peoples in India we are likewise told that if one of the brothers who have a wife in common brings a new wife, he has to share her with the other brothers. In Ceylon, according to the Níti-Nighanduva—a compilation of the native customary law made in 1818 by a commission of respected Sinhalese at Kandy—it was not only frequently the custom for one man to have at the same time a number of wives and for one woman to have at the same time a number of husbands, but it was "also a frequent custom for two or three men to have two or three wives in common."

There can be no doubt that in these cases group-marriage has arisen as a combination of polygyny with polyandry. This is implied or even directly said in the statements made by several of our authorities, and may in other cases be inferred from the fact that both in Tibet and in India polyandry is much more prevalent than group-marriage; that the latter occurs there nowhere except side by side with polyandry; and that the occasional combination of polygyny with polyandry, when the circumstances permit it, is easy to explain, whereas no satisfactory reason has been given for the opinion held by some sociologists that polyandry has developed out of an earlier stage of group-marriage.

It is possible that Cæsar's well-known statement about the marriages of the ancient Britons likewise refers to a combination of polygyny with polyandry. He says: "In their domestic life they practise a form of community of wives, ten or twelve combining in a group, especially brothers with brothers and fathers with sons. The children born of such wedlock are then reckoned to belong to that member of the partnership who was the first to receive the mother as a bride into the household." The latter passage almost suggests that the community of wives spoken of—provided that it really existed—had a polyandric origin. So far as the Celtic population of Britain is concerned, the accuracy of Cæsar's statement has been doubted or denied. Sir John Rhys observes that "in the first place, one might suppose that he had heard and misunderstood some description of the families of the Britons to the effect that it was usual for ten or twelve men, with their wives and children, to live together under the *patria potestas* or power of one father and head, a kind of undivided family well known to the student of early institutions, and marking a particular stage in the social development of most Aryan nations. In the next place it is probable that the Britons of the south-east of the island, and some of the Gauls of the Continent, had heard of tribes in the remoter parts of Britain whose view of matrimony was not the one usual among Aryan nations." Professor Zimmer has no doubt that Cæsar's statement refers to the non-Aryan inhabitants of Britain; but Sir William Ridgeway maintains that "the theory of a non-Aryan population in the British Isles rests on no other evidence, historical, social, or linguistic, than a few rash assumptions." Statements more or less similar to Cæsar's were subsequently made by Strabo with reference to the Irish, by Dio Cassius and St. Jerome with reference to the people of Scotland, and by the Irish interpolator of Solinus with reference to the pauper king of the Hebrides and the inhabitants of Shetland Mainland.

Genuine group-marriage has, so far as I know, been found only side by side with polyandry. But there are peoples who have a kind of sex communism, in which several men have the right of access to several women, although none of the women is properly married to more than one of the men. The fact that some of our authorities apply the term "group-marriage" to relations of this sort should not deceive us as regards their true nature.

Certain Australian tribes are of particular interest in this connection, since their "group-marriage" has been the subject of much discussion and led to far-reaching conclusions. The best known of these tribes are the Dieri—inhabiting part of the Barcoo delta on the east and south-east of Lake Eyre, in Central

Australia—whose marriage customs have been most fully described by Dr. Howitt. They are divided into two exogamous moieties, whose members may freely intermarry, subject only to restrictions dependent on kinship. We are told that they have two kinds of marriages: the *tippa-malku* or individual marriage, and the *pirrauru* or group-marriage. As regards the individual marriage Dr. Howitt informs us in his latest book that it is usually brought about by betrothal in infancy or childhood, whereas the *pirrauru* relation "arises through the exchange by brothers of their wives. When two brothers are married to two sisters, they commonly live together in a group-marriage of four. When a man becomes a widower he has his brother's wife as *pirrauru,* making presents to his brother. A man being a visitor, and being of the proper class, is offered his host's *tippa-malku* wife as a temporary *pirrauru.*" Moreover, if a man is in great favour with the women, "a woman might even ask her husband to give her such or such a man as a *pirrauru.* Should he refuse to do this, she must put up with it; but if he agrees to do so, the matter is arranged." In order to make the *pirrauru* relation legal a ceremony is performed by the head of the totem, or heads when there are more than one totem concerned. A man may have several *pirrauru* wives and a woman several *pirrauru* husbands, but no woman can have more than one *tippa-malku* husband at the same time, although a man can have more than one *tippa-malku* wife. The *tippa-malku* wife takes precedence over the *pirrauru* wife; and the rights granted to a *pirrauru* husband are much inferior to those possessed by the *tippa-malku* husband. He has marital rights over the wife only if the *tippa-malku* husband is absent. While the *tippa-malku* husband and his wife form a real household, it is only in his absence that she lives with any of her *pirraurus,* enjoying his protection. And from a statement made by Mr. Gason it appears that the *tippa-malku* husband recognises all the children of his wife as his own and treats them with the same kindness and affection.

In the Urabunna tribe, whose territory adjoins that of the Dieri on the north, Messrs. Spencer and Gillen have found an institution very similar to the *pirrauru* relation. A man can only marry women who stand to him in the relationship of *nupa,* that is, are the children of his mother's elder brothers (own or tribal), or, what is the same thing, of his father's elder sisters. But while he has one or perhaps two of these *nupa* women who are specially attached to him and live with him in his own camp, he has in addition to them certain other *nupa* women to whom he stands in the relationship of *piraungaru.* To the latter he has access under certain conditions only: "if the first man be present, with his consent or, in his absence, without any restriction whatever." A woman's elder brothers will give one man a preferential right to her and other men of the same group a secondary right, but in the case of the *piraungaru* the arrangement must receive the sanction of the old men of the group before it can take effect. A woman may also be *piraungaru* to a number of men, and as a general rule men and women who are *piraungaru* to one another are to be found living grouped together.

It may be seriously questioned whether the *pirrauru* or *piraungaru* relation should be called marriage at all.

GROUP-MARRIAGE

It almost exclusively implies sexual licence, and is therefore essentially different from the *tippa-malku* relation or the ordinary Australian marriage, which, as Dr. Malinowski observes, cannot be detached from family life, but is defined by "the problems of the economic unity of the family, of the bonds created by common life in one wurley, through the common rearing of, and affection towards, the offspring." But, as we have seen, even from the purely sexual point of view there is no comparison between the rights of the individual husband and those of a *pirrauru*.

The *pirrauru* or *piraungaru* relation is of particular interest on account of the support it is considered to give to the hypothesis of ancient group-marriage in Australia, according to which the men of one division or class had as wives the women of another division or class. Marriages of this sort do not exist anywhere in Australia at the present time. In the case of the so-called group-marriage of the Dieri and the Urabunna the term "group" only means a number of persons who stand in a certain relationship to another number of persons, whereas in the theory of group-marriage the same term is applied to a portion of a tribe distinguished by a class name and term of relationship. Nor is this the only difference between the two kinds of "group-marriage." No person becomes a *pirrauru* or *piraungaru* as a matter of course on account of his or her status. An agreement must be made with the *tippa-malku* husband, and the *pirrauru* may have to pay for it (in the case of a widower), and in spite of the rule "once a *pirrauru* always a *pirrauru*," the relation may even be of very short duration (in the case of a visitor) ; whilst the *piraungaru* requires the consent of the woman's elder brothers. Considering, further, that the *tippa-malku* spouse in every respect takes precedence over the *pirrauru,* I find no reason to accept Dr. Howitt's view that the *tippa-malku* marriage is an innovation and "an encroachment upon the *pirrauru* group-right." On the contrary, it seems to me much more probable that the *pirrauru* relation is an engraftment on individual marriage, and that, partly at least, it owes its origin to circumstances not unlike those which have led to more or less similar customs in other parts of the world.

From various parts of Australia we hear of the difficulty the young native has in getting a wife on attaining manhood. While many men are thus compelled to remain unmarried for a considerable length of time or are married to women who must be more or less distasteful to them, tribal custom may provide them with certain means of gratifying their sexual desires outside the ordinary marriage relation. One such method, which is found among both West and Central Australian tribes, is to give to the bachelor a boy-wife; and in other instances the *pirrauru* or *piraungaru* custom may serve as a substitute for regular marriage in the case of young men who have to remain unmarried or who have only got old women as wives. But it is also evident that the old and influential men largely make use of that custom to their own advantage. Dr. Eylmann was told by members of the Dieri and other tribes that it chiefly benefited the old men, because it gave them an excellent opportunity to have sexual intercourse with young women without transgressing the rules of tribal morality, though it was only with the greatest reluctance that the younger men let them have access to their wives. Nor is the sexual gratification the only benefit a man derives from having many *pirraurus*. Howitt observes that "it is an advantage to a man to have as many *pirraurus* as possible. He has then less work to do in hunting, as when they are with him they supply him with a share of the food they procure, their own *tippa-malku* husbands being absent. He also obtains great influence in the tribe by lending his *pirraurus* occasionally, and receiving presents from the younger men who have no *pirraurus* with them, or to whom none has yet been allotted." It should be remembered that the Australian natives are ruled by a system of customs the tendency of which is to give everything to the strong and old to the prejudice of the young and weak. If the old men keep for themselves the best and fattest pieces and marry the most attractive women, it is only natural that they also should favour an institution like the *pirrauru* relation, which gives them sexual enjoyment and at the same time increases their influence. I am therefore inclined to believe that the *pirrauru* custom is a consequence of the comparative scarcity of women and of the selfish tyranny of the old men. But we must also remember another fact, which we have met with before in connection with polyandry, namely, the necessity of a married woman to have a protector and guardian during the temporary absence of her husband. It is significant that a man has sexual rights over a woman who is *pirrauru* or *piraungaru* to him chiefly, if not exclusively, while her husband is away, and on such occasions only does she live with him, enjoying his protection. That the need of protection and guardianship has something to do with the *pirrauru*

[273]

custom is also suggested by a statement for which I am indebted to Mr. Frank P. ("Bulman") Brown. He tells me that among the Kacoodja, on the South Alligator River in the Northern Territory, if a man goes away for some time he hands over his wife to some other man of his own class, who during his absence is entitled to have sexual intercourse with her. In case she were left alone she would probably be seized by somebody else, or she might herself invite somebody to have connection with her.

I cannot, then, regard the *pirrauru* or *piraungaru* custom as evidence of a prior state of group-marriage; and the same is the case with various other customs which have been supposed to give support to the group-marriage theory, such as the lending or exchange of wives, the sexual intercourse to which a girl is regularly subject before her marriage, the licence allowed at the performance of certain ceremonies when the ordinary rules of morality are more or less suspended, the levirate, or the use of classificatory terms of relationship which group together under single designations many distinct degrees and kinds of relationship. Lack of space prevents me from repeating the arguments which I have brought forward in my detailed criticism of these supposed survivals in my book *The History of Human Marriage*. Much stress has been laid on the fact that the term applied to the "special wife" is also applied to all the other women of her group "whom it is lawful for a man to marry and outside of whom he may not marry." But there is no reason whatever to look upon the common term as a relic of group-marriage, as it is easily explained by the fact that the women who may be a man's wives and those who cannot possibly be so stand in a widely different relation to him. Nor can I in the least agree with those writers who regard group-marriage as the earliest form of marriage out of which the others have gradually developed.

CHAPTER XI

THE DURATION OF MARRIAGE AND THE RIGHT TO DISSOLVE IT

IT is the general rule that marriage is contracted for an indefinite length of time or for life, although even in the latter case it may very frequently be dissolved, for some reason or other, during the lifetime of the partners.

Among a few uncivilised peoples marriage is said to be indissoluble or divorce unknown, and among many others divorce is said to be rare or marriage as a rule to last for life; but there are also many tribes in which divorce is reported to be of frequent occurrence or marriage of very short duration. Owing to the defective character of the information at our disposal it is impossible to say anything definite about the comparative prevalence of lifelong unions and of divorce among the lower races in general, or about the duration of marriage at the different grades of economic culture compared with one another. But the universal or almost universal prevalence of lifelong unions among some of the lower hunters and incipient agriculturists, such as the Veddas of Ceylon, the Andamanese, the Orang Mamaq and Orang Akit of Sumatra, and the "pure" tribes of the Malay Peninsula, is certainly very striking.

Somewhat more definite than the information we

possess of the actual prevalence of divorce among the simpler peoples are the statements as to the circumstances in which their customs allow it to be practised. Among a large number of tribes the husband is said to be able to dissolve the marriage at will or on the slightest grounds or pretexts, and in the majority of these cases a similar right is granted to the wife. This is borne out by my own materials as well as by the figures given by Messrs. Hobhouse, Wheeler, and Ginsberg. Of certain tribes we are only told explicitly that the wife can leave at will; and although in some or most of these tribes, the husband presumably possesses the same power, this is not the case among all of them. But among many of the simpler peoples marriage can be dissolved only by mutual consent, unless it be for some very cogent reason, or one of the parties is said to be unable to effect divorce against the will of the other; and although in such cases the husband's consent is probably more often required than the wife's, there are also many cases in which the wife's wishes have to be consulted.

We are frequently told that a man must not divorce his wife and a wife not separate from her husband without just or good cause. The ideas as to what constitutes such a cause vary among different tribes. The most generally recognised ground for divorce is probably adultery on the part of the wife, and in many cases it seems to be the only or almost the only ground; but on the other hand we also hear of uncivilised peoples who do not consider a man justified in repudiating his wife on account of adultery, even though he may do so for some other cause. Among some peoples the wife is said to have the right to divorce an unfaithful husband. A very frequent cause of divorce is barrenness in the wife, while the birth of a child may make marriage indissoluble; and sometimes we are told that the wife can effect divorce if the husband proves impotent. There are a variety of other recognised grounds for divorce more or less frequently found in the savage world. A man may divorce his wife if she is lazy or neglectful; if she does not cook his food properly; if she is bad-tempered or quarrelsome, disobedient, thievish, or suspected of witchcraft; if she suffers from a foul or incurable disease; if she becomes too old; if all her children die; or, of course, if she deserts her husband. The wife, again, may dissolve the marriage if the husband neglects or ill-treats her or is guilty of gross misconduct; if he is lazy and will not do his fair share of work; if he deserts her or is long absent from home; or, sometimes, if she has a strong repugnance to him. Among some natives of Eastern Central Africa the wife may divorce a husband who neglects to sew her clothes. Among the Shans of Burma, should the husband take to drinking or otherwise misconduct himself, the wife has the right to turn him adrift and to retain all the goods and money of the partnership.

A divorce without good reason very often entails economic loss for the party who effects it, whereas a divorce for good reason entails loss for the party who is at fault. Thus a husband who puts away or abandons his wife without satisfactory cause forfeits the price he paid or the presents he gave for her, or he has to pay a fine or give up some portion of his property; but if he divorces her because she has been unfaithful or proved barren or otherwise affords sufficient cause for divorce, the price paid for her is returned. So also it is generally returned if the wife dissolves the marriage; but if she does so for some fault of her husband the bride price is in many cases not given back to him.

Sometimes the party whose conduct affords good cause for divorce loses the children in consequence; but the general rule seems to be that the fate of the children is little influenced by the question which of the parents is to blame. If they are very young they naturally remain with the mother; but they may afterwards have to be given to the father, who among very many peoples is considered to have a right to his children. This is particularly often said to be the case in Africa, where marriage by genuine purchase is prominent. We are often told that the children are divided between the parents, and in such cases the boys may be taken by the father and the girls by the mother. But among a large number of peoples all the children generally follow the mother. This is especially the case where descent is matrilineal, and among the native tribes of North America it seems to be the general rule. Among various West African tribes, where the mother retains her children, she is liable to her husband for a certain sum to compensate him for what he has paid for their maintenance; but this arrangement is often compromised by the mother allowing her sons to remain with their father. In some cases the children may themselves choose whether they will go with their mother or remain with their father.

Among some simple peoples a woman who has been divorced by her husband must remain unmarried. On the other hand, among the Brazilian Karayá a man who has divorced his wife cannot take another, although he is allowed to engage a woman to keep house for him. Among the Tepehuane of Mexico, if either husband or wife should prove unfaithful, they immediately separate, the guilty one is severely punished, and neither of them is permitted to marry again.

Among the peoples who have reached a higher degree of culture the stability of marriage is not less variable than it is among the lower races. There are in this respect very marked differences among the different nations of ancient civilisation, in the New World as well as in the Old.

The Aztecs of Mexico looked upon marriage as a solemn and binding tie which should be dissolved by death only. We are told that a man was permitted to divorce his chief, or real, wife only for malevolence, dirtiness, or sterility, whilst an adulteress was not divorced but punished with death; and not even a "less legitimate wife," or concubine, could be repudiated without good cause and the sanction of a court. Among the Maya nations, on the other hand, divorce was obtained with great facility. In Nicaragua an adulteress was discarded and could not marry again; but if the wife deserted her husband, she was neither punished nor reproved, and he usually refrained from fetching her back. In Guatemala the wife could leave her husband on the same slight grounds as the man could leave his wife.

According to Chinese law a husband can divorce his wife, but only on certain conditions. It is said in the Penal code that if he repudiates her "without her having broken the matrimonial connection by the crime of adultery or otherwise, and without her having furnished him with any of the seven justifying causes of divorce," he shall in every such case be punished with eighty blows. The seven causes in question are: barrenness, lasciviousness, disregard of the husband's parents, talkativeness, thievish propensities, envious and suspicious temper, and inveterate infirmity. Yet none of these causes will justify a divorce if the wife has mourned three years for her husband's parents, if the family has become rich since the marriage after being poor previously, or if the wife has no parents living to receive her back again; the first two provisions are due to the idea that the wife has suffered privation enough with her husband to give her a claim to his lasting regard. A wife who has been convicted of adultery is not protected by any of these saving clauses; indeed, the husband is liable to punishment if he retains such a wife. Marriage can, moreover, be dissolved by mutual consent. The same prescriptions also apply to the "inferior wives," or lawful concubines, with the difference that if the husband transgresses the law his punishment is reduced. In practice, however, the husband's power of divorce was no doubt greater than it was according to the letter of the law. On the other hand, it does not seem that either law or public opinion justified a wife in deserting her husband or demanding a separation from him. The divorce law of the Japanese Taihō code was substantially the same as that in China, but practically a wife could be divorced at the pleasure of her husband under any slight or flimsy pretext, the most usual being that she did not "conform to the usage of his family." As in China, the wife had no legal right to demand a divorce from her husband on any ground. This was the case till the year 1873, when a law was enacted which for the first time allowed the wife to bring an action of divorce against the husband; and the new Civil code, promulgated in 1896–1898, went further in the same direction. Professor Hozumi, in his commentaries on this code, says that it places husband and wife on an equal footing with regard to the right of divorce; but I fail to see that mere adultery on the part of the husband gives the wife the right to divorce him, although he can divorce an unfaithful wife. Divorces are very frequent in Japan, but since the new code came into force their number has rapidly decreased. In 1897 the proportion of divorces to marriages was 34 per cent., in 1900 it was 18.5 per cent.

Among Semitic peoples the husband has had, or still has, the legal right of repudiating his wife at will. In Babylonia, according to the Laws of Ḥammurabi, however, the wife and even a concubine had certain pecuniary guarantees against arbitrary divorce, and she might also herself in certain circumstances claim a divorce, or at least separation. The right of the husband to divorce his wife at his pleasure is the central thought in the entire system of Jewish divorce law; and the Rabbis neither did nor could set it aside, although they gradually tempered its severity by numerous restrictive measures. Two restrictions are already found in the Deuteronomic code—the husband shall not put his wife away all his days if he has falsely accused her of ante-nuptial incontinence or if he has ravished her before marriage; but his loss of the right to divorce her in these cases was really a penalty inflicted upon him on account of his own offensive behaviour. To these restrictions the Mishnah added three others by providing that the husband could not divorce his wife if she had become insane, if she was in captivity, or if she was a minor too young to take care of her bill of divorce. But in the period of the Mishnah the very theory of the law was challenged by the school of Shammai, who held that according to Deuteronomy the husband cannot divorce his wife unless he has found her guilty of sexual immorality. The ancient doctrine was strongly supported by the school of Hillel, who went so far as to say that a man can divorce his wife even for the most trivial reason, for instance, for spoiling his food or if he sees another woman who pleases him better. Both schools based their opinions on the same passage in the Deuteronomic text (xxiv. 1), which they interpreted differently. In legal respects the opinion of Hillel prevailed, but at the same time divorce without good cause was morally disapproved of by the Rabbis in general. The theoretical right of the husband to divorce his wife whenever it pleased him to do so ceased to exist in practice, and was at last, in the earlier part of the eleventh century, formally abolished, although he retained the right to divorce her where a good cause could be shown. In the Old Testament it is nowhere said that a marriage could be dissolved at the will of the wife, and the Jewish law has never given her a right to divorce her husband. But the Mishnah allowed her to sue for divorce, and if the court decided that she was entitled to be divorced the husband was forced to give her a bill of divorce, although he was supposed to give it of his own free will and accord. When the right of the wife to demand a divorce had been once established, the causes for which it could be exercised gradually became more numerous. At Jewish law the wife may demand a bill of divorce from her husband if he repeatedly ill-treats her, if he is guilty of notorious dissoluteness of morals, if he wastes his property and refuses to support her, if he suffers from some loathsome chronic disease contracted after marriage, if he is physically impotent, and for a few other reasons. For divorce by mutual agreement no specific causes are required. According to a principle of Rabbinical law, the court has no right to interfere when both parties declare that their marriage is a failure and they desire to dissolve it.

As the ancient Hebrews, so the pagan Arabs permitted the husband to repudiate his wife whenever he pleased, and subsequently this unlimited customary right was crystallised in Muhammad's law. And at Muhammadan, as at Jewish, law the wife can never divorce her husband, although she may take steps leading to the dissolution of her marriage. When she desires a divorce, she may obtain from him a release from the marriage contract by giving up either her settled dower or some other property; and when the husband is guilty of conduct which makes the matrimonial life intolerable to the wife, when he neglects to perform the duties which the law imposes on him as obligations resulting from marriage, or when he fails to fulfil the engagements voluntarily entered into at the time of the matrimonial contract, she has the right of preferring a complaint before the judge and demanding a divorce by authority of justice. The power of the judge to pronounce a divorce is founded on the express words of Muhammad: "If a woman be prejudiced by a marriage, let it be broken off." But the facility with which Muhammadan women can effect a dissolution of their marriage is influenced by local custom. So also the frequency of divorce differs considerably in different parts of the Muhammadan world. In some parts it is practised to an extent which is almost without parallel. In Cairo, according to Lane, there were not many men who had not divorced one wife if they had been married for a long time, and not a few men in Egypt had in the course of two years married as many as twenty, thirty, or more wives. Burckhardt knew Arabs about forty-five years old who had had more than fifty different wives; and I once had in my service a Berber from the south of Morocco who told me that he had divorced twenty-two wives. On the other hand, among the Muhammadans of India, according to Mr. Gait, the husband seldom exercises his right to divorce his wife without any special reason. This may be due to Hindu influence.

With orthodox Hindus marriage is a religious sacrament which cannot be revoked. A woman convicted of adultery may be deprived of her status and turned out of her caste, but even in this case divorce in the ordinary sense is an impossibility; she cannot form a new connection and, often at least, remains in her husband's house on the footing of a slave. Again, the only remedy which a blameless wife has against an offending husband is to obtain a decree for her separate maintenance, such decree being practically equivalent to a decree for judicial separation. The law, however, was not always equally stringent. At present the orthodox Hindu law of divorce is more or less disregarded by certain low castes in the north of India and by many castes, both high and low, in the south, among whom usage has superseded texts; agreeably to such usage the granting of a divorce, or the recognition of a divorce as one properly made, is the duty of the caste. Where it is allowed by custom, a divorce by mutual agreement is also recognised by law. It may be said that, as a rule, the degree in which divorce prevails in India is in direct ratio to the degree in which the respective castes have imitated Brahman habits.

When passing to the so-called Aryan peoples of Europe we find that among the Greeks and Romans in early days, as among the Hindus, marriage evidently was a union of great stability, although in later times, contrary to what was the case among the Aryans of India, it became extremely easy and frequent. Among the Greeks of the Homeric age divorce seems to have been almost unknown; but afterwards it became an everyday event in Greece. According to Attic law the husband could repudiate his wife whenever he liked and without stating any motives, but he was compelled to send his divorced wife back to her father's house with her dowry. The wife could demand a divorce by appealing to the Archon and stating the motives for her demand.

A Roman marriage was perhaps at no time indissoluble, but the specifically patrician kind of marriage, by *confarreatio,* was at any rate very nearly so. The other forms of marriage, not being of the same mystical and sacramental character, could be dissolved without difficulty. A husband might discharge, that is, emancipate, his wife from his power in the same way as he might discharge his child. In the old law a wife *in manu* was as little a free party to the act of divorce as a child was a free party to that of emancipation. She had neither the power to require, nor the power to prevent, a divorce; and the husband's legal authority in regard to the dissolution of a marriage with *manus* was as absolute as it was in regard to the other incidents of such a marriage. Yet in practice the husband's right was no doubt more or less checked by public opinion and, as it seems, even by the Censors; it was said that for five hundred years no one took advantage of the liberty of divorce, which at any rate shows that in earlier times divorce must have been rare in Rome. In regard to a "free" marriage, which implied that the wife did not fall under the *manus* of her husband, the rule of divorce was very different. The dissolution of such a marriage could be brought about either by mutual agreement between both parties or by the will of one party only; but it should be noticed that when the wife remained in the *potestas* of her father, the latter could, in the exercise of his power, take his daughter from her husband against the wishes of both. His right of interference, however, was restricted by some imperial constitutions. Moreover, the rules of divorce which were recognised in the case of a free marriage were afterwards practically extended to marriages with *manus,* and in the end marriages with *manus* fell into disuse altogether. Towards the end of the Republican era and during the Empire divorce was very frequent among the upper classes. Almost all the well-known ladies of the Ciceronian age were divorced at least once; and Seneca said that some women counted their years, not by consuls, but by their husbands.

In the law-books of Celtic peoples we find various

rules relating to divorce, from which we may draw the conclusion that separation of married couples was by no means an uncommon occurrence. In ancient Ireland it might take place either by mutual consent or as the outcome of legal proceedings; and with reference to the latter kind of separation, one of the Brehon law tracts specifies seven different causes for which a married woman may separate from cohabitation without losing her dowry. In ancient Wales either husband or wife might, practically, separate whenever one or both chose. According to the old customary law of the Teutonic peoples a marriage could be dissolved by agreement between the husband and the woman's kin; and the husband was entitled to repudiate his wife if she was sterile or guilty of conjugal infidelity and perhaps for some other offences. If he did so without good cause, the marriage was dissolved, but he exposed himself to the revenge of her kindred or had to pay a fine or suffered some other loss in property. The wife had originally no right to dissolve the marriage.

Christianity revolutionised European legislation with regard to divorce. In the New Testament there are various passages bearing upon the question. A man who puts away his wife and marries another commits adultery against her, and a woman who puts away or deserts her husband and is married to another is guilty of the same crime. A man shall cleave to his wife, "they twain shall be one flesh"; and "what God hath joined together, let not man put asunder." There are, however, two exceptions to this rule. Like Shammai and his school, Christ taught, according to

St. Matthew, that a man might put away his wife for
fornication, but for no other reason; and St. Paul lays
down the rule that if a Christian is married to an unbeliever and the latter departs, the Christian "is not
under bondage in such cases." A man who married
the divorced adulteress was himself guilty of adultery,
but there is no indication whatever that the innocent
husband was prohibited from remarrying. Yet, in
accordance with the ascetic tendencies of early Christianity, it seems to have been the general opinion
among the Fathers of the first three centuries that no
such remarriage was allowed; if a second marriage
was disapproved of as adultery even in the case of a
widower or widow, how could it be permitted while
the first spouse was still alive? Subsequently laxer
views were expressed, but, largely under the influence
of St. Augustine, the Church gradually made up her
mind to deny the dissolubility of a valid Christian
marriage, at least if it had been consummated. Such a
marriage is a sacrament and must consequently remain
valid for ever. On the other hand, a Christian marriage
which has not been consummated is not indissoluble; it
is only by consummation that it becomes a sacrament
and a symbol of the union between Christ and the
Church. Nor is non-Christian marriage a sacrament,
even though consummated; hence it is in certain circumstances dissoluble, in accordance with the rule laid
down by St. Paul. While asserting the indissolubility
of Christian marriage, however, the Church admitted
an "imperfect divorce" or a "separation from bed and
board," which discharged the parties from the duty of
living together for a determinate or an indeterminate
period, but at the same time left them husband and

wife and consequently unable to marry any other person.

Yet in spite of the theory of the indissolubility of Christian marriage, the Roman Catholic doctrine gives ecclesiastics a large practical power of dissolving marriages which may have appeared perfectly valid. The Church recognised a legal process which was popularly, though incorrectly, called a divorce "from the bond of matrimony," in case the union had been unlawful from the beginning on the ground of some canonical impediment, such as relationship or earlier engagement of marriage. This only implied that a marriage which never had been valid would remain invalid; but practically it led to the possibility of dissolving marriages which in theory were indissoluble. For, as Lord Bryce observes, "the rules regarding impediments were so numerous and so intricate that it was easy, given a sufficient motive, whether political or pecuniary, to discover some ground for declaring almost any marriage valid."

The doctrine of the Western Church profoundly influenced the secular legislation of the countries in which she was established. For a long time, however, it was not accepted in full by the legislators. The Christian emperors laid down certain grounds on which a husband could divorce his wife and a wife her husband without blame, and after some legislation on the subject Justinian resettled the grounds of divorce. He prohibited divorce by mutual consent, which until then seems to have taken place without any legal check whatever; but his prohibition of this kind of divorce was repealed by his successor. The facility of divorce by mutual consent also remained in the Roman codes of the German kings, and a man might besides divorce his wife for certain offences. Those subjects of the Western rulers who elected to live under the old Teutonic systems of law seem to have had an equal facility; thus the dooms of Aethelbirht, Christian though they be, suggest that the marriage might be dissolved at the will of both parties or even at the will of one of them. Even the Anglo-Saxon and Frankish penitentials allow a divorce in various cases. Only in the tenth century the ecclesiastical rules and courts gained exclusive control of this branch of law in Germany. At a somewhat earlier date the provisions of the Roman law had been superseded by new rules enforced by the Church in the regions where the imperial law had been observed. But while the Western Church in the matter of divorce at last completely triumphed in the countries under her sway, the Eastern Church, instead of shaping the secular law, was, on the contrary, greatly influenced by it: the enactments of the emperors and princes as to the grounds of divorce never met with an ecclesiastical contradiction. The grounds of divorce with the right of remarriage are those admitted by the laws of Justinian with certain modifications introduced in later times.

The canonical doctrines that marriage is a sacrament and that it is indissoluble save by death were rejected by the Reformers. They all agreed that divorce, with liberty for the innocent party to remarry, should be granted for adultery, and most of them regarded malicious desertion as a second legitimate cause for the dissolution of marriage. The latter opinion was based on St. Paul's dictum that a Christian married to an unbeliever "is not under bondage" if the unbeliever depart, which was broadened by Luther so as to include

malicious desertion even without a religious motive.
He also admitted that the worldly authorities might
allow divorce on other strong grounds, and several
reformers went farther than he. These views exercised
a lasting influence upon the Protestant legislators both
in Germany and in other continental countries.

The Fathers of English Protestantism as a body were
more conservative than their brethren across the
Channel. They were unanimous, however, in allowing the husband to put away an unfaithful wife and
contract another marriage, and prevailing opinion
appears also to have accorded a similar privilege to the
wife on like provocation. A general revision of the
ecclesiastical code, with special attention directed to the
law of divorce, was contemplated in the earlier days of
the Reformation. A commission of leading ecclesiastics
was for this purpose appointed by Henry VIII. and
Edward VI. The commissioners drew up the elaborate
report known as *Reformatio Legum,* in which they
recommended that "divorces from bed and board,"
which had been rejected by nearly all the English
reformers of the sixteenth century as a papist innovation, should be abolished, and in their place complete
divorce, with liberty for the innocent party to marry
again, should be allowed in cases of adultery, desertion,
and cruelty. The whole scheme, however, fell to the
ground; but the principle represented by it was
carried out in practice in the well-known case of Lord
Northampton, whose second marriage was declared
valid by an Act of Parliament. This decision seems to
have been deemed good law until 1602, when, in the
Foljambe case, it was decided that remarriage after
judicial separation was null and void. After this

revival of the old Canon law, says Jeaffreson, "our ancestors lived for several generations under a matrimonial law of unexampled rigour and narrowness. The gates of exit from true matrimony had all been closed, with the exception of death. Together with the artificial impediments to wedlock, the Reformation had demolished the machinery for annulling marriages on fictitious grounds. Henceforth no man could slip out of matrimonial bondage by swearing that he was his wife's distant cousin, or had loved her sister in his youth, or had before his marriage stood godfather to one of her near spiritual kindred."

In the latter part of the seventeenth century a practice arose in England which in a small degree mitigated the rigour of the law. While a valid English marriage could not be dissolved by mere judicial authority, it might be so by a special Act of Parliament. Such a parliamentary divorce, however, was granted only for adultery in certain circumstances, and could be obtained only through the expenditure of a fortune sometimes amounting to thousands of pounds. In the civil divorce law of 1857 the legal principle of the indissolubility of marriage was at last abandoned, though only after stubborn resistance. In Scotland, on the other hand, the courts began to grant divorces very soon after the Roman connection had been repudiated, and in 1573 a statute added desertion to adultery of the husband or the wife as a ground for divorce.

On the Continent a fresh impetus to a more liberal legislation on divorce was given in the eighteenth century by the new philosophy with its conceptions of human freedom and natural rights. If marriage is a contract entered into by mutual consent it ought also to be dissolvable if both parties wish to annul the contract. In the Prussian "Project des Corporis Juris Fridericiani" of 1749, "founded on reason and the constitutions of the country," it is admitted that married people may demand with common consent the dissolution of their marriage. The "Project" never became law; but in practice divorce was freely granted by Frederick II. *ex gratia principis* at the common request of husband and wife, and in the Prussian "Landrecht" of 1794 divorce by mutual consent is admitted if the couple have no children and there is no reason to suspect levity, precipitation, or compulsion. In France the new ideas led to the law on divorce of 20th September, 1792. In the preamble of the new law it is said that facility in obtaining divorce is the natural consequence of the individual's right of freedom, which is lost if engagements are made indissoluble. Divorce is granted on the mutual desire of the two parties, and even at the wish of one party on the ground of incompatibility of temper, and on many other grounds. The new law was certainly very popular: in the year VI the number of divorces in Paris exceeded the number of marriages. But six years later, in 1804, the law of 1792 was superseded by the new provisions in Napoleon's "Code Civil des Français," which made divorce more difficult, and at the Restoration in 1816 divorce was abolished in France. It was reenacted by a law of 1884, which again introduced the divorce law of the Napoleonic code, but with important changes; thus divorce by mutual consent, even with the restrictions laid down in that code, has disappeared. In the course of the nineteenth century or later divorce was made legal in several Roman Catholic countries even in the case of marriage between Catholics. In the United States, South Carolina stands alone in granting no divorce whatsoever, which is the more remarkable as no State has fewer Roman Catholic citizens. It is the only Protestant community in the world which nowadays holds marriage indissoluble.

According to the laws of those European and American States in which divorce is permitted, the most general grounds for divorce are offences of some kind or other committed by either husband or wife and entitling the other party to demand a dissolution of the marriage. In this respect the two spouses are as a rule on a footing of perfect equality; but there are some exceptions to the rule. While any act of adultery in the wife is everywhere a sufficient cause for dissolving the marriage, there are still countries in which adultery only in certain circumstances gives the wife a right to demand a divorce. Desertion, or "malicious" desertion, or desertion "without just cause or excuse," is very frequently mentioned as a ground of divorce, especially in Protestant law-books. In most countries in which divorce is allowed, ill-treatment of some kind is a sufficient reason for it. An extremely frequent ground of divorce is the condemnation of one of the parties to a certain punishment on his or her being convicted of a certain crime. And there are yet some special offences that in some law-books are mentioned as causes for divorce, such as the husband's neglect of the duty to support his wife although he is able to do so (in many jurisdictions of the United States), drunkenness, inveterate gambling habits, and ill-treatment of the children.

There are certain other circumstances recognised as

grounds of divorce, which may or may not involve guilt in one of the parties but in all cases are supposed to make marriage a burden for the other spouse, such as impotence in the husband or wife, some loathsome disease, and insanity or incurable insanity. The Swiss code contains a provision to the effect that, even though none of the specified causes for divorce exists, a marriage may be dissolved if there are circumstances seriously affecting the maintenance of the conjugal tie.

Divorce by mutual consent—which, as we have seen, had been permitted in the Roman Empire even in Christian times, and was reintroduced as a legal practice by the French law of 1792 and, though with important limitations, by the Prussian code of 1794—is at present allowed on certain conditions in several countries. Such a condition is separation *de facto,* by mutual consent or otherwise, for a certain period. In Sweden a judicial separation may, upon the application of either husband or wife, be converted into a divorce after one year. In the new Russian "Soviet Law of Marriage and the Family" no such formalities are required. It goes, in fact, even further than the French law of 1792 by simply stating that "the grounds for divorce may be either the mutual consent of the parties or the desire of one of them."

A large number of law-books that permit divorce also permit judicial separation either for life or for a definite or an indefinite period, which implies that neither party can contract another marriage before the death of the other or before the marriage is dissolved by divorce. In some of these law-books the grounds for separation are more or less different from those for divorce; whereas according to others separation is not, as in England, intended as a minor remedy for minor offences, but as an alternative enabling petitioners to obtain universal relief without a complete severance of the marriage tie. In those Roman Catholic countries which still prohibit divorce the grounds for judicial separation are generally very similar to, though not infrequently somewhat more extensive than, the grounds for which divorce may be obtained in other countries.

In the countries of Western civilisation, as elsewhere, a dissolution of marriage entails certain economic consequences, which vary in different countries. It seems, however, that according to all modern laws on divorce a guilty husband, or a guilty wife as well, may in certain circumstances at least be compelled to furnish an innocent spouse with a maintenance. The question of innocence or guilt may also influence the disposal of the children, although in this respect more or less discretion is generally given to the court. In England the discretion given is great. It is the first duty of the court to tend the welfare of the children, and, subject to that principle, if it is not to be anticipated that the giving of the custody of a child to a guilty parent will be the cause of its being injured morally, the court may award custody both to a guilty husband and, in extremely rare circumstances, even to a guilty wife.

When we pass from laws to practice we find that the divorce rate varies greatly in the different countries of the West. In Europe it is highest in Switzerland, but in the United States it is higher than in any European country and the number of divorces probably exceeds that in all European countries put together. In nearly all the countries for which statistics are available divorce has been steadily increasing during recent years. Both in Europe and in America there are, comparatively speaking, more divorces in towns than in the country. With reference to the United States, Dr. Willcox observes that in about 95 per cent. of the cases the divorce rate of a large city is greater than that in the other counties of the State.

The duration of marriage and the customs or laws by which it is regulated depend on such a variety of circumstances that our explanation of the facts stated above must necessarily be very incomplete. All that I can do is to make some general observations as to the influences which tend either to prolong or to shorten the unions between the sexes, and as to the rules which either prevent or control their dissolution.

Marriage, as we have seen, is by its very nature a relation which lasts beyond the mere act of propagation. It seems to be based upon a primeval habit. We have found reasons to believe that even in primitive times it was the habit for a man and a woman, or several women, to remain together till after the birth of the offspring, and that they were induced to do so by an instinct which had been acquired through natural selection because the offspring were in need of both maternal and paternal care. In other species having the same habit the period during which the union lasts varies greatly. Among many birds it lasts for life, whereas among mammalian species the same male and female very seldom seem to live together longer than a year. Among the man-like apes family groups containing young ones of different ages have been found; but we cannot, of course, be certain that in such cases the latter have the same father. It is remarkable that among some of the lowest races of men marriage is regularly a lifelong union; but this by no means proves that it was so among our earliest human ancestors. We may assume that if man originally made love at a certain season only, but subsequently began to pair throughout the year, there came a new inducement for the mates to remain with one another, which must have had the tendency to make their union more durable. But apart from the purely sexual instinct, conjugal affection may keep man and wife together even after their marriage has fulfilled its original aim. And conjugal affection has certainly become more durable in proportion as love has been influenced by mental qualities.

Parental feelings exercise a similar influence, and they do so longer than is necessary for the rearing of the progeny. Marriage not only came into existence for the sake of the offspring but often becomes a lasting union through the presence of children. Among many of the simpler peoples the birth of offspring is the best guarantee for the continuance of the marriage tie, while childless marriages are often dissolved; and the same is the case among many peoples who have reached a higher level of civilisation. Even among modern civilised nations, who do not recognise barrenness as a sufficient ground for repudiating a wife, divorces are more frequent in cases where there are no children. Dr. Willcox thinks it fair to conclude that in the United States childless marriages are between three and four times as likely to end in divorce as marriages with children, and statistics from the middle of the last century showed a similar tendency in France. It has been noticed that in Switzerland two-fifths of the total number of divorces take place between married people who have no children, while the sterile marriages only amount to one-fifth of the number of marriages.

The marriage tie is further strengthened by economic considerations. The dissolution of it deprives the woman of a supporter and the man of a helpmate and in many cases of a drudge. The man may have to provide his divorced wife with the means of subsistence, and very frequently he is obliged to give her what she brought with her into the house, and even a certain proportion of the common wealth. If the marriage is dissolved the husband may lose the price he paid for his wife, or her family may, on the other hand, have to return the price received for her. Both the custom of providing a daughter with a marriage portion and the purchase of wives undoubtedly tend to make marriage more durable.

The economic factor has in various ways proved an obstacle to divorce in civilised communities. In the United States depressions in trade have had a tendency to decrease divorces as well as marriages. "In the great mass of the population," says Dr. Willcox, "they have discouraged change, have compelled men and women 'in whatsoever state they were, therewith to be content,' or at least to abandon or postpone the idea of change." He adds that in England, on the other hand, the number of divorces has not fallen off, but rather increased, in the years in which the number of marriages has been diminished by hard times; and in explanation of this he conjectures that the expense and delay involved in procuring a divorce in England are so great that only somewhat wealthy persons, who do not feel so severely the burden of a financial crisis, can afford to go into court. There can be no doubt that the cost of carrying a suit through has been a very important reason for the remarkably small number of divorces in England and Wales; in the days of parliamentary divorce, which was exceedingly expensive, the number of divorces was infinitesimal. On the other hand, the recent increase of divorce in England, while very largely a consequence of certain circumstances arising from the war, is also undoubtedly connected with the fact that a divorce may now be obtained more cheaply than before.

While there are thus various factors that tend to make marriage durable, there are others that have the very opposite tendency. To these belong certain peculiarities of the sexual instinct. The physical qualities in men and woman which act as sexual stimulants are not imperishable, and the loss of the attractive quality may put an end to the union. We often hear of savage men repudiating wives who grow old or ugly; and it has been noticed that in Switzerland marriage is much more frequently dissolved through divorce when the wife is the husband's senior than when the reverse is the case. Moreover, the sexual desire is dulled by long companionship and excited by novelty. According to von Oettingen, the statistics of divorce and remarriage in Europe show that the taste for variety is often the chief cause of the dissolution of marriage; and I believe it is a matter of ordinary experience that in countries where divorce is of common occurrence, sexual indifference and a desire for new gratifications of the sexual instinct are potent causes of it.

[301]

The custom of marrying without previous knowledge of the partner, which is found in many countries, must also, of course, be injurious to the stability of marriage. The facility of Muhammadan divorce is a necessary consequence of the separation of the sexes. "A man would never embark in the hazardous lottery of Eastern marriage if he had not the escape of divorce from the woman whom he has never seen, and who may be in every way uncongenial to him." The frequency of divorce in ancient Athens and among some of the similar peoples has been attributed to a similar cause.

But however carefully the partner is selected, marriage is always something of an adventure. Where two persons are brought into so close contact with, and into such constant dependence on, each other it would be little short of a miracle if their wills always acted in complete unison. In modern civilisation, where life is becoming richer in interests and individual differences are getting more accentuated, the causes of disagreement are multiplied and the frictions are apt to become more serious and, consequently, more likely to end in a rupture of the marriage tie. The idea that it is a right, or even a duty, to assert one's own individuality is characteristic of our age. As Lord Bryce observes, "the desire of each person to do what he or she pleases, to gratify his or her tastes, likings, caprices, to lead a life which shall be uncontrolled by another's will—this grows stronger. So, too, whatever stimulates the susceptibility and sensitiveness of the nervous system tends to make tempers more irritable, and to produce causes of friction between those who are in constant contact. . . . It is temper rather than unlawful passion that may prove in future the most dangerous enemy to stability of the marriage relation." There is also the spread of a spirit of dissatisfaction in our time, which has been called "the age of discontent." It has been noticed that the rates of divorce and of suicide—the highest expression of discontent—show a close and constant relation. Both are much more common among Protestants than among Catholics, among the Teutons than among the Celts, and in cities than in the country; both are rapidly increasing, and the proportion of suicides among divorced persons is abnormally large. The emancipation of women, too, has its share in the increasing instability of marriage. It is natural to find divorce most frequent where a woman finds it most easy to earn her bread. In the United States nearly two-thirds of the divorces are granted on demand of the wife.

It is impossible to doubt that the number of divorces is also influenced by the rules laid down by custom and law, although the effect of legal restrictions may often have been exaggerated. Dr. Willcox even maintains that "the immediate, direct, and measurable influence of legislation is subsidiary, unimportant, almost imperceptible." In support of this opinion he points out that in New York, in spite of its more stringent divorce law, the rate of divorces was higher than in New Jersey and only a little lower than in Pennsylvania. This means that more divorces for adultery were granted in New York, in proportion to the population, than for adultery and desertion in New Jersey, and almost as many as for adultery, desertion, cruelty, and imprisonment in Pennsylvania. From this he draws the conclusion that "limiting the causes increases the number of divorces in those which remain, but without materially affecting the total number. A certain proportion of the married couples in the three States desired divorce and were willing to offer the evidence required in order to obtain the decree." In Europe, also, the rates of divorces are certainly not proportionate to the facility with which divorce may be obtained according to law; Norway, for instance, has a more liberal divorce law, but at the same time fewer divorces, than several other continental countries. Yet I believe that Dr. Willcox has somewhat underrated the influence of legal obstacles. He argues that restrictions on divorce and on remarriage after divorce have been tried in various places and at various times and have proved of little effect. This contention is by no means borne out by recent experience in Japan, where the introduction of the new Civil code, which made divorce considerably more difficult than it had been before, was accompanied with a sudden and great decrease in the number of divorces. Much depends, of course, on the manner in which the law is administered. It seems that the exceptionally great divorce rates in the United States are largely due to the laxity of procedure which has grown up there. One wife alleges that her husband has never offered to take her out "riding" (= driving) ; another, that he does not come home till ten o'clock at night, and when he does return he keeps plaintiff awake talking.

Laws and rules of custom, while undoubtedly influencing conduct, are themselves influenced by it, and have largely originated in behaviour which has been habitual in the community. Hence the circumstances which tend either to preserve or to dissolve the unions of men and women have also made themselves felt in the establishing of rules relating to divorce. But there are other influences that have been at work as well. The dissolution of a marriage is not a matter which concerns the interests of one person alone, and individual desires may for this reason also be checked by the public sentiment of the community.

The nature of the restrictions to which divorce is frequently subject generally discloses the causes from which they have sprung. They are in the first place intended to prevent the infliction of an injury on a spouse who does not desire a dissolution of the marriage. But in certain circumstances this regard for his or her interests ceases to act as a check, namely, if the spouse is guilty of offensive behaviour, or if the preservation of the marriage tie for some other reason—such as impotence or insanity or disease—would entail undue suffering for the party who is desirous of dissolving it. The rules relating to divorce have thus in a large measure originated in the tendency of the community to sympathise with the sufferings of its members as long as they behave without reproach. This tendency, as I have tried to show elsewhere, is the main cause of moral rules as expressed in customs or laws. On the one hand, marriage is a contract which grants rights and imposes duties, but on the other hand it "gives either party an extraordinary power of injuring the other." The community tries to protect the interests of both parties, or of one of them, and provides divorce as a remedy if the marriage proves a failure. It may certainly be anything but impartial in laying down its rules of divorce; but this is only another instance of that inequality of rights which so often characterizes the legal relations between the sexes.

Husband and wife are not the only persons whose interests are affected by a divorce. The welfare of the offspring has also been considered in the rules controlling the dissolution of marriage. There are not only provisions for safeguarding the children's future, but in some cases, as we have seen, the birth of a child makes the marriage indissoluble. Among ourselves the interests of children are often appealed to by those who oppose changes in the existing laws on divorce, however little the children may have been thought of when the laws were framed.

In many cases the rules of divorce have been greatly influenced by religion. In some countries, as Japan and ancient Greece, this influence has been in favour of divorce in certain circumstances, particularly in the case of a barren wife. In other instances religion has, on the other hand, acted as a bar to divorce in all circumstances. Although Jesus, like the school of Shammai, simply prohibited a man from putting away his wife for any other reason than adultery and a woman from deserting her husband, the Christian Church established the dogma that a valid marriage can never be dissolved, and that in the case of adultery on the part of the wife the innocent husband is not allowed to take another wife. This draconic legislation is undoubtedly due to the ascetic tendencies of the Church, which made her insensible to the misery caused by unhappy marriages. So thoroughly did she succeed in impressing her views upon the minds of Christian legislators that to this day even many Roman Catholic countries which have introduced civil marriage obstinately refuse to permit divorce in any circumstances whatsoever. In other countries, where the principle of the indissolubility of marriage has broken down long ago and even the express injunctions of Christ are no longer followed, the rigid attitude of the Church has left behind sentiments which put obstacles in the way of the most needful reforms.   Legislators are still imbued with the idea that a marriage must inevitably end in a catastrophe, either by the death or some great misfortune of one of the consorts or by the commission of a criminal or an immoral act.   New motives are found for old restrictions, new wine is poured into the old bottles.   It would seem that a contract entered into by mutual consent also should be dissolvable by mutual consent.   But it is argued that marriage cannot be treated as an ordinary contract, and that its dissolution should be permitted only on very serious grounds. It is said that few things can be more harmful to the moral well-being of the offspring than the divorce of their parents.   This may be perfectly true, but constitutes no valid argument against divorce.   The interests of children are obviously out of the question where the marriage is childless, and where it is not so, there is every reason to believe that it is rather better than worse for the child to live peacefully with one parent alone than to live with two parents who cannot agree or who, for some reason or other, wish to break up their home.   Moreover, if the regard for the children's welfare were the real cause of the prohibition of consensual divorce, why should it be prohibited in so many countries which allow consensual separation?   We have seen that divorce by mutual consent has already been introduced by some modern law-books, and it is not known that any evils have resulted from this concession.   Where such divorce is not allowed by law it is nevertheless easily obtained in practice; and it is strange that any legislator should persist in regarding crime or immoral conduct on the part of one of the spouses as a more proper ground or excuse for dissolving the marriage than the mutual agreement of both.

It is a widespread idea that divorce is the enemy of marriage and, if made easy, might prove destructive to the very institution of the family. This view I cannot share. I look upon divorce as the necessary remedy for a misfortune and as a means of preserving the dignity of marriage by putting an end to unions which are a disgrace to its name. The existence of marriage does not depend on laws. If the main thesis of this work is correct, if marriage is not an artificial creation but an institution based on deep-rooted sentiments, conjugal and parental, it will last as long as these sentiments last. And should they ever cease to exist, no laws in the world could save marriage from destruction.

INDEX

ABORS (Assam), 55

Adoption, a bar to intermarriage, 94

Adultery, as a ground for divorce or separation, 1, 277, 278, 280-283, 285, 288, 289, 291-293, 295, 303, 306; punished, 18

Africa, marriage by capture in, 112; marriage arranged by the young man's parents or father, 126; marriage by service, 158; marriage by consideration, 160, 161, 163; marriage rites, 224, 227; monogamy and polygyny, 230, 240-242, 244 *sq.*; polyandry, 251; divorce, 279

——, Central, 148

——, East, 148

——, Eastern Central, 241, 278

——, Equatorial, 240 *sq.*

——, South, 35

——, West, 147, 279

Age, marriage, ch. ii. *See* Old age, Seniority.

Agricultural tribes, mother - right among, 23; supporting of a family easy, 33; women's liberty of choice, 128; marriage by purchase, 128, 129, 163; monogamy and polygyny, 230

Aith Saddĕn (Morocco), 131 *sq.*

Aith Yusi (Morocco), 192

Akamba (British East Africa), 115

Akikúyu (British East Africa), 244

Albania, marriage by capture in, 113; marriage by purchase, 171

Aleut, 251

Algeria, consent to marriage in, 136

Algonkin, 22

Amzmiz (Morocco), 207

Anabaptists, polygyny advocated by the, 236

Ancestor-worship. *See* Dead, cult of the.

Andaman Islands, 229, 276

Anglo-Saxons, consent to marriage

among the, 142; marriage by purchase, 170; bride price becoming the property of the bride, 176 *sq.*; morning gift, 177; polygyny, 234; divorce, 291

Animals, peculiarity of the pairing instinct in, 82-84, 102; in-breeding among, 99-103, 106-109

Antilles, marriage restriction for Frenchmen in the, 53

Ants, "marriage flight" of winged, 82, 102

Apes, anthropoid, relations between the sexes and paternal care among the, 4, 6 *sq.*; long period of infancy, 6 *sq.*; not gregarious, 6 *sq.*; diet of the, 6, 25, 27; masculine jealousy among the, 18; duration of the unions between the sexes, 298 *sq.*

Arabs, proverb regarding love among the, 82; divorce, 285

——, ancient, marriage inside the village among the, 56; cousin marriage, 70; marriage with a half-sister, 87; marriage between housemates held indecent, 87, 96; marriage by capture, 112; curses, 153; marriage by consideration, 167; gift offered by the bride-groom to the bride, 167, 174; bride price given to the bride, 174; polygyny, 233; polyandry, 255 *sq.*; divorce, 284

—— of Moab, 123 *sq.*

Araucanians (Chili), 119 *sq.*

Argyllshire, marriage rite in, 190

Aristotle, 180

Aryans, ancient, views on celibacy among the, 41; marriage by purchase, 168; marriage rites, 193, 206; consummation of marriage supposed to have been deferred, 219; "raising up seed," 255

Ashanti, 231

INDEX

Asia, mock capture of the bride among the nomads of Central, 120; absence of marriage rites among several tribes in, 227

Athenians, ancient, marriage with a half-sister among the, 68, 87; dowry, 180, 286; marriage rite, 203; concubinage, 180, 235; divorce, 286, 302.

Atkinson, J. J., 78

Australian aborigines, paternal authority among the, 21; mother-right, 21, 23; social condition of the, 26; excess of males over females among the, 34, 238, 273; polygyny of the old men, 34, 242 *sq.*; difficulties in procuring wives, 34, 36, 130, 157, 242, 243, 272; betrothal of infants, 36, 129 *sq.*; exogamous rules, 71, 72, 77, 78, 157; marriage by capture, 112, 114, 156; marriage arranged by the community, 127; consent to marriage, 127-130; exchange of women for wives, 129, 130, 156 *sq.*; authority of the old men, 129, 130, 148, 242, 272 *sq.*; elopement, 132, 133, 156; levirate, 156, 269, 274; absence of marriage rites, 227; monogamy and polygyny, 229, 238; absorbing passion for one, 247; "group-marriage" and group-relations, 268-275

Austria, marriage rate in, 47; marriages between Christians and Jews, 57 *sq.*; prohibition of marriage between cousins, 70; consent to marriage, 145

Avebury, *Lord,* 12, 14, 18, 33, 78

Aztecs, ancient. *See* Mexico.

BABYLONIA, paternal authority in, 135; consent to marriage, 135; marriage by consideration, 166; presents given by the bridegroom to the bride, 173; bride price given to the bride, 174; marriage portion, 174, 179; monogamy, polygyny, and concubinage, 232, 233, 282

Baganda, 35

Bagesu (British East Africa), 32

Bain, Alex., 246

Balmoral, marriage rite in the neighbourhood of, 37

Banks Islands, 126 *sq.*

Barea (North-East Africa), 153

Barrenness in the wife, a cause of polygyny or concubinage, 233, 234, 239 *sq.*; a cause of divorce, 278, 280, 281, 288, 299, 300, 306

Barton, G. A., 55

Basuto (Bechuana tribe), 188

Bathing, as a marriage rite, 202 *sq.*

Bats, 6

Beating, at weddings, 197, 199, 206 *sq.*

Beauty, the sexual instinct stimulated by, 239; short duration of female, at the lower stages of civilisation, 239

Bechuanas, 24, 188

Bedouins, 64, 136

—— of Sinai, 120 *sq.*

Bees, "marriage flight" of, 82, 102

Belford, marriage rite in, 212

Belgium, marriage between uncle and niece and between aunt and nephew in, 69

Bengal, purchase of bridegrooms in, 183; marriage rite, 198

Benin, 231

Berbers of Morocco, marriage inside the village among some, 56; sexual indifference between cousins, 81; ceremonial reluctance to give a daughter in marriage, 118; differences between the speech of men and women, 125; *'ār* and the liberty of married women to change their husbands, 131 *sq.*; marriage by purchase, 168; marriage rites, 192, 199, 207; polygyny and the blood-feud, 240; divorce, 285

Bernard, M., 143

Bestiality, 89 *sq.*

Best-man, 212, 214, 219

Betrothal, 184-186

Bhuiyas (Orissa States), 111

Bhutan (Eastern Himalayas), 259, 265

Birds, relations between the sexes and parental care among, 3, 5; duration of the unions between the sexes, 3, 298; absorbing passion for one, 246

INDEX

Blemmyans (Ethiopia), 8
Blessings, of strangers, 15; of parents, 150-154
Bloch, Iwan, 86, 89
Blood-feud, the, 97, 239
Bodin, Jean, 144
Bogišić, M., 140
Bogos (North-East Africa), 153
Bohemia, marriage rite in, 214
Boloki (Upper Congo), 34
Brahmans, exogamy among the, 73
—— of Eastern Bengal, marriage rite among the, 198
—— of South India, 207-209
Brand, John, 37, 204, 215, 218
Brazilian Indians, 89, 96, 110, 114
Bread, in marriage rites, 193 sq.
Breaking of objects, in marriage rites, 190-192
Brehm, A. E., 3, 246
Bridal procession, barring the, 117, 119
Bride, the, deflowered by extra-matrimonial intercourse, 12-14; resistance made to the bridegroom by the family of, 115-119; regarded as queen, 117 sq.; resistance made or grief expressed by, 119-123, 187, 210, 214, 220; lifted over, or prevented from stepping on, the threshold, 125, 216 sq.; veiling of, 125, 212 sq.; throwing a shoe after the bridegroom and, 125, 217 sq.; gift presented by the bridegroom to, 165, 173-178; supposed to be in a dangerous condition and also dangerous to others, 199, 200, 222-224, see Prophylactic or purificatory marriage rites; holiness attributed to, 214. See Marriage rites.
Bridegroom, the, reluctant to deflower the bride, 13; resistance made to, by the bride's people, 115-119, 210; regarded as king, 117 sq.; resistance made to, by the bride, 119-123; "captured," 122 sq.; resistance made to, by the female friends of the bride, 123 sq.; throwing a shoe after the bride and, 125, 217 sq.; return gift presented to, by the bride's people, 164, 165, 172 sq.; gift presented by,

to the bride, 165, 173-178; purchased, 183; supposed to be in a dangerous condition, 199, 200, 222-224, see Prophylactic or purificatory marriage rites; holiness attributed to, 214. See Marriage rites.
Bridesmaids, 201, 208, 212, 219
Bridesmen, 121, 123, 202, 212
Brisay, Marquis de, 82
Britons, group-marriage among the, 267 sq.
Brittany, marriage rites in, 190, 210; consummation of marriage deferred, 219
Brother, consent of the, essential to a girl's marriage, 127; the bride's, receives part of the bride price, 161. See Fraternal love.
Brown, Frank P. ("Bulman"), 274
Bryce, James, Lord, 290, 302
Bukhāri (Al-), 255
Bulgaria, marriage rate in, 47; local exogamy, 78; marriage rite, 187
Burckhardt, J. L., 285
Burma, stopping the bridegroom's procession in, 116
Burne, Charlotte Sophia, 185
Burra Isle (Shetland Islands), 104
Burton, Sir Richard F., 82, 240
Bushmen, 89, 96, 114, 229
Butterflies, effects of in-breeding upon, 101 sq.
Büttner, C. G., 153

CÆSAR, C. J., 179, 267 sq.
Cairo, 217, 285
Californian Indians, 53, 110
Cambodia, marriage by service in, 159
Canadian Indians, 33
Candles, in marriage rites, 204
Canelos Indians (Ecuador), 222
Caribs, 124
Carver, J., 159
Caste endogamy, 59 sq.
Catholic Church, the Roman, views on marriage and virginity in, 46; celibacy of its clergy, 46; marriage age according to, 46; religious endogamy, 58 sq.; prohibitions of marriage between relatives, 74, 75,

INDEX

79; between relatives by alliance, 76; "spiritual relationship," 76, 77, 98, 293; consent to marriage, 141 *sq.*; marriage portion, 182; betrothal and wedding, 185; continence after marriage prescribed by, 219 *sq.*; marriage regarded as a sacrament, 225, 289; religious marriage ceremony prescribed, 225; its attitude towards polygyny, 236, 248; towards divorce, 289, 290, 306; separation from bed and board according to, 289, 290, 306 *sq.*

Catholics, Roman, consent to marriage among, 143; divorce and suicide, 303

Cattle, effects of in-breeding upon, 101

Caucasia, marriage by capture in, 113

Celebes, 208

Celibacy, prevalence and causes of, and views held about, ch. ii. *passim*; of the secular and regular clergy in Roman Catholicism, 46

Central America, marriage restriction for Spaniards in, 53

Ceylon, polyandry in, 253, 259, 266; proportion of the sexes, 259; group-marriage, 266

Charlemagne, polygyny and concubinage of, 236

Charlevoix, P. F. X. de, 22

Chastity, pre-nuptial, among uncivilised peoples, 10 *sq.*; child-betrothal a means of preserving a girl's, 36, 42

Cheremiss, marriage rite among the, 214 *sq.*

Chiefs, deflowering brides, 12-14

Child-birth, conjugal abstinence after, 238, 239, 248

Chimpanzees, 4, 6, 7, 27

China, aboriginal tribes of, marriage by service among the, 158

Chinese, treatment of the children of concubines and domestic slaves among the, 2 *n.*, 232; children married in order of seniority, 37; frequency of marriage and marriage age, 38; marriage regarded as a duty, 38 *sq.*; exogamous rules,

72, 76; paternal authority and filial piety, 134, 149; consent to marriage, 134; views on ghosts, 148 *sq.*; marriage by consideration, 165 *sq.*; return gifts, 172; presents given by the bridegroom to the bride, 173; the money given to the bride's parents spent in outfitting her, 173; marriage rites, 189, 190, 213, 215 *sq.*; concubinage, 232, 281; milk eschewed, 239; divorce, 280 *sq.*

—— of Canton, marriage rite among the, 192

—— of Foochow, marriage rite among the, 215

—— of Swatow, marriage rite among the, 204

Chittagong hill tribes, 112

Christians, the early, views on marriage, continence, and virginity among, 44-46; views on marriage with non-Christians, 58 *sq.*; religious marriage ceremony, 225; their attitude towards polygyny, 235, 248; towards divorce, 288 *sq.*; towards remarriages, 289

Chukchee, 89, 110 *sq.*

Cicero, 43, 61

Circumambulation, as a marriage rite, 205 *sq.*

Clan, coincidence between a territorial group and a, 96 *sq.*; antagonism between the family and the, 154 *sq.*

—— exogamy, ch. iv. *passim*

Class endogamy, 60-62, 64 *sq.*

Classes, age for marriage among different, 50; origin of, 62 *sq.*

Classificatory terms of relationship, 274 *sq.*

Codrington, R. H., 21, 118

Coins, ritual use of, 177, 178, 193, 203, 205, 207, 216

Colenso, William, 82

"Communal marriage." *See* Promiscuity.

Concubinage, ch. ix. *passim*; the term, 231

Confucius, 38

Congo, 241, 242, 245

Conjugal affection, 245-247, 299. *See* Marital instinct.

INDEX

Conjugal duties, 1. *See* Marital care and duties.

Consent as a condition of marriage, ch. vi.

Consummation of marriage, the publicity of, 186; rites intended to ensure or facilitate, 190-192; supposed to be impeded by magical influences, 191; deferred, 212, 219-222; views of the Roman Catholic Church on, 289

Continence, required of bride and bridegroom, 219-222; of married men at certain periods, 238 *sq.*

Cos, marriage rite in ancient, 208

Cossacks, Zaporog, polyandrous relations among the, 262

—— of Little Russia and the Ukrainia, marriage by capture among the, 113

Cousins, marriage between, 69, 70, 95, 96, 103, 104, 106 *sq.*

Crampe, *Dr.*, 106

Cranbrook (Kent), marriage rite in, 215

Crawley, A. E., 124, 209, 228

Croatians, marriage arranged by the parents among the, 140; marriage rite, 197

Cromarty, marriage rite in, 203

Crooke, W., 210

Cross-cousin marriage, 70

Cruelty, as a ground for divorce, 278, 292, 295, 303 *sq.*

Cruickshank, B., 247

Curses of visiting strangers, 15; of parents, 150-154; of old people, 153 *sq.*; of dying persons, 153; of superiors, 153 *sq.*

Customs as rules of conduct, 28 *sq.*

DALTON, E. T., 55

Dalyell, J. G., 216

Dancing, at weddings, 227

Darwin, Charles, 18, 26, 99, 105, 246

Darwin, G. H., 106

Dead, cult of the, 32, 38, 39, 41, 43, 148, 149, 154, 155, 239

Defloration of a bride, the, performed by somebody else than the bridegroom, 12-14; means of ensuring, 190-192

Delivery, rites intended to ensure an easy, 196 *sq.*

Demnat (Morocco), 199

Denmark, consanguineous marriages in, 104 *sq.*; isolated communities, 105; marriage rites, 208, 217; ceremonial throwing of shoes, 217 *sq.*

Desertion, as a ground for divorce, 278, 280, 288, 289, 291-293, 295, 303, 306

Dieri (South-East Australia), 269-274

Dio Cassius, 268

Dionysius of Halicarnassus, 113

Disguises at marriages, 207-212

Divorce, ch. xi.; 1, 17, 52, 137, 165, 174, 176, 180-182

Djidda, 64

Dogs, the sexual instinct of, dulled by companionship, 83; effects of in-breeding upon, 100

Doves, the sexual instinct of, 82

Dowry, 165, 173-183, 300

Dravidians, marriage age among the, 42; milk eschewed, 239; freedom of women, 262

Drinking together of bride and bridegroom, 189 *sq.*

Ducks, excited by strangers, 83 *sq.*

Dunlop, R. H. W., 258

Durham, county of, marriage rite in the, 201

Durkheim, Émile, 78, 85, 98

Du Vair, 144

EATING together of bride and bridegroom, 188 *sq.*

Eggs, in marriage rites, 190-192, 196; used to promote fecundity, 196

Egypt, *ṣadāq* and marriage portion in, 179; marriage rites, 212, 217; monogamy and polygyny, 240; divorce, 285

——, ancient, brother-and-sister marriage in, 68, 89, 103; monogamy and polygyny, 232

Ehrenfels, Christian von, 249

Ekenäs (Finland), marriage rite at, 192

Elephants, 6

Ellis, Havelock, 80

Elopement, 132, 133, 163

Embe (East Africa), 148

INDEX

Emin Pasha, 230
Endogamy, ch. iii.
England, reminiscences of the rule of daughters marrying in order of seniority in, 37; marriage rate, 47-49; marriage age, 48; aristocracy of, 62; prohibited degrees, 69, 75; marriage with a deceased wife's sister, 76; consanguineous marriages, 105 *sq.*; barring the wedding procession, 117; consent to marriage, 142, 145 *sq.*; marriage rites, 190, 193, 194, 201, 203-205, 212, 213, 215-218; religious and civil marriage, 226; divorce, 292, 293, 297, 300 *sq.*; judicial separation, 292, 297. *See* Anglo-Saxons.
Erinyes, 151-154
Eskimo, 251
—— about Bering Strait, 32
Essenes, 44
Esthonia, marriage rites in, 208-210, 213
Euripides, 180
Europe, prostitution in, 12; illegitimate births in some towns of, 12; frequency of marriage and marriage age in, 47-52; exogamous rules, 69, 79; cases of incest, 87-89; isolated communities, 104-106; barring the bridal procession, 117; ceremonial crying of the bride, 121 *sq.*; sexual separation influencing popular language, 124; consent to marriage, 141-146; marriage portion, 182 *sq.*; betrothal and wedding, 185; marriage rites, 188-190, 193, 201-206, 213, 216, 228; the consummation of marriage supposed to be impeded by magical influences, 191; consummation of marriage deferred, 219 *sq.*; civil marriage, 226; soldiers not encouraged to marry, 262; grounds for divorce, 295 *sq.*; grounds for judicial separation, 296 *sq.*; consequences of a divorce, 297; prevalence of divorce, 297, 298, 304; divorce caused by the taste for variety, 301
Evil eye, the, 15, 195, 200, 209, 212, 213, 216
Ewald, G. H. A. von, 96

Ewart, J. C., 101
Ewhe-speaking peoples (Slave Coast), 21, 118 *sq.*
Exchange of bride for bride, 129, 130, 156 *sq.*
—— of gifts. *See* Return gifts.
—— of wives, 19, 274
Exogamy, ch. iv.; 53, 125
Eylmann, Erhard, 272

Fahlbeck, Pontus, 50
False bride, the, 210
Fasting of bride and bridegroom, 218
Father. *See* Parental care, Parents, Paternal authority, Paternal care and duties, Paternal instinct.
Father-right, 16, 17, 23
Father's sister, consent of the, essential to a young man's marriage, 126 *sq.*
Felkin, R. W., 35
Fertility, marriage rites intended to promote, 192-196, 224, 227
Fez (Morocco), 175, 179, 196, 208, 209, 211 *sq.*
Fiji, 31, 244 *sq.*
Filial love and regard, 92, 147
—— rights and duties, ch. vi. *passim*
Finland, marriage rate in, 48; sexual indifference between lads and girls educated in the same school, 81; marriage rite, 192
Fire, in marriage rites, 203-206
Fish, used for reproductive purposes, 195; in marriage rites, 195 *sq.*
Fishes, lack of parental care among, 5
Florida (Solomon Islands), 164
Fosterage, a bar to intermarriage, 93 *sq.*
Foula (Shetland Islands) consanguineous marriages in, 104 *sq.*
France, guests supplied with temporary wives in mediæval, 15; marriage rate in, 47; marriage age, 48; class endogamy, 61; aristocracy of, 62; marriage between uncle and niece and between aunt and nephew in, 69; incest, 87 *sq.*; barring the wedding procession, 117; consent to marriage, 143-145; notions of paternal rights and fil-

INDEX

INDEX

ICELAND, marriage rate in, 48
Igorot (Luzon), 224
Illegitimate births, in Europe, 12
—— children, treatment of, 2
Impotence of the husband, a ground for divorce, 278, 284, 305
In-breeding, effects of, 99-109
Incest, ch. iv. *passim*
India, marriage regarded as a duty in, 41; marriage age, 41 *sq.*; hypergamy, 42, 60; infant-marriage, 42; caste endogamy, 59 *sq.*; origin of caste, 62 *sq.*; marriage between an uncle and niece and between an aunt and nephew, 69; exogamy, 73, 78, 81, 82, 95; large households, 95; crying of the bride, 121; filial reverence, 139, 149 *sq.*; consent to marriage, 139 *sq.*; marriage by purchase, 168 *sq.*; bride price given to the bride, 176; property of married women, 179; purchase of bridegrooms, 183; marriage rites, 187, 188, 193, 202-205, 210, 211, 217, 224, 228; monogamy and polygyny, 234, 245; marriage regarded as a sacrament, 285; divorce, 285 *sq. See* Muhammadans of India.
——, aboriginal tribes of, frequency of marriage among the, 33; marriage age, 33; exogamy, 73, 78; marriage by capture, 111 *sq.*; marriage arranged by parents, 126; marriage by service, 158; polyandry, 252-254, 258-267; group-marriage, 265-267
——, ancient, marrying in order of seniority in, 37; views on celibacy, 41; marriage age, 42; marriage by capture, 112 *sq.*; crying of the bride, 121; parental authority, 138 *sq.*; consent to marriage, 139; filial piety, 139, 149 *sq.*; marriage by consideration, 168; return gifts, 172; bride price given to the bride, 176; marriage portion, 179; marriage rites, 188, 193, 202-207, 213, 217, 224; consummation of marriage deferred, 219-221; polygyny, 234, 239 *sq.*; polyandry, 255; divorce, 285
——, Northern, tree-marriages in,

210 *sq.*; polyandry, 252, 258-260, 265; group-marriage, 265
India, South, polyandry in, 252-254, 258-263, 265-267; group-marriage in, 265-267
Indian Archipelago, marriage by capture in, 112; marriage by service, 158; marriage rite, 193; monogamy and polygyny, 229; polyandry, 251
Indo-China, marriage by service among the uncivilised tribes of, 158; marriage rite in, 193
Infanticide, female, 78
Infants, betrothal of, 36, 42, 126, 129 *sq.*
Invertebrates, relations between the sexes and lack of parental care among, 3, 5
Ireland, marriage upon trial in, 10; daughters marrying in order of seniority, 37; marriage rate, 48, 51; mock capture of the bride, 117; betrothal and wedding, 184; marriage rite, 194
——, ancient *jus primæ noctis* in, 14; guests supplied with temporary wives, 15; paternal authority, 140 *sq.*; marriage by consideration, 171; bride price partly given to the bride, 178; marriage portion, 179, 180, 288; polygyny and concubinage, 235 *sq.*; divorce, 288
Iroquois, 22, 147, 241 *sq.*
Isæus, 43, 180
Isle of Man, marriage rites in, 205, 217
Italy, marriage age in, 48; marriage between uncle and niece and between aunt and nephew, 69; consent to marriage, 145; marriage rite, 190

JACOBS, Joseph, 58
Jamieson, G., 166
Japan, frequency of marriage in, 39; celibacy denounced, 39; marriage with a half-sister in ancient, 68; authority of a housefather in, 134; consent to marriage, 134 *sq.*; reverence for parents, 149; marriage by capture, 166; marriage by purchase, 166, 173; presents given by

INDEX

the bridegroom to the bride, 173;
exchange of gifts, 173; marriage
rite, 190; concubinage, 232, 239;
divorce, 281, 282, 304, 306
Jeaffreson, J. C., 293
Jealousy, masculine, 18-20, 79, 264;
feminine, 244 *sq.*
Jews, marriage regarded as a religious duty among the, 40; marriage age, 40; religious endogamy,
56 *sq.*; marriage with Christians,
57 *sq.*; with a niece, 69; between
cousins, 70; parental consent to
marriage, 135 *sq.*; betrothal by
kaseph, 167; *kethūbhāh*, 174 *sq.*;
betrothal and wedding, 184; marriage rites, 190, 191, 213, 277;
polygyny, 233, 235; divorce, 282-
284
——, German, marriage rite among
the, 196
——, Oriental, marriage rite among
the, 195 *sq.*
——, West Russian, marriage rite
among the, 196
—— of mediæval Egypt, marriage
rites among the, 208
—— of Morocco, marriage rite
among the, 196
Jochelson, W., 118, 159, 164
John of Damascus, 45 *n.*
Joining of hands, as a marriage rite,
187
Jones, Ernest, 85, 90 *sq.*
Josephus, 44
Jounsar district (Punjab), 258
Jovinian, the monk, 46
Jung, C. G., 85
Junod, H. A., 35
Jus primæ noctis, 12-14

Kachins (Burma), 31
Kacoodja (Northern Territory of
Australia), 274
Kafirs, 24, 31, 161
——, Xosa, 126 *sq.*
Kalmucks, 111
Kamilaroi (New South Wales), 157
Kaniagmiut (Alaskan coast), 251
Karayá (Brazil), 280
Karlowa, Otto, 170
Karsten, Rafael, 13, 119, 222
Kashmir, polyandry in, 252

Kavirondo, Bantu (East Africa),
186
Keith, A. B., 139
Kings, deflowering brides, 12-14
Kinship, origin of the social force of,
91-93
Klovborg (Denmark), marriage rite
at, 208
Kohler, Josef, 95
Koppenfels, H. von, 4
Koryaks (Siberia), 159
Koschaker, Paul, 174
Kovalewsky, Maxime, 178
Krause, Fritz, 125
Kunáma (North-East Africa), 153
Kurnai (Gippsland), 77, 132 *sq.*
Kutchin (Déné), 34 *sq.*

Ladakh, polyandry in, 252, 259
Lancerote (Canary Islands), 251
Lane, E. W., 240, 285
Lang, Andrew, 78
Language of women, 124 *sq.*
Lasch, Richard, 124
Le Bon, Gustave, 249
Lengua Indians (Paraguayan Chaco),
82
Leroy-Beaulieu, Anatole, 147
Letourneau, Ch., 130
Levirate, 156, 233, 264, 265, 269, 274
Lewin, T. H., 112
Livingstone, David, 244
Livonians, marriage rite among the,
212
Loango, 231
Lobi (French West Africa), 21
London, cousin marriages in, 106
Lopez de Castanheda, Fernão, 262
Love between the sexes, connection
between jealousy and, 19; the ab-
sorbing character of the, 246 *sq.*
See Conjugal affection, Marital in-
stinct, Sexual instinct.
Love-birds, 246
Low, David, 100
Lubbock, *Sir* John. *See* Avebury,
Lord.
Luiseño Indians (California), 110
Luther, Martin, 142, 225, 236, 291
Lyø (Denmark), 105

Macdonnell, A. A., 139
McDougall, William, 78

[318]

INDEX

INDEX

INDEX

INDEX

by purchase, 128, 129, 163 *sq.*; monogamy and polygyny, 230

Paternal authority, ch. vi. *passim*; among matrilineal peoples, 20-22
—— care and duties, ch. i. *passim*
—— instinct, the, 5, 25, 28, 29, 92, 299 *sq.*

Patrilineal descent. *See* Father-right.

Patrilocal marriage, 17, 56

Pennsylvania, divorce in, 303

Pentecost Island (New Hebrides), 118

Persia, polygyny in, 240, 245
——, ancient, views on marriage and procreation in, 42 *sq.*; next-of-kin marriage, 103

Perthshire, marriage rite in, 205 *sq.*

Peru, marriage between uncle and niece and between aunt and nephew in, 69
——, ancient, brother-and-sister marriage in, 67 *sq.*; paternal authority, 133 *sq.*; parental consent to marriage, 134

Philo Judæus, 149

Picts, marriage by capture among the, 113

Plato, 43, 81, 151 *sq.*

Plinius Secundus, C., 8

Plutarch, 208

Polak, J. E., 245

Poland, marriage rite in, 187

Pollock, *Sir* Frederick, 177

Polterabend, the German, 190, 191, 201

Polyandry, ch. x.; 19, 20, 33, 34, 36, 229

Polygyny, ch. ix.; a cause of celibacy among the men, 11, 34 *sq.*; connection between mother-right and, 17; increasing the number of married women, 35; combined with polyandry, 265-268

Polynesia, class distinctions and endogamy in, 60

Portugal, marriage rite in, 187

Pottery broken at weddings, 190-192

Powers, Stephan, 53

Prague, 58

Pregnancy, 238, 248

Priests, deflowering brides, 12-14

Primitive men, pairing season of, 20, 299; social conditions of, 25-27; the family among, 27, 107; avoidance of incest, 107; durability of the unions between the sexes, 298 *sq.*

Promiscuity, the hypothesis of primitive, 7-20, 263; peoples said to live or to have lived in a state of, 7-9; customs interpreted as survivals of ancient, 9-17; outside marriage, 9-12

Prophylactic or purificatory marriage rites, 195, 199-224

Prosperity or abundance, marriage rites intended to promote, 194, 195, 216

Prostitution, in Europe, 12; of wives by their husbands, 19 *sq.*; caused by a paucity of marriageable women, 264

Protestants, marriages with non-Protestants among, 59; prohibited degrees, 75; parental consent to marriage, 142 *sq.*; sacerdotal nuptials, 225 *sq.*; divorce, 292, 295, 303; suicide, 303

Protozoa, effect of in-breeding upon, 102

Prussia, marriage portion in, 182; divorce, 294

Psycho-analysis, 84, 85, 90 *sq.*

Ptolemies, consanguineous marriages of the, 103

Punjab, marriage rites in, 201, 210 *sq.*

Purificatory or prophylactic marriage rites, 195, 199-224

Pygmies of Central Africa, 229

QUATREFAGES, A. de, 54

RABBITS, effects of in-breeding upon, 101 *sq.*

Racial endogamy, 53-55, 64 *sq.*

Rats, effects of in-breeding upon, 101, 102, 106

Reade, W. Winwood, 241

Red colour, the, in marriage rites, 190, 192, 215

Reformers, the, on parental consent to marriage, 142; on

[322]

INDEX

divorce, 291 *sq.*; on judicial separation, 292. *See* Luther, Melanchthon.

Relatives by affinity, marriage prohibited between, 75, 98

Religious endogamy, 56, 59, 64 *sq.*
—— marriage rites, 224-226

Reptiles, lack of parental care among, 5

Return gifts presented by the bride's people, 164, 165, 172 *sq.*

Réunion, marriage restriction for Frenchmen in, 53

Rhine, marriage rite on the, 217

Rhys, *Sir* John, 267

Ridgeway, *Sir* William, 62, 268

Rif, marriage inside the village in the, 56

Rings, betrothal and wedding, 125, 188

Rivers, W. H. R., 126, 148, 253, 258, 266

Romance peoples, barring the bridal procession among, 117; notions of paternal rights and filial duties, 143 *sq.*; feeling in favour of dotation, 182 *sq.*; "the false bride," 210

Rome, ancient views on marriage in, 43 *sq.*; marriage age, 44, 46; endogamy, 53-56, 60 *sq.*; origin of class distinctions, 62; prohibition of marriage between kindred, 73, 74, 95; on account of "spiritual relationship," 76; households, 95; marriage by capture, 113; resistance made by the bride, 121; paternal authority, 137, 138, 141, 287; consent to marriage, 137, 138, 141; reverence for parents, 150; curses of parents and of offended guests, 152; *coëmtio* and *arrha sponsalitia*, 169, 170, 176; *confarreatio*, 169, 170, 186, 188, 189, 224, 225, 286; *dos*, 180-182; betrothal, 184 *sq.*; marriage rites, 186-189, 192, 193, 203-205, 213, 216, 224 *sq.*; polygyny prohibited, 235; concubinage, 235, 262; soldiers forbidden to marry, 262; divorce, 286, 287, 290

Roro (British New Guinea), 115 *sq.*

Rosehearty (Aberdeenshire), marriage rite in, 194

Rossbach, A., 95

Routledge, *Mrs.* Katherine, 244

Royal families, consanguineous marriages in, 67, 68, 89, 103

Rumania, marriage rate in, 47

Russell, R. V., 81

Russia, frequency of marriage and marriage age in, 47, 51; marriages between Jews and Christians, 57; prohibition of marriage between cousins, 70; local exogamy, 78; marriage by capture, 113; crying of the bride, 121; paternal authority, 140, 147, 150; reverence for old age, 147; parental curses, 152; marriage by purchase among the peasantry of, 171; marriage rites in, 190, 197, 200, 208; divorce, 296
——, ancient, paternal authority in, 140; marriage by purchase, 170 *sq.*

Russian Empire, tribes of the former, marriage by capture among the, 111

Russians, Great, paternal authority among the, 140; bride price partly given to the bride, 178; marriage rite, 198 *sq.*
——, White, marriage rites among the, 204, 212

Saalfeld country (Saxe-Meiningen), marriage rite in the, 190

St. Augustine, 289

St. Jerome, 268

St. Paul, 44, 58, 225, 289, 291

Sakellarios, Ph., 113

Salsette (near Bombay), 217

Salt, in marriage rites, 190, 199, 216

Samerberg district (Bavaria), marriage rite in the, 210

Samoyeds, 111

Samter, Ernst, 119

Santa Cruz Islands, 126 *sq.*

Santals (Bengal), 31

Sapper, Carl, 124

Savage, T. S., 6

Scandinavia, class endogamy in, 61; marriage rites, 188, 204, 213, 216

Scandinavians, ancient, marriage by

INDEX

INDEX

Thomas, N. W., 89

Thomas Aquinas, 45 *n.*

Threshold, lifting of the bride over, or preventing her stepping on, the, 125, 216 *sq.*; carrying of the bridegroom over the, 217; the fear of the, 217

Thurnwald, Richard, 157

Tibet, polyandry in, 252, 258-261, 265; proportion of the sexes, 258; group-marriage, 265, 267

Tikopia (Santa Cruz Islands), 126 *sq.*

Tlingit, 251

Tobias, continence of, 220

Tocqueville, A. de, 63

Todas (Nilgiri Hills), 253, 258, 259, 265 *sq.*

Tonga Islands, 154

Torches, in marriage rites, 204

Torres Straits, Western islands of, 164

Totemism, 72, 79, 98, 269

Troels-Lund, T. F., 204

Tunis, consent to marriage in, 136

Turkomans, 120

Tying of something to the bride and the bridegroom separately, 187 *sq.*

Uganda, 231

Ugro-Finnic peoples, marriage rite among, 214

Ujfalvy, K. E. von, 103

Ulster, *jus primæ noctis* in ancient, 14

Unchastity, prenuptial, 9-12

United States, racial endogamy in, 54; marriage with a niece or a nephew mostly prohibited, 69; parental consent to marriage, 146; divorce, 295, 297, 298-300, 303 *sq.*

Unmarried people, ch. ii. *passim*

Unyoro, 230 *sq.*

Urabunna (Central Australia), 270-274

Uruguay, marriage between uncle and niece and between aunt and nephew in, 69

Variety, taste for, 239, 247, 301

Veddas (Ceylon), 229, 253, 276

Veiling of the bride, 125, 213

Vertebrates, lower, lack of parental care among the, 3, 5

Vienna, 57 *sq.*

Virginity, child-betrothal as a means of preserving a girl's, 36, 42; men's preference for, 36, 42, 161; Christian enthusiasm for, 44-46; price paid for a bride's, 162, 177 *sq.*

Votyaks, 111

Waguha (West Tanganyika), 35

Waldron, George, 205

Wales, marriage upon trial in, 10; reminiscences of the rule of daughters marrying in order of seniority, 37; marriage rate, 47 *sq.*; marriage age, 48; barring the wedding procession, 117; mock capture of the bride, 117; marriage rites, 198, 216; divorce, 301

——, ancient, the exogamous joint family in, 96; consent to marriage, 141; marriage by consideration, 171; return gifts, 172 *sq.*; marriage portion, 173, 180; morning gift, 178; divorce, 288

Wallace, A. R., 4, 101

Walruses, 6

Wapokomo (British East Africa), 24

War, among savages, 114; causing a disproportion between the sexes, 248

Warega (Belgian Congo), 245

Wärmland (Sweden), 198

Water rites, at weddings, 202-204

Weapons, at weddings, 197, 199, 201 *sq.*

Wedding feasts, 186

Weddings, dancing at, 227; sexual licence, 227. *See* Marriage rites.

Weeks, John H., 34, 241

Wheeler, G. C., 10, 128, 163, 230, 277

White, J. Claude, 265

White things, in marriage rites, 196

Whitethorn, in marriage rites, 204

Widowers, dangers supposed to be connected with the remarriage

INDEX

of, 210 *sq.*; weddings of, 223; remarriage of, disapproved of, 289

Widows, bride price paid for, 161; dowry of, 174 *sq.*; morning gift sometimes given to, 177; weddings of, 223 *sq.*; remarriage of, disapproved of, 289. *See* Levirate.

Willcox, W. F., 298-300, 303 *sq.*

Williams, Thomas, 244

Winternitz, M., 206

Wives, custom of supplying guests with temporary, 14, 15, 19, 269, 271, 274; exchange of, 19, 274; prostituted by their husbands, 19 *sq.*; rights of, 162 *sq*, *see* Marital care and duties; as labourers, 241, 244, 249; position of, among the lower races, 245 *sq.;* classificatory terms for, 274 *sq.*

Women, the declining tendency to marry partly due to the in-creasing economic independence of, 51; more particular in their choice than men, 54; language spoken by the, 124 *sq.*; their liberty of choosing their husbands, ch. vi. *passim*; short duration of their youthfulness at the lower stages of civilisation, 239; divorce rate influenced by the emancipation of, 303. *See* Wives.

Wood, Andrew, 105

YAHGANS (Tierra del Fuego), 110

Yakuts, 161

Yukaghir (Siberia), 24, 118, 164

ZIMMER, Heinrich, 268

Zoroastrianism, marriage and pro-creation according to, 42 *sq.*

Zulus, 241